PRINCE CHARLES
Horseman

FRONTISPIECE *Congratulations ... words are superfluous as Prince Charles kisses the Queen's hand, after his England II side beat a Brazilian team in the International Day at Smith's Lawn in 1985*

PRINCE CHARLES
Horseman

MICHAEL CLAYTON

Stanley Paul

LONDON   MELBOURNE   AUCKLAND
JOHANNESBURG

For Jane

Stanley Paul & Co. Ltd
An imprint of Century Hutchinson Ltd
62–65 Chandos Place, London WC2N 4NW

Century Hutchinson Australia (Pty) Ltd
PO Box 496, 16–22 Church Street, Hawthorn, Melbourne,
Victoria 3122, Australia

Century Hutchinson New Zealand Limited
PO Box 40–086, Glenfield, Auckland 10, New Zealand

Century Hutchinson South Africa (Pty) Ltd
PO Box 337, Bergvlei 2012, South Africa

First published 1987
© Michael Clayton 1987
Set in Linotron Sabon
Printed and bound in Great Britain by
Butler & Tanner Ltd, Frome and London

British Library Cataloguing in Publication Data
Prince Charles: horseman
1. Prince of Wales——Knowledge ——
Horsemanship 2. Horsemanship——Great Britain
I. Title
798.2'0924   SF284.52.C5

ISBN 0 09 166340 7

Designed by Humphrey Stone

Contents

Author's Introduction

'It is possible, but supremely unlikely, that anyone with even the slightest association with horses has survived the experience without suffering at least a minor accident. In many cases I suspect that one such accident is very often the last, and the end of a promising equestrian career. Some optimists tend to assume that, once you have learned the lesson that horses bite at one end and kick at the other, there is nothing further to worry about. No such luck, I am afraid. That is only lesson one in a learning process which will go on as long as you are mug enough to continue to associate with horses.'

These are some reflections of the Duke of Edinburgh on the noble art of horsemanship. They are certainly relevant to the riding career of his eldest son, the Prince of Wales.

The never ending 'learning process' is part of horsemanship's charms. Prince Charles has embraced this challenge from the start of his serious involvement in learning to ride successfully. He admits with a candour not demonstrated by many horsemen that he had to overcome considerable youthful fears.

Jumping fences was something he 'missed out on' in his boyhood riding experiences. His self-imposed task in overcoming his apprehension to the extent of becoming a bold and skilled rider across country strikes a chord of sympathy and interest in any horseman who has discovered what a lonely place a saddle can be if you have not struck up a rapport with the animal underneath it – and you are about to take on a large, black fence.

Perhaps some apology is due for what appears to be an aspect of royal biography which throws undue emphasis on merely one sporting activity. It must be read in the context of the extraordinary breadth of public life and interests in which the Prince of Wales partakes. His achievements as a rider are all the more extraordinary in the light of those many other responsibilities which he undertakes so diligently and with manifest success.

If we may know a man by his friends, we also learn a great deal by his recreations, and the enthusiasm and persistence with which he pursues them. Such light as may be thrown on Prince Charles's character in this book is simply produced by His Royal Highness's own actions in tackling some of the most demanding forms of equestrianism.

His achievement in becoming one of Britain's leading high-goal polo players is all the more remarkable when recounted chronologically against the background of his development from university to Service life, and subsequent full-time role as Heir to the Throne.

There are more than a few mysteries associated with horses, and especially with the subject of fox-hunting. I hope that this account of the Prince's explorations in these areas will dissolve some of the misunderstandings and prejudices attached to these sports. One central fact should come through: horsemanship is for fun, and those who do not regard the horse merely as a creature to be exploited, but who have a sympathetic liking for the horse and pony in all forms, will derive far more pleasure from them. Prince Charles is easily identified as someone who enjoys horses for their own sake.

This is not an 'official' book in any sense, but I have been infinitely privileged to receive generous and helpful cooperation from its subject. 'Putting something back' is an essential part of royal participation in any activity, and Prince Charles's contributions to the equestrian sports he has enjoyed are warmly appreciated.

If this account of his riding activities in some minor way helps to document adequately the Prince's contribution to some of the most enduring and rewarding aspects of what can only be called 'the British Way of Life', then it has been worthwhile.

Apart from my deepest gratitude to His Royal Highness, thanks are due to others who include Lt Col Sir John Miller, the Crown Equerry; Major Ronald Ferguson, Prince Charles's polo manager; and *Horse and Hound's* racing correspondent, Lord Oaksey, and polo correspondent, Major William Loyd.

I

WHY HORSES?

Don't give your son money. As far as you can afford it, give him horses.
No one ever came to grief – except honourable grief through riding horses.
No hour of life is lost that is spent in the saddle.

WINSTON S. CHURCHILL

High summer ... there is an amazing contrast amid the afternoon sunshine at Smith's Lawn, that delightful plateau of new mown grass in Windsor Great Park.

On the polo ground eight men are battling it out in one of the fastest ball games in the world. When play swirls to the sides of the ground you can see the polo ponies sweating, their eyes staring, legs ready to skid to a halt or drum away at amazing acceleration ... the urgent shouts of the players as they seek to wrest possession of the polo ball from each other ...

All around is languid calm; ice chinks in glasses in the Guards Polo Club bar, panama hats are perched forward to keep the sun out of the eyes of semi-reclining figures, and ladies in shimmery summer dresses stroll between the open stands and the clubhouse.

Only the occasional roar of a Jumbo gaining altitude from the all too close Heathrow runways provides a reminder that this is the late twentieth century.

The game of skill, speed and nerve on the polo grounds is derived from ancient Asia's recreations. Riding spirited horses while trying to hit a ball travelling at speeds of up to 100mph is anything but a new problem.

In the thick of the hectic play is the Prince of Wales: a four handicap high-goal polo player, exhibiting abilities in controlling his horse and hitting

the ball accurately and effectively which can only be acquired after much dedication and application.

He is a truly modern Prince of Wales; possessor of a pilot's licence, able to drive vehicles at speed; qualified as a parachutist, and an experienced diver, concerned and involved in any number of important projects from industry to the arts.

Why is he spending an afternoon on a horse in a seemingly anachronistic sport?

Deep winter ... the frost has only just come out of the ground in a Midlands landscape of undulating pastureland and occasional arable tillage. Neat black thorn bushes divide the enclosures; small woodlands and copses dot the sweeping landscape.

There is a splash of colour in a narrow lane leading to a red brick farmhouse. Scarlet coats are to be seen above hedgerow level as a huntsman and two whippers-in trot smartly along the lane amid the waving sterns of eighteen and a half couple of white, tan and black foxhounds.

Other horsemen and women join them in the farmhouse yard. There is much touching of caps, and a welter of friendly greetings. Just after eleven o'clock the huntsman leads hounds from the farmyard followed by a throng of mounted followers.

They pause when they enter a grass field near the farmhouse – and a slim figure in dark blue cap and matching coat, with scarlet cuffs, canters across on a compact, workmanlike strawberry roan mare.

'Morning, Michael,' the Prince of Wales greets the huntsman.

'Morning, Sir,' is the response from the huntsman and from the Joint Masters.

Others in the mounted field doff their hats, but the Prince is not approached unless he speaks first to an individual. He turns his mare and canters alongside the huntsman as hounds are taken to draw the first covert.

A day's foxhunting is under way; a sport over 250 years old in broadly its present form, and deriving from one of man's oldest activities – hunting a wild animal in its own environment with the aid of hounds.

Even as dusk draws on at the end of a grey winter's afternoon, this Hunt will still be galloping across the winter pale green of the Shires. Horsemen following the sweet cry of hounds, and the sound of the huntsman's horn, jumping hedges guarded by broad ditches, and stout timber fences when they bar the route across country.

Another ancient sport? Another anachronism? What is the appeal of a risk sport dependent on cooperation with a horse?

Destiny and tradition may have much to do with Prince Charles's development as a fine horseman in summer and winter. Yet he had many other options, a wealth of alternative choices of recreation.

Up to the end of the 1985–86 season he had hunted with forty-six packs of hounds the length and breadth of Britain – a remarkable record for any hunting man.

An attempt to tell the story of 'Prince Charles – Horseman' should convey a little about the tastes and character of our future King.

Yet even a Prince cannot be a horseman without somewhere eminently suitable to ride. This account of a royal equestrian adventure is, if anything, a tribute to the extraordinary versatility of our people and our small, crowded group of islands which is still the finest country in the world for horses and horsemanship.

LEFT *A Prince who relishes a game of skill, speed and nerve*

2

EQUESTRIAN INHERITANCE

England's past has been borne on his back.
All our history is his industry.

RONALD DUNCAN
(The Horse)

Although Prince Charles was a 'late starter' in widening his riding experience, his love of horses is anything but surprising if ancestry and family background shape one's life-style.

Yet such is the gigantic volume of equestrian influence in the Royal Family past and present that it would not have been impossible for a 20th century Prince to be 'turned off' the subject completely.

If you have ever been to a horsey house party and observed the one member of the party who has *not* just been hunting, racing, eventing or whatever – and, worse still, could not care less which end the oats go into a horse – you can easily understand the plight of a non-equestrian child in a formidably horse-minded family.

It says much for the good sense of the Royal Family that there is absolutely no evidence that any of the royal children were pushed into horsemanship. Opportunities were ample, but there was no pressure, and it was a home where so many other major topics and interests filled conversation and shared activities.

Prince Charles's own alternative sports make an awesome list: flying, fishing, shooting, water-skiing, scuba diving, wind surfing, skiing, parachuting have all been identified with the public persona of the Prince of Wales. At one time the popular press regularly referred to him as Action Man.

It has been said, mildly critically, that all his sports are solo activities. This overlooks completely the team spirit in polo, an area of the game where Prince Charles has always shone. He also proved himself a great team man in the hazardous sport of team 'chasing, as we shall see.

The historical background of riding in the Royal Family, and the present day equestrian interests of the Queen and her husband and children, are well known, but tend to be seen in fragmented form. When observed overall, the extent of equestrian connections in British royalty makes Richard III's famous battlefield appeal, as interpreted by Shakespeare, seem something of an understatement: 'A horse! A horse! my kingdom for a horse!'

It is a marvellous element of British racing that it goes hand in hand with a deep interest in the breeding of that miracle, the Thoroughbred horse.

Our monarchs and other members of the Royal Family have often been to the fore in the excitements of the racecourse, and the pleasures associated with selecting and nurturing the greatest horse breed in the world. Henry VIII had royal studs at Hampton Court, at Eltham in Kent, at Tutbury in Staffordshire and at Malmesbury, Wiltshire. Imports of Arab blood, sometimes through the Court of Spain, provided the endurance, quality and speed which the Thoroughbred should always possess.

The first Queen Elizabeth went racing at Salisbury on the eve of the Spanish Armada; not on the present course, but on one much nearer the banks of the River Avon, close to Salisbury Cathedral.

Elizabeth's successor, James I, founded Newmarket as a great racing centre, and built stables there. The tragic Charles I endowed the first cup race at Newmarket in 1634, and clearly adored horsemanship on the Turf and in the Chase.

It has been said that 'he preferred the pleasure of hunting from county to county to the tedium of state visits, with long addresses from petty worries.' *

The luckless King travelled the length and breadth of his kingdom on horseback during the Civil War. Despite his cares, 'the prospect of a journey, particularly to one of his own castles, cheered the King.'

Charles II's image did not please some later monarchs. 'We do not care for Charles II,' Queen Victoria is said to have told one of her officials. Yet his impact on the quality of English life was profound – and all horsemen owe him a special debt for greatly advancing racing and Thoroughbred breeding. He adored racing, which had been banned in Cromwellian England but had survived unofficially. He made Newmarket his own.

'He enjoyed and increasingly valued its informality, which allowed him to "put off" the King. He built himself a house opposite the Maidens' Inn, and established a string of Arab horses which he fed personally on bread soaked in beer and fresh eggs. Then, dressed in the plainest of country clothes, he would gallop across the heath with the other jockeys, often first past the winning post to the accompaniment of drums and trumpets acclaiming him victor.'†

Charles II developed racing as competitor and organizer. His favourite horse, Old Rowley, gave his name to racing's best known 1600-metre course, the Rowley Mile. The King rode the winner of the Newmarket Town plate in 1667, having founded the race two years earlier. The first two Classics of the modern English flat racing season are still run on the Rowley Mile course: the 1000 Guineas and 2000 Guineas.

Hampton Court was revived as a Royal Stud by

William and Mary. William III certainly supported racing, but it was his successor, Queen Anne, who made the greater contribution as the founder of Ascot Races in 1711. Like all the Stuarts, she was passionately fond of hunting, and followed hounds in a specially built horse-drawn chaise which she drove herself. It was after a gallop behind her Royal Buckhounds, which she established at Swinley Bottom, near the water jump at Ascot, that the Queen decided to have a racecourse built on Ascot Heath. Her name is commemorated in racing by the Queen Anne Stakes at Royal Ascot.

The Royal Buckhounds originated much earlier. Long before William the Conqueror brought strict laws to the conduct of the Chase, English kings had ridden to hounds as a natural element in the life of the Court. The office of Master of the Buckhounds dated from the reign of Henry II (1154–89). From the ancient royal Hunts there developed the pack which hunted deer in Berkshire and Buckinghamshire until 1901, covering the areas west of London.

George I and George II mainly confined their hunting to the parks, but George III especially enjoyed hunting during his long life (1738–1820). As an adult he rode at 19 stone and yet covered great tracts of country in all directions around Windsor. He was once driven home to Windsor Castle in a butcher's cart, after a run to Aldermaston, ten miles beyond Reading.

The Royal Buckhounds hunted carted deer. They were red deer stags, kept in paddocks at Swinley, and about three times a season each stag was set loose near a meet, with hounds being put on the line fifteen minutes later. Long, exciting runs resulted, and at the end, the stag – totally untouched by hounds – would stand at bay, and would then be haltered and taken back to the paddocks, completely unharmed.

George IV was a devoted staghunter and foxhunter, and adored horses. He once turned to an official at a great state function and asked in an audible aside: 'Which do you fancy – the horse or the mare?' The Royal Buckhounds, and the Turf, flourished under his rule.

---

* *Charles I, the Personal Monarch*, by Charles Carlton.
† *Charles II, Portrait of An Age*, by Tony Palmer.

William IV was not a natural horseman, but cheerfully kept up the royal connection with hunting and racing. At the Goodwood Cup in 1830 he was asked which of his three horses should run, and ordered – in appropriate manner for the naval man he was – 'start the whole fleet!' All three ran, and finished first, second and third.

Alas, Queen Victoria was not a racing enthusiast, and allowed the Royal Stud at Hampton Court to be dispersed. Fortunately, on the advice of the Prince Consort, she revived it fifteen years later. Sanfoin, winner of the Derby in 1890, was bred at Hampton Court, and another notable success from the stud was Memoir who won the Oaks and the St Leger in the same year.

Albert Edward, Prince of Wales, the future King Edward VII, had ample opportunity to include the Turf among his many pleasures during the years awaiting his accession late in life in 1901. He started his own stud at Sandringham in the 1880s. There he bred Persimmon who won the Derby for him in 1896, and his second Derby winner, in 1900, Diamond Jubilee. That same year the Prince won the Grand National with Ambush, ridden by Algy Anthony.

As a young man, Albert Edward was an intrepid horseman, and a keen rider with the Royal Buckhounds who were already finding the spread of urban London something of an embarrassment. This eventually led to the closure of the pack, and its conversion to the Berks and Bucks Farmers Staghounds who continued to hunt carted deer much further west of Windsor, from 1901, hounds being kennelled at Wallingford, Berkshire.

In 1868 the Prince of Wales experienced a run from Denham Court, Buckinghamshire, to Harrow Hill, Wormwood Scrubs and on to Paddington goods station where the deer was captured.

Afterwards the Prince rode through Hyde Park and down Constitution Hill to Marlborough Hill in hunting dress. This could well have been the last time a Prince of Wales rode through the centre of London at the end of the hunt.

The Prince wore scarlet when out with the Royal Buckhounds, also known as the Queen's Hounds at that time. He summered his hunters at Cumberland Lodge where he also kept a pack of harriers, which he afterwards gave to the farmers of the Queen's country.

His heyday as a hunting man was the 1860s and 1870s. One hunt ended at Harrow, and the Prince's horse – a favourite mare named Firefly – caught cold and died within a day or two. In another run the Prince was reported to have ridden 'hard and well' throughout the arduous route from Taplow, near Maidenhead, to St Albans.

One of the Prince's favourite hunters was a grey, QC, on which he was mounted by the eighth Duke of Beaufort when staying at Badminton. The Prince liked the horse so much that he persuaded the Duke to sell him.

(Prince Charles remarked at the Masters of Foxhounds Association Centenary Dinner in 1981 that he had ridden a hunter of the tenth Duke of Beaufort's which he had particularly liked. Mock ruefully he recalled the story of QC and reflected that he had not been able to repeat the deal, remarking with a sigh, ' . . . those were the days.')

After his succession, King Edward VII's sporting life reached a climax with his third Derby win, in 1909, when Minoru was victorious for the King after a tremendously exciting finish, beating Louviers by a head. Minoru, who was ridden by Herbert Jones and trained by Richard Marsh, had also won the 2000 Guineas.

King George V, although a 'Sailor King' who had spent many years at sea, rode regularly and maintained the royal racing connection; his filly Scuttle, bred at Sandringham, won the 1000 Guineas in 1928, ridden by Joe Childs. It was the first time a reigning monarch had both bred as well as owned the winner of one of the five Classic races in England.

Prince Charles's immediate predecessor as Prince of Wales revived the tradition of competitive royal riding, mainly in point-to-points. He was a keen and dashing rider to hounds – and his brothers also hunted regularly in the Shires, although most public attention naturally focused on the Heir to the Throne.

The dashing Prince of Wales, later briefly Edward VIII, adored polo and hunting – and the accompanying social whirl between the wars. Here, the Prince in top hat, chats with King Alfonso XIII of Spain at an international polo match in 1921

The Prince of Wales, later Edward VIII, started hunting in the Shires – the name given to the packs which hunt wholly or partly in Leicestershire – in 1923.

He took a suite at Craven Lodge in Melton Mowbray which had been a hunting box of Mr Craven in 1863, but which was founded and conducted as a club by an ex-officer, Major General John Vaughan, in the 1920s and 1930s. It was the focal point of the whirl of social activity in Melton Mow-

bray. The Prince gave dinner parties and dances, and it was the 'done thing' to be invited.

Edward, Prince of Wales, was a bold horseman, but not an especially polished one. In the hunting field he 'went like a bomb' says Ulrica Murray Smith, Joint Master of the Quorn for twenty-six years, who hunted in Leicestershire in the 1930s.

At the Quorn's annual meeting in 1932, the Prince of Wales attended as a subscriber and made a suggestion which would have changed the Hunt considerably. He proposed that it would be very convenient for people who could only get up to Leicestershire at weekends if the Friday country could be hunted on Mondays, and the Monday country on alternate Saturdays.

Not a natural rider, but bold and immensely enthusiastic: Edward, Prince of Wales, tackles a cut and laid fence while 'hailing a cab' in a 1921 competitive cross-country ride

The following season the Saturday meets were held in the Monday country for a short time, and then the arrangement was quietly dropped. An outbreak of foot and mouth disease closed the Friday country early in that season anyway.

There was some public controversy about the Prince of Wales riding in point-to-points. He was an enthusiastic, fearless race rider, and King George V and Queen Mary watched him win a race at the Household Brigade meeting at Hawthorn Hill, near Bracknell in Berkshire.

Public fears about the future King's safety increased, and he was forbidden to steeplechase again – presumably by King George V – after a heavy fall in 1924. The Prince was riding his horse Little Favourite at a point-to-point at Arborfield, Berkshire, when it fell at the first fence, and he was concussed.

Nevertheless, the Prince of Wales continued to hunt enthusiastically in Leicestershire. His brothers, Prince George (Duke of Kent) and Prince Henry (Duke of Gloucester) also stayed at Craven Lodge and hunted intermittently in Leicestershire.

The Duke of York, who was to succeed his brother to become King George VI, was regarded by reliable witnesses to have been the most polished horseman among the royal princes. Prince Charles's grandfather had a deep love of horses and of country life. After his marriage to Lady Elizabeth Bowes-Lyon, in 1923, the Duke of York kept up his riding on the polo ground and in the hunting field for some years.

The Duke and Duchess took a hunting box at Naseby Woollies in the Pytchley country for several seasons. The Pytchley was an especially formidable country to cross before the Second World War. It was still a great grazing area, much of it in Northamptonshire, entering Leicestershire at the northern end. The enclosures were stoutly fenced with thorn hedges, often guarded by the famous Pytchley oxers: strong wooden rails erected to keep fly-maddened cattle from crashing into the hedges during the summer months. The oxer is nowadays seen in a formalized fashion in front of show jumps.

The great Frank Freeman hunted the Pytchley hounds with tremendous expertise for twenty-five years until 1931, and great sport was shown over this formidable country. The future King George VI had his hunting arrangements in the hands of the much respected dealer Mr Bert Drage. King George VI and Queen Elizabeth are still recalled throughout the Pytchley country with special affection. Their grace and ease of manner in communicating with individuals from all walks of life, later to earn the love of their people throughout the King's reign, is especially remembered in the Pytchley farming community.

The then Duke of York made a special point of buying forage for his horses locally which was much appreciated in those days. Princess Elizabeth, the future Queen, was taken to Pytchley meets on a leading rein by her mother. Lord (Reggie) Paget, QC, a member of one of the best known Pytchley families, and a former Joint Master, has a Lionel Edwards water-colour of Frank Freeman's last day in April 1931. It shows Freeman taking hounds away from Pitsford past Princess Elizabeth, who is riding a pony led by the Duchess of York, with Reggie Paget's father, Major Guy Paget, just behind.

In his *History of the Pytchley Hunt*, Guy Paget wrote of 'one April evening in 1931. This day will be ever remembered by a certain little lady, who one day may be the greatest in the land, HRH Princess Elizabeth of York. She had come out on her pony to see Freeman hunt his last fox; and it had been arranged that the afternoon draw should be Mr Drummond's Boughton Wood.

'Here, with her mother, she took up her position by the bridle gate at the Pitsford corner. Hounds had not been long in the covert before they spoke, and a minute or two later a fox jumped on to the wall not 20 yards from Her Royal Highness.

'He gave her a good look over, and then crossed the field; so she was able to see the whole thing, fox, hounds and horsemen, for several fields.'

Just how much hunting meant to the future King George VI is revealed in a letter he wrote to Bert Drage on 17 September 1931, from Glamis Castle, family home of the Queen Mother in Scotland, where the Yorks stayed regularly with her family:

Dear Drage,

Thank you for your letter and for your kind suggestion re my hunting this year. I fear that it will not be possible, and I must tell you the tragic news that I am going to sell all my horses at Leicester on October 31st. It is very sad for me as I do really enjoy my hunting, and after all you have done for me it seems such an ungracious thing to do.

I will send you my card giving particulars when it is printed, and you may perhaps know of some possible buyers of really tried out horses.

I shall miss my hunting more than I can say, and this winter will be a long and depressing one for me.

Again so many thanks for your kind suggestion.

Yours very sincerely
(*signed*) ALBERT

OPPOSITE *A passion for horses usually influences childhood games in equestrian families. The future King George VI (right) is seen with his brother, the future King Edward VIII, during a Victorian childhood in which horses were a normal part of life. George VI was later regarded as a more polished horseman than his brothers*

The letter, which was published in Mr Bert Drage's autobiography (*Reminiscences of Bert Drage*), indicates how close the hunting tradition is in Prince Charles's direct ancestry. Note the reference to 'really tried out horses'.

Economies deemed necessary in the 1931 financial crisis which hit Britain had prompted the Duke of York to give up hunting and sell his horses. However, as we shall see, King George VI and Queen Elizabeth maintained close connections with horses through their love of racing.

In the early 1930s they lived at 145, Piccadilly, in London, but in 1931 King George V also gave them a permanent home out of town with gardens round it, the Royal Lodge in Windsor Great Park where Queen Elizabeth the Queen Mother still maintains a delightful residence. The future King and Queen created a marvellous country home at Royal Lodge. Eloquent tributes have often been paid to their success in establishing a remarkably happy family life for their daughters, in which horses, dogs and so many other aspects of country life played an essential part. This was to set a pattern which has influenced the Royal Family's way of life ever since.

A contemporary impression of Lady Elizabeth Bowes-Lyon at the time of her marriage to the Duke of York casts more than a little light on some of the inherited characteristics of her eldest grandson.

'Her tastes are chiefly for an outdoor life. She rides and goes well to hounds, although she has not hunted nearly so much as she would have liked ... she has much fondness for reading and music.'

Despite his accession occurring only some three years before the outbreak of the Second World War, followed by the immediate postwar years of grey austerity, George VI nevertheless managed to maintain continuity in the royal racing establishments. The royal stud was at a low ebb, however, and it became the practice to lease some yearlings from the National Stud each season and to race them in the King's name, returning them to the National Stud at the end of their racing careers.

Two of these, Big Game and Sun Chariot, won four of the five Classic races for King George VI in 1942. They were trained by Fred Darling at Beckhampton, and the sixteen-year-old Princess Elizabeth went with the King to watch Sun Chariot and Big Game on the gallops.

Wartime had prevented the Princess from going to the races, but she was already forming an intense interest in bloodstock breeding and the Turf. Tradition, and the influence of both parents, had ensured that Princess Elizabeth and Princess Margaret rode, and drove, ponies at an early age. With only a skeleton staff at the Royal Mews at Windsor during the war, the sisters largely looked after their own ponies.

By the time she was twenty the future Queen had made regular visits to the Royal Stud at Hampton Court, and knew her father's mares and their progeny well before they came into training. The Queen first watched the Derby in 1945, when it was still run under wartime conditions at Newmarket instead of Epsom.

Despite her premier interest in the Flat, the Queen has shared Queen Elizabeth the Queen Mother's pleasure, and some acute disappointments, in National Hunt racing. Encouraged by the late Lord Mildmay, Princess Elizabeth and her mother became joint owners of the steeplechaser Monaveen. Trained by Peter Cazalet, Monaveen gave the Princess her first win as an owner, at Fontwell Park, near Chichester, in 1949.

Monaveen won four steeplechases that season, but was killed in a fall at the Hurst Park water jump. Princess Elizabeth had already been given the flat race filly Astrakhan as a wedding present when she married Prince Philip in 1947. After Monaveen's death, the Princess concentrated on flat racing, with her mother continuing to give royal patronage to the winter sport of steeplechasing and hurdling which has benefited so much from the Queen Mother's unflagging interest.

In 1953, her Coronation year, the Queen's Aureole, by Hyperion, was second in the Derby, ridden by Harry Carr. The winner was Sir Victor Sassoon's Pinza, ridden amid much acclaim by the newly knighted Sir Gordon Richards: his first Derby victory achieved in his 50th year. The Derby came just four days after the Coronation, and legend

The Queen, as Princess Elizabeth (left), and Princess Margaret largely looked after their own ponies during the war. They were riding these greys in the grounds of Royal Lodge, Windsor, in April, 1940

relates that, when asked by one of her ladies-in-waiting on the morning of the crowning if all was well, the Queen replied, 'Oh yes, the Captain has just rung to say Aureole is really well.'

The Captain was Sir Cecil Boyd Rochfort who took over as royal trainer in 1943. Before retiring in 1968 he had trained 136 winners for the Queen. His greatest triumph for King George VI had been in winning the 1946 1000 Guineas with Hypericum.

Aureole was a most difficult three-year-old to train, but was treated by a London neurologist, Dr Charles Brook, who had already calmed several over-excitable horses used in the Queen's Coronation. The Queen agreed that Brook's treatment, which consisted of a laying on of hands, should be tried on Aureole, and certainly he produced a brilliant season as a four-year-old, culminating in his great victory in the King George VI and Queen Elizabeth Stakes at Ascot.

Although a Derby victory has so far eluded the Queen, she has enjoyed a remarkably consistent level of success in over thirty years as an owner-breeder. Her knowledge of bloodstock and the Turf is formidable.

Under the able direction of Lord Porchester as general racing manager, with Michael Oswald in charge of the bloodstock breeding side, the Queen's achievements have included all the other four English Classic races. Her brood mares are kept at her three studs – at Sandringham, and at Wolverton and Polhampton in Hampshire. At Sandringham there stands Shirley Heights, the leading Thoroughbred sire in Britain, and Bustino . . .

In 1982 the Queen purchased the West Ilsley Stables, near Newbury, where the great trainer Dick Hern is her tenant and shares the training of the Queen's horses with Ian Balding at Kingsclere in Berkshire. Major Hern's dreadful hunting injury, in which he suffered paralysis after breaking his neck during a Quorn Friday in 1984, was an appalling reminder of the inevitable risk factor in all forms of riding. The Royal Family were among the Major's warmest admirers when he so gallantly continued to administer his training yard in 1985, despite his severe handicap.

The Queen's long experience and perception as a horse breeder are by no means confined to Thoroughbreds. If her close interest in flat racing and bloodstock has so far not been actively shared by Prince Charles, his riding has been enormously assisted by the Queen's aid in breeding polo ponies and hunters.

As we shall see, breeding polo ponies in Britain from Thoroughbred stock at a level capable of competing with South American-bred ponies is a remarkable achievement. The hunters, bred by the Queen, which Prince Charles has ridden, were in fact intended as eventers, and were ridden by Princess Anne before being passed on to the Prince of Wales for the hunting field.

The Queen has always taken a close interest in the carriage horses kept in the heart of London behind Buckingham Palace in the Royal Mews, and in the Royal Mews at Windsor. Some thirty carriage horses are in the charge of the Crown Equerry, Lt Col Sir John Miller, and his staff. About ten or twelve are greys, and the remainder bays. Of these, six are kept mostly at Windsor for Prince Philip's use in competition carriage driving, but they all fulfil ceremonial duties as well, whenever required. Most of the carriage horses have Cleveland Bay blood – the Cleveland Bay is the only British breed of carriage horse – although there have been many Dutch, German and other foreign horses in the Royal Mews, as well as Irish importations.

Again, this is part of a breeding as well as purchasing project, in which the monarch's own knowledge of horses plays an important part. Some of the mares are kept in the Royal Paddocks at Hampton Court, where the Queen has maintained tradition by using the former Royal Stud mainly for various breeding projects, even though the main Thoroughbred enterprise is now elsewhere.

Some of the Queen's horse breeding, including the polo pony production, has been carried out at her stud at Old Windsor. There is a splendid collection of hacks at Windsor which the Queen and other members of the family enjoy riding in the Great Park. Highland, Fell and Haflinger ponies at Balmoral in Scotland; Arab horses elsewhere, and a project to breed suitable drum horses for the Household Cavalry ... the Queen's equestrian interests are amazingly diverse and are in evidence at all the royal estates. Gifts from foreign heads of government have often taken the form of recruits for the royal stables.

The Queen rides regularly when she is out of London, and during May and June, prior to the Birthday Parade at Horseguards, she rides side-saddle in the Riding School or the garden at Buckingham Palace. The Queen's current riding horses are Greenshield, by the Queen's own stallion, College Green. Greenshield is a bay gelding foaled in 1970 at the Royal Stud, at Sandringham. The dam was Betaway, one of the most famous of Prince Philip's polo mares. Greenshield was ridden by Prince Charles on the polo field, but the horse has a particularly long back and proved difficult to turn and manoeuvre during a game. Greenshield was therefore taken back for the Queen's own use as a hack.

Another hack ridden regularly by the Queen is Reneau, a chestnut gelding foaled in 1973. This is an Arab/Barb from Algeria, presented to Prince Philip by President Boumedienne. Reneau is a delightful ride, and is a favourite mount of Prince Edward.

A clue to the Queen's polo pony breeding policies is her hack, Sanction, a brown gelding foaled in 1978 by her Thoroughbred polo pony stallion Sanbal out of an extremely good Argentine mare called Carnarita. Sanction is a full brother to three of Prince Charles's high-goal polo ponies, and is a most comfortable and pleasant ride.

Earl Mountbatten of Burma, 'Uncle Dickie' in the Royal Family, was a life-long polo enthusiast, and encouraged Prince Philip and Prince Charles to play. He is seen about to change polo ponies during a 1936 match

The most famous of the Queen's riding horses is her black mare, Burmese, a gift from the Royal Canadian Mounted Police. Burmese, who was twenty-four years old in 1986, has carried the Queen faithfully on her Birthday Parade for the last seventeen consecutive years, and was deemed fit to do so again in 1986. The mare is a great favourite of the Queen's, and knows the ceremonial procedures of the Birthday Parade as well as anyone on the famous parade ground. Centenial, the Queen's second black Canadian horse, lives at Windsor and travels to the other royal residences. He was sixteen in 1986. He is a big horse of about 17 hands and has an impeccable temperament. Prince Charles has ridden Centenial on parades.

The weight of equestrian tradition from the House of Windsor, and previous British royalty is obvious, even from an outline survey. Yet the most immediate riding influence to make much impact on Prince Charles's life was from his father. And the original source of encouragement came from one of the most persuasive, active, and distinctive personalities in public life, Admiral of the Fleet, Earl Mountbatten of Burma. Prince Philip was chiefly instrumental in encouraging his son to take up polo, but Lord Mountbatten provided even further encouragement.

'Uncle Dickie' had his first game of polo at Jodhpur when replacing an absent player during the Prince of Wales's tour of India in 1921. An Army officer mischievously suggested the correct way to mount a polo pony was to take a flying leap and vault over its tail into the saddle. Only when this had failed disastrously did Mountbatten manage to mount correctly. He said later that during this game he only succeeded in hitting the ball three or four times, but a lifetime's passion for polo was truly born.

Lord Mountbatten applied his extraordinary powers of concentration and enthusiasm, and although not a natural rider, became a top-class player. Typically, he devised and patented an oval-shaped head to the polo stick which gave 'loft and length'. Better still, he wrote the definitive text book, *An Introduction to Polo* by 'Marco'. It was first published in 1931, and ran into seven editions, the last appearing in 1982. The author sent a copy to the Editor of *Horse and Hound*, accompanied by a personal letter, emphasizing the book's relevance to modern polo. Prince Charles contributed a Foreword in which he recalled:

'Lord Mountbatten thrust a copy of his book into my hand (over 15 years ago) and wrote in the front page – "from Great Uncle Marco". I read the book several times and learnt a great deal from it. It was designed to make the aspiring polo player think a bit harder about the mechanics of the game and, as such, is still thoroughly applicable to today's players. Lord Mountbatten, I know, would have been immensely gratified by such clear recognition of his authoritative hand book on polo and we are all indebted to him for the extraordinary amount of thought and hard work which went into its compilation. I hope it will give encouragement and instruction to countless generations of polo players.'

The copyright of the book was vested in the Royal Naval Polo Association, later amalgamated with the Royal Naval Saddle Club. Lord Mountbatten had played much of his polo in Malta and elsewhere abroad as a Naval officer.

The most notable young player to be influenced by Lord Mountbatten was his nephew, Prince Philip, son of Mountbatten's sister, Princess Alice and Prince Andrew of Greece.

Prince Philip later recalled: 'I had just got as far as wielding a stick in a polo pit and doing some stick and ball practice on a pony before the war broke out. It was twelve years before I started again in Malta under the eye of my uncle, the great "Marco" himself ... '

After returning to Britain from Naval service in 1952, following the Queen's accession, Prince Philip recalled enjoying some 'wonderful seasons playing at Cowdray, and even more important, on Cowdray ponies.' Lord Cowdray was instrumental in helping to revive the game in postwar Britain on his Sussex estate. Noticing how many Household Cavalry and Household Brigade officers were playing, Prince Philip provided the impetus for the formation of the Household Brigade Polo Club at Smith's Lawn in 1956. Cirencester, re-opened in 1952 by Earl Bathurst, still forms, together with Windsor and Cowdray, the Big Three of the polo world.

Prince Philip shared his uncle's deep affection for the game, and applied himself enthusiastically to polo's disciplines to become one of the best eight players in Britain. His handicap was highest at five.

He summed up his attitude to the game: 'I suppose every games player thinks his particular game is far better than any other. I am no exception. I have no objection whatever to others enjoying their particular game, but give me polo every time.'

In *The Horseman's Year*, edited by Dorian Williams, Prince Philip also provided an assessment of the sport, with some evidence of the cutting edge to his humour, for which he is renowned:

'I dare say every sport has its characters and its problems, although I sometimes find it hard to believe that any do as well as polo in this respect. There seems to be more opportunity in polo for dramas. For one thing, as a team consists of four players, if one of them defects a quarter of the team disappears, and if by chance he owns most of the ponies, the rest are up a gum tree.

Then there is the system of handicapping, which works in the opposite way to golf handicaps. Endless permutations and computations go into the business of getting a team together and further complications can arise as handicaps may be altered in the middle of the season.

As if that wasn't enough the game is played on ponies, so the whole glorious world of horse-coping comes into it. As almost every horse deal puts a very great strain on, if it doesn't wholly break up, the oldest and strongest friendships, these can have a dramatic influence on team solidarity.

Prince Philip, captaining the Windsor Park team in a Combermere Cup match in 1965

This is also one of the fields in which wives like to take a part and whoever it was who said that "the female of the species is more deadly than the male" must have been a horse-coper. Wives have also been known to have very firm views about the way both their husbands and other players conduct themselves on the polo ground.'

There speaks one who really knows! It is just possible that Prince Philip may have been referring to the tendency towards 'straight talking' between players at moments of stress – which can all too easily waft over to the spectator area, including the royal pavilion.

Prince Philip captained teams at Windsor throughout the fifties and sixties. With little more than 500 people playing polo regularly throughout Britain at that time, the Prince became personally known to many people throughout the sport. He visited many of the smaller clubs, such as Toulston, Cheshire, Tidworth and Kirklington, and he

remarked, 'Whenever I have managed to get away and play on some of these grounds, I have had a wonderful time ... the hospitality offered to visiting teams does nothing to improve the standard of play.'

Typically, he made a firm decision to give up polo whilst still a formidable player. This was due partly to a recurring wrist problem; he has since been prone to extol the virtues of the controversial anti-inflammatory drug phenylbutazone for horses, by tapping his wrist and saying, 'Well, *I* take bute – and it has done a lot for me.'

Far more significantly, Prince Philip remarked when he stopped playing polo in 1970, 'I reckoned fifty was quite old enough for that game.' He is to be seen watching Prince Charles at Smith's Lawn and taking immense pleasure in his son's prowess. Not too many fathers in any walk of life gain the satisfaction of an eldest son clearly delighting, and excelling, in their favourite sport.

Lord Mountbatten was on many occasions an equally happy spectator at Smith's Lawn when Prince Charles was playing – until the murder of the former First Sea Lord by the IRA in August 1979. Lord Mountbatten's beneficial influence on and assistance to the Royal Family in so many ways throughout his remarkable life has been well documented. If the sporting life of the Prince of Wales is even a footnote to history, it should be recorded that royal involvement in one of the greatest equestrian sports in the world was due originally to the indefatigable enthusiasm of 'my uncle, the great "Marco" himself ...'

A similar branch of enthusiasm and application has always marked Prince Philip's attitude to work and play.

It was fortunate for the horse world when Prince Philip was elected President of the FEI (International Equestrian Federation) in 1964. As he remarked, his equestrian knowledge was mainly confined to polo, but he knew enough about horsemanship 'to understand what they were all talking about', and he was able to be a totally neutral chairman between the different factions in show jumping, dressage and horse trials.

Prince Philip has achieved much as a leading competitor in world-class competition carriage driving. He is tackling the marathon phase of the Royal Windsor Horse Show's International Driving Grand Prix in Home Park, Windsor, in 1974. The horses are from the Royal Mews where their main role is in royal ceremonial driving functions

Prince Philip threw himself with characteristic energy into the ramifications of re-writing out-of-date rules, and tackling the detailed problems of international travel and veterinary problems associated with the above named sports.

It was his FEI work which led to Prince Philip taking up competition carriage driving. He assisted greatly in making combined driving an official FEI sport, and 'after a bit of arm twisting' helped to ensure that Britain saw the sport for the first time as an adjunct to the Royal Windsor Horse Show in 1971.

Prince Philip took up the sport in 1973, using five bays from the Royal Mews, and he trained himself at Sandringham, with help from Major Tommy Thompson, former Riding Master of the Household Cavalry.

Since then, Prince Philip has put the sport on the map in Britain and abroad. Its exciting marathon phase across country involves horrendous obstacles which can lead to spectacular upsets for carriages. All this produces 'good television', and the sport has had plenty of publicity in its own right as an exciting challenge, and not simply because of its royal connection. Prince Philip has excelled as a four in hand driver (known as a 'whip') and his successes have included membership of Britain's team which won the World Carriage Driving Championships in 1980 at Windsor. He was also in Britain's bronze medal team in the European Championships at Zug, Switzerland, in 1981.

Royal Windsor Horse Show is a focus for the equestrian background into which Prince Charles was born. The show started in 1943 as a wartime Wings for Victory week event. Its chairman and founder, Windsor businessman Geoffrey Cross invited the Royal Family – and they not only attended, but also took part. Geoffrey has also performed prodigious services as former Secretary of the Guards Polo Club.

Watched by King George VI and Queen Elizabeth, the Princesses won the single private driving class. Princess Elizabeth drove Hans, a Norwegian pony, to a pony phaeton with Princess Margaret as passenger. Later Princess Margaret was the driver to win the wartime utility driving class, with the King's Fell pony Gypsy between the shafts.

King George became Patron of the Royal Windsor Horse Show Club which has run the show annually in May ever since. Geoffrey Cross remains Chairman of this great equestrian occasion, and the Queen has continued as Patron since King George's death in 1952.

It is not too much to claim that the show has become part of the Royal Family's way of life. Prince Charles first attended with his parents as a six-year-old. He has since ridden his polo ponies in a main ring competition, and has competed in a triathlon jumping and obstacle class. His mount in the latter was Candlewick. This former eventer mare – which we shall meet later – jumped brilliantly, but let down her royal rider when she declined to be led between two narrow pieces of fencing on the course.

The Queen, Prince Philip, and their Windsor Castle house party, brave the windiest, coldest weather which May can so easily produce, to watch the Services Team Jumping, tent pegging and other classes in the main ring of the show on the final Sunday afternoon.

The Patron also attends one of the floodlit evening performances, which can be distinctly chilly, but which are well worth visiting for the grand climax: the Musical Drive of the King's Troop Royal Horse Artillery, performed with tremendous pace and precision in the flood-lit ring in Home Park, with the illuminated walls of Windsor Castle as a backdrop.

Princess Anne has competed at Royal Windsor since childhood, and has won the combined dressage and jumping contest on her great eventer, Doublet.

Major sponsorships have arrived in recent years, and Royal Windsor in 1986 could proudly claim to be the largest outdoor show in Britain devoted entirely to horse classes.

Ancestry, tradition, parental influence certainly add up to a formidable equestrian bias in the Royal Family. Princess Anne emerged from this background as one of the world's leading horse trials riders.

In all equestrian families at least one son or daughter completely fails to fall under the spell of the animal which Prince Philip so aptly described as 'the great leveller'. In the Royal Family Prince Andrew clearly finds fulfilling interests and recreation outside the horse world. He suffers hay fever from horses, and riding was not suitable as his sport. Prince Edward rides well, but so far his lifestyle has hardly permitted him much opportunity for competitive riding. He has hunted a little, and enjoys riding for its own sake as a form of exercise and relaxation. He has been seen riding in the park at Badminton during the annual three-day event, while viewing his brother-in-law Mark Phillips's performance on the cross-country course.

Prince Charles has followed royal traditions in becoming increasingly keen on horsemanship in its most daring forms. Despite the weight of tradition, and example, he can justifiably sum up his riding career with the popular song title: I did it my way ...

3

'I RATHER GOT PUT OFF...'

Princes learn no art truly, but the art of horsemanship. The reason is,
the brave beast is no flatterer. He will throw
a Prince as soon as his groom.

BEN JONSON

Prince Charles was to learn the last of these points early in childhood. It would not have been surprising if he had, like many other boys, decided that horsemanship was not to be the sport for him, and turned instead to more mechanical forms of transport.

As he recalls it, the early attempts to gain his full interest in riding were anything but a success.

'I rode, and had lessons first, at the age of four. Later I went for the Pony Club, gymkhana activities. Then I found I was one of only about three boys in the Garth Pony Club, and I thought "Hell, there's something wrong here". So I thought I had better not go on with that any more.

I was a bit put off jumping as well, because I had a pony at that time – Bandit – which used to stand up on its hind legs in the collecting ring, and all that sort of thing.

Not being nearly as brave as my sister – which very often happens – I rather got put off.

My father had an old pony which he let me have, and he introduced me to polo at about the age of thirteen.

Like all these things, a lot depends on what your parents are interested in. Neither the Queen nor Prince Philip jumped their horses, nor raced, nor went hunting. So there was not that natural tradition, but I dare say that if my parents had been particularly keen on hunting, I would have gone

into it from a much earlier age. My father played polo, and in a game like that one tends to follow one's father.

I did not do dressage, but I had all the good basic stuff in my early lessons. I dare say I could still do with a refresher course. When I first started, I did fiddle about, helping to look after my ponies. Then somehow I didn't do this any more; there were always people around to do it, and things got too busy. Now I rather regret not really knowing all that much about that side of horsemanship.'

The grey pony Bandit on which Prince Charles had his first competitive experience belonged to Mrs Cynthia Pitman, sister of the Queen's Crown Equerry, Lt Col Sir John Miller. The pony did misbehave sometimes, but it cannot be entirely blamed for Prince Charles's confession that 'the whole idea of taking off scared me stiff in those days; so when my father suggested I took up polo I was all for it. At least you stay on the ground.'

Bandit continued to play a part in other children's early riding experiences, and survived to enjoy a happy retirement in Gloucestershire to well over the age of thirty.

There had been other ponies before Bandit. Most of the Prince's early riding was at Windsor, Balmoral or Sandringham. He first rode a completely 'bomb proof' pony called Fum, and later an equally tractable Welsh pony called William.

ABOVE *Prince Charles holds his pony William, and Princess Anne takes a somewhat firmer hold of Greensleeves. The Queen and Prince Philip were on holiday with their children at Balmoral in August, 1955*
BELOW *A horse for the infant Prince Charles at Clarence House in 1951 – and could that be a hunting horn?*

Windsor was a particularly important area for the Royal Family's private equestrian activities – and still is. The Home Park, below the Castle walls, provides a spacious, but protected area of grassland, tracks, streams and a private path alongside the Thames. It is usually closed to the public, but they are allowed in on special occasions, such as the annual International Carriage Driving Grand Prix, associated with Royal Windsor Horse Show in May.

Prince Charles and Princes Anne were taken for rides in the Home Park, and later graduated to the wider open space of Windsor Great Park, one of the most superb areas for pleasure riding in Britain. By special arrangement with the Royal Parks authorities, members of the general public also ride on the grass, woodland and heathery stretches of this 'lung' of open country which relieves the pressures of ex-urbia west of London's sprawl.

Because the royal children were at Sandringham for the Christmas holidays, most of the Pony Club activities in the Garth branch were in the Easter holidays. They took part in very few junior competitions – Princess Anne says she could probably count the number 'on the fingers of one hand' – and their most exciting riding experiences were venturing into Windsor Great Park to ride with the Queen, who knows 'every inch' of the terrain.

During Royal Ascot week the Queen and other members of the Royal Family used to hack across the Park from the Royal Mews at Windsor Castle to the racecourse. They would canter down the course in front of the main grandstand under the watchful gaze of the bowler hatted Bernard, Duke of Norfolk, who was the Queen's Representative in charge of racing at Ascot.

Princess Anne showed early signs of the adventurous interest in riding which was to take her to the top level in international horse trials. She also rode Bandit, and confirms Prince Charles's memory that he had a mind of his own.

'Once he'd done one bending race he wouldn't do another. It was the same with show jumping,' recalled the Princess. 'He'd do one round, but if you wanted to go into the ring again you had to back him in.

'I have an impression of one very large grey cob and two rather small grey ponies, all of them plaited and absolutely spotlessly white from head to foot,' recalls Princess Anne. 'Miss Sybil Smith was on the cob in the middle; Charles and I were on either side on the ponies. We were both on a leading rein and we were *towed* around a cinder ring, but the fastest we ever went was a trot. I'm afraid I thought it was a most grisly waste of time.'

Miss Smith, who was in her eighty-fifth year in 1986, has always maintained a discreet silence about her royal equestrian connections, but it is clear that she has made a significant contribution. Her family firm, W. J. Smith, kept horses in London, and had branches at Roehampton, High Wycombe, and at Holyport, near Maidenhead, where the manager of their hunting stables was the father of Dick Francis, the famed jockey and thriller writer.

Miss Smith, a kindly but formidable lady, taught most members of the Royal Family to ride in the early stages. She used to take ponies to Buckingham Palace to give lessons to the sisters Princess Elizabeth and Princess Margaret. Pansy was the pony on which the Queen was taught to ride.

The Holyport stables were sold in 1972 and developed for housing, but Sybil lives nearby and continued into her eighties to be a much liked and respected figure in the Berkshire equestrian scene. She judged pony classes for well over half a century.

She once said, 'You know, I thought I'd never have the patience to teach, but I'm told I'm *very* patient.'

OPPOSITE *The redoubtable Miss Sybil Smith who gave Prince Charles and Princess Anne their first riding lessons*
BELOW *As a twelve-year-old in 1961 Prince Charles rides in Badminton Park during a visit to the Duke and Duchess of Beaufort for the annual Badminton Horse Trials. Nowadays the Pony Club insists that its members wear safety hats with chin-straps, even when hacking*

Patient or not, it must be admitted that the early riding instruction given to Prince Charles merely enabled him to acquire the basics of rising to the trot, sitting down to a canter and giving a pony some direction in steering and, hopefully, some braking ability when required – except when the pony happened to be Bandit!

It was essential for a royal prince to include horse riding as an accomplishment, if only for future ceremonial purposes, but no one assumed that the infant Prince Charles was a natural horseman who would go far in competitive riding. There were so many other priorities in education and training for a future king.

Certainly there is every reason to think that he could have overcome his fear of jumping his ponies much earlier in life if there had been more time and opportunity to concentrate on this problem during his boyhood. As a prep schoolboy he was inclined to be plump, and was somewhat sensitive on this subject. He soon developed into a lean, muscular teenager, with an ideal physique for a horseman.

He did not relish jumping his ponies as a child, but Prince Charles always looked forward to the prospect of playing polo one day. At Windsor Great Park in 1957 when he was eight, the Prince bends forward, apparently to get an inside tip from a polo pony at Smith's Lawn, Windsor Great Park, where Prince Philip was playing

He has none of the disadvantages of the man who is cursed with round limbs, especially the thighs, nor the tall man with a long back which usually suffers from strains during a strenuous riding career.

Prince Charles's medium height (5 feet 11 inches), wiry frame, and a life-long regime of hard exercise, frugal eating and drinking, and non-smoking are ideal for the tough demands of polo and the hunting field. He has always shown an extraordinary resilience in taking crashing falls on the polo ground, or later in pursuit of hounds, during team 'chases and steeplechasing.

Although Prince Philip clearly had ambitions for his son as a polo player – which were to be more than justified – there was not much evidence that the schoolboy Prince Charles would later devote so much of his leisure time to horsemanship.

Princess Anne graduated to her first 14.2 hands pony High Jinks at the age of eleven, and went on to compete in hunter trials. At Benenden School for Girls she was able to make progress with her riding through weekly sessions at the nearby Moat House stables.

For Prince Charles there was no regular organized riding at his preparatory school, Cheam, at Headley on the Berkshire Downs. There were the conventional games at Cheam, plus some camping and wild-life study, and there were regular athletic sessions in the school gymnasium.

There was great emphasis on physical development at his next school, Gordonstoun, near Elgin. The usual schoolboy games were augmented by rigorous activities such as a fire service, mountain rescue, and surf life saving. Canoeing and sailing were skills the Prince developed during his Gordonstoun years, and in 1963 he travelled alone to Bavaria for a winter-sports break with Prince Ludwig of Hesse and his family. There he began to learn skiing.

Yet his connection with horsemanship was retained through Prince Philip's example on the polo field. Prince Charles and Princess Anne watched their father play during the summer months at Cowdray and at Smith's Lawn, Windsor Great Park. They were given ponies to hold between chukkas; they sometimes assisted in saddling and bridling; above all, they absorbed the drama and excitement of one of the fastest, toughest and most competitive games man has ever devised.

During his early school days Prince Charles was thought to be somewhat reserved, and shy. This was probably an exaggerated public judgement, but the Prince admitted that it was his later spell at Geelong school in Victoria, Australia, which 'conquered my shyness...'

He was based at Geelong's country outpost, Timbertop, some 200 miles to the north of Melbourne.

Cross-country hikes and runs, tree chopping, swimming and climbing were all part of a strenuous but thoroughly arduous regime. The down-to-earth Aussie approach to life in general, and especially in human relationships, helped Prince Charles overcome any trace of self-consciousness. He learned rapidly to adjust to any company, any style of living, and his later experiences at university and in the Services put this ease of manner fully to the test.

Yet it was overlooked that, even before leaving Gordonstoun, Prince Charles had begun a lasting passion for a rugged team game which develops decision, nerve, and aggression.

It was in 1964, at the age of fifteen, that Prince Charles began to play polo more seriously; he was in his fourth year at Gordonstoun, where his talents in artistic as well as athletic areas were providing more than a clue to the immense versatility of the young man who had yet to be subjected to the full glare of the world media.

His mentors in polo, as described earlier, were his father and Lord Mountbatten; a formidable combination of influences in any pursuit. Prince Charles recalls that he liked playing polo tremendously from the start – and he had the great good fortune of starting the game on a superb pony, given to him by Prince Philip.

'She was called San Quinina, and she was marvellous, knew an awful lot about the game; she was a sort of Maltese Cat.*

My father was a very good instructor, and he gave me the basic techniques. Lord Mountbatten used to add all sorts of things to my training as well. He had originally encouraged my father to play polo, of course. Lord Mountbatten showered me with endless advice; he was a great encourager. He gave me his book, *An Introduction to Polo*, by Marco.

After Quinina I had Sombra, which was a present from Lord Cowdray. She really was the classic Maltese Cat. She was twenty-one years old, and knew so much about the game. When you went to take a backhander, she would turn before you hit the ball.

* Rudyard Kipling's famous story of a polo pony of that name

So I was permanently going over her nose! She was a really wise old bird; a great school teacher in so many ways.'

Before taking part in matches, Prince Charles went through the preliminary training faced by all polo players. Learning to strike the ball was accomplished on a wooden horse, as described by Lord Mountbatten in his invaluable book. Ideally,

'My father ... introduced me to polo at about the age of thirteen ...' Here, the Prince is undertaking essential stick and ball practice in 1962

the wooden horse is placed in a pit dug in the ground, with a flat centre. When the ball is hit by the novice sitting on a saddle, on the wooden horse, the ball travels up a slope, is stopped by a net, and rolls down again towards the striker, giving him practice, while mounted on a stationary horse, at hitting a moving ball.

In the school holidays on the lawns of Windsor Castle Prince Charles also started the years of stick-and-ball practice sessions on a live pony which he would need in his climb to the international high-goal game.

Horsemanship *is* vital to succeed in polo, and although the game calls for different applications of riding skills from equestrian sports involving jumping, the same essential aids are necessary for instant control. A polo pony's powers of acceleration, manoeuvring and stopping are incredible.

Prince Charles admits that when he began to play the game he found the intricacies of positional polo at high speed one of his main problems. Two teams, each comprising four players, seek to win by scoring goals – hitting the ball through the goal posts erected at each end of the 300-yards long ground.

First-time spectators, and novice players, find their bewilderment increased because the teams change end every time a goal has been scored through the 10-feet high goal posts. This is said to lessen the advantage of one side benefiting from a strong prevailing wind.

In each team, numbers one and two are the forwards, number three is the half-back, and number four is the back. The game is divided into periods of play called 'chukkas' after the original Indian expression. The Persians and Turkomans were playing the game about 600 BC, and it was the British conquest of India which brought the game to the United Kingdom in the nineteenth century.

The British game is divided into a maximum of six chukkas, each timed to last seven minutes, with an interval of three minutes, and five minutes at half time. At the end of the play in each chukka a bell is rung, but the chukka does not actually end until the ball goes out of play.

In important matches there are two mounted umpires on the field of play, and a referee is appointed, who watches the game off the field of play, and who arbitrates to make the final decision if the umpires disagree.

Polo players are handicapped in an ascending order of merit from minus two to a maximum of ten. There are only about fifty-five players with handicaps of three and above in the Hurlingham Polo Association Handicap list, out of a total of 655 players in twenty-three clubs – including the Cyprus Polo Association, and the All Ireland Polo Club.

In matches played under handicap conditions the higher handicapped team concedes to the lower handicapped team the difference in the handicaps divided by six and multiplied by the number of periods of play of the match. Where this results in fractions they always count as 'half a goal'.

We shall be referring frequently to high-goal, medium-goal and low-goal teams. Teams playing high-goal in tournaments must each have a total handicap of between seventeen and twenty-two goals; medium-goal, an upper limit of fifteen; and low-goal, limits of nought to four, six or eight, depending on the rules of each tournament. There is also an intermediate tournament level of no more than twelve goals.

No one can play in a high-goal tournament with less than a personal handicap of one, and not more than two sponsored foreign players may be included in each high-goal team. (See Appendix II for more detailed description of polo's rules and history.)

Positional play is vital in polo, and although a brilliant individual is highly sought after, unless he can exhibit the virtues of a real team player he is of little use in helping his side to victory.

OPPOSITE ABOVE LEFT *Dressed for driving – the Prince of Wales has the all-round horseman's ability to drive a team, although he much prefers riding*
OPPOSITE TOP RIGHT *Riding is an essential skill for a British monarch, faced with such commitments as the annual Trooping the Colour at the Queen's Birthday Parade. The Queen is riding Burmese, the black mare presented to her by the Royal Canadian Mounted Police*
OPPOSITE BELOW *Relaxation between chukkas at the beautiful Cirencester ground in Gloucestershire*

LEFT *Aged nineteen, and already a dedicated polo player, the Prince already had to fit his recreation into a strenuous programme of commitments. He was preparing for his investiture as Prince of Wales the following year*

OPPOSITE *With Lord Mountbatten, a life-long polo enthusiast, who warmly encouraged the young Prince to improve his play*

BELOW *Prince Charles appears regularly amid the panoply of International Polo Day, organized at Windsor as a great annual event by his polo manager, Major Ronald Ferguson, since 1972*

TOP *Often playing at back, Prince Charles is an excellent defender*

LEFT AND ABOVE *The Princess of Wales in supportive role on the polo ground. She denies that she dislikes the game*

OPPOSITE *Prince Charles adds a face-guard to his well insulated polo helmet, far safer than most other forms of riding headgear*

ABOVE *Another special 'facility' on the polo ground at Palm Beach: glamorous cheerleaders – an aspect which is missing from the British game!*

RIGHT *Electric scoreboard at Palm Beach – a refinement you won't find on a British polo ground*

OPPOSITE *Palm Beach in 1985 – playing before enthusiastic American spectators during the official visit of the Prince and Princess of Wales to the United States*

One of the most important rules in polo concerns the 'right of way' of a player in seeking to hit the ball. The chances of a collision are so high when players attempt possession of the ball that transgressions across the right of way are penalized by the umpires with a range of penalties. These range from the award of a penalty goal to the opposing side, to a series of free-hits at the rule-breaker's goal from varying distances, according to the severity of the penalty.

Some of the roughness and toughness of polo is seen most frequently in the practice of 'riding off' an opposing player. This involves marking your opposing back, if you are a forward, and impeding his opportunities to get a shot at the ball. The arm and the elbow can be used in 'riding off', as in a soccer charge, but the elbow must be kept close to the side. Players can also prevent each other from hitting the ball by hooking each other's sticks with their own.

At school at Cheam, Prince Charles played rugger and soccer. He was captain of the First XI soccer team, but his game was marked by a lack of aggression. He was said to have caused some amusement by apologizing chivalrously to anyone he felled with a perfectly proper tackle.

Polo was to demand considerable reserves of aggression and competitiveness. There was to be more than ample evidence that the Prince possesses these qualities in abundance, although, modestly, he will smilingly remark, 'I am not sure that I have got *enough* aggression in my play, even now.'

Of his first impression of polo he confirms Lord Mountbatten's advice to the absolute beginner: 'Few polo players, even first-class ones, will claim that they were not completely bewildered in their first game; so don't be depressed if you get thoroughly lost the first time you play.'

Prince Charles summed up his initial experience thus:

'At first I found the most difficult thing was where to put myself – and to understand what was going on; what the rights of way were; and all that side of it. It can still, I think, be quite confusing when you are playing.

Everybody begins playing up the front, and I was a forward at number one. Then suddenly I found myself ending up at back; only because I think I have a more defensive outlook, rather than an attacking one. However, I do love playing at number two occasionally, because it gives me a chance to get really stuck into the game.'

Getting 'stuck into the game' proved to be almost an understatement. Apart from the excitements and satisfactions of the game itself, and the many friendships it has brought, polo gives Prince Charles a vital respite from his gruelling summer round of official engagements at home and abroad. He does not take his polo for granted, but he values it enormously.

'I have to squeeze it in. I rush about, and then I dash out to play polo. Then I have to come back for something in the evening, and to do some things in the morning. It is the only way I can survive in the summer. Otherwise the summer would be a total nightmare – there are permanently things happening all the time. If I didn't get the exercise – or have something to take my mind off things – I would go potty.'

OPPOSITE *A Prince in his element: Charles enjoying himself hugely during a brief visit to sample continental polo at Deauville. He played for Guy Wildenstein's Les Diables Bleus in the French polo championships*

4

THE BEAUTIFUL CHESNUT
LADY – AND OTHERS

'He quivered his little flea-bitten withers just to show how satisfied he felt; but his heart was not so light. Ever since he had drifted into India on a troopship, taken, with an old rifle, as part payment for a racing debt, the Maltese Cat had played and preached polo to the Skidars' team on the Skidars' stony polo-ground. Now, a polo pony is like a poet. If he is born with a love for the game he can be made. The Maltese Cat knew that bamboos grew solely in order that polo balls might be turned from their roots, that grain was given to ponies to keep them in hard condition, and that ponies were shod to prevent them slipping on a turn. But, besides all these things, he knew every trick and device of the finest game in the world...'

Rudyard Kipling's classic story, *The Maltese Cat*, describes the crucial role of a polo pony, which had once pulled a vegetable cart in Malta, in an Indian Army polo match in the 1890s.

When Prince Charles describes one of his ponies as 'a Maltese Cat' it is the highest accolade. He is more than aware that pony power is an essential key to success in a game which demands so much acceleration, and the ability to manoeuvre in a flash throughout every chukka.

When the Prince was learning polo as a schoolboy from his father, most of the polo ponies used at the top end of the game in Britain were imported from Argentina.

'In those days a really good pony cost about seven hundred pounds. The price is a problem nowadays.

People say that imported ponies are costing twelve to twenty thousand pounds. I think this is absolutely ludicrous. Some of the breeders abroad are making far too much money. I just don't believe the ponies are worth it in any way. They try to sell you ponies which are too young, for a start. In my experience a polo pony is only really any good when it is about seven years old.'

Although Prince Charles has used imported ponies, he has been fortunate to have his string augmented by ponies home-bred by the Queen. Although called a pony, the animal used in polo is technically a horse. The official limitation of pony size in British equestrianism is 15 hands, and polo ponies usually exceed this.

The original regimental game in India, founded in the mid-nineteenth century, benefited from the availability of cheap, small ponies. It was the annual arrival of not only players but also polo ponies from the Argentine which helped lift the standard of post-war polo in Britain.

Prince Philip has paid tribute to the Argentinians as 'a most powerful factor in the revival, and indeed in the high standard of polo ... they have been the most delightful people to play with, almost without exception, and they have brought a very special character and cosmopolitan atmosphere to the polo seasons. A most directly practical benefit is that they sell all their ponies here at the end of the season.'

South American polo ponies owe much to their origins as the mount of the Gaucho who herded his cattle and fought the indigenous Indians. The original Indian's pony was the Petizo, a small, short-legged cobby type of pony up to 13.2 hands. Then came the Criollo, a cross-bred, owing much to the influence of pure Arabian and Barb stallions brought into South America by the conquering Spaniards.

Polo came to Argentina in the 1880s and the owners of the great grazing farms, or estancias, bred and reared ponies cheaply in excellent conditions, picking the best for polo, and using the others for herding cattle.

Since then the Argentinians have used English Thoroughbred stallions to produce more speed and quality, as well as to give the animal more height. Yearly importations into Britain from the Argentine were taking place before the First World War, and resumed between the wars.

The Falklands War of 1982 caused English polo to cease importations of Argentine polo ponies – and players. (See also Chapter 6) Referred to genially as 'hired assassins' the leading Argentinian players had been a regular feature of the top teams in Britain, as described by Prince Philip.

There was a marked increase in British Thoroughbreds brought out of racing to make up for the shortage of imported ponies. Some were imported from the United States and New Zealand instead of Argentina. By 1985 the trade ban was over, but those who had been breeding successfully at home had benefited considerably.

The Queen began breeding polo ponies, using Thoroughbred stallions, about fifteen years ago. Her Majesty's long experience of bloodstock, and her knowledge of Thoroughbred lines, clearly produced excellent results. The foundation mare of the polo lines bred by the Queen appropriately goes back to a mare bred by Lord Mountbatten. This was a mare named Mayling, foaled in 1944, having been sired by the Thoroughbred stallion Riverdale. The dam was an Argentine polo pony mare, Golondrina.

The dark brown filly, having been bred by Lord Mountbatten, and registered in the National Pony Stud Book, was one of the first polo ponies which he gave to his nephew, Prince Philip.

When Mayling was nineteen years old, in 1963, she produced a brown filly foal called Mayfly. The Queen decided to use the Thoroughbred stallion Doubtless II. Although he was an English Thoroughbred, he had been foaled in the Argentine and imported into this country. Doubtless II proved to be an excellent sire of polo ponies, and such experts as Jack Gannon and Mike Holden-White used him to breed polo ponies.

Mayfly has produced two of Prince Charles's ponies: Mayfair, a grey mare foaled in 1977; and Samphire, also by Sanbal, and foaled in 1979. Mayfly has also produced the gelding Rise, by Rapid Pass, born in 1981, and likely to make a useful hunter or event horse.

Lord Mountbatten, the great polo enthusiast, would indeed have been delighted that his mare, born over forty-two years ago, has begun such a useful line of stock, good enough to be played by the Prince of Wales in modern high-goal polo. Mayling's daughter, Mayfly, lived until she was nineteen, in 1982. It is hoped that her daughter, Mayfair, will continue at stud, after playing polo, to become a highly useful broodmare, producing polo ponies of proven stock.

The other foundation mare used by the Queen was Suerte, an Argentine mare from Eduardo Rojas Lanusse. The chesnut gelding which the mare produced, when put to Doubtless II, was intended for the polo field, but he grew somewhat too large, reaching 16.2 hands. This was indeed a happy outcome for Princess Anne. She was given the chesnut for eventing. He was called Doublet – and was the Princess's partner in winning the individual European Championship at Burghley in 1971.

Breeding polo ponies successfully is far from easy. Finding a suitable stallion is a major difficulty, and it is then vital to have nagsmen skilled and experienced in this specialist area who can break and train polo ponies. One of the main problems is producing small, tough, horses with sufficient speed to excel in the game.

One of the great successes in the Queen's polo breeding venture was the small Thoroughbred stallion, College Green. He was small because he was born a twin, but fortunately he does not sire large stock.

The Crown Equerry, Lt Col Sir John Miller, found College Green living very comfortably in a railway wagon near Scarborough, the property of a local butcher. When Sir John went to see the stallion, a boy jumped up on his back and rode him bareback round a field. Clearly, this was a stallion of equable temperament. His conformation seemed to suit, too; he was purchased for £250 in 1968.

At the grand old age of twenty-four College Green was still thriving – residing on the Queen's Wolferton Stud on the Sandringham estate, and being used as a teaser (the stallion used to prepare a mare for service by another stallion intended for breeding). College Green is by Royal Palm, out of Alkapuri by Panorama. This is a Thoroughbred line bred for sprinting, and illustrates the value of speed in the ancestry of successful polo ponies. Hapanui was the sire of two of Prince Charles's most successful polo ponies, Pan's Folly, bred in 1971, out of the mare Molly's Folly; and Happiness, foaled in 1974, out of the mare Inez.

Prince Charles describes his mare Happiness as 'a total dream'.

'She is the most beautiful chesnut lady there has ever been, I think; a once-in-a-lifetime horse. I don't think I will ever have another pony like her; she is just fantastic. She puts up my handicap by another two goals. I can do anything on her. She is a dream machine ... she obviously loves her polo because she gets in a real lather before a game. I have to play her in the first chukka always because she gets so excited otherwise. And I have to go back into the polo lines to get on to her.

When I first started playing her, she used to stand up and spin round; incredible. Then a year later she

began to improve, and she has proved to be the fastest pony I have had. I can overtake everybody. I just worship that horse.'

Prince Charles's fondness for his polo ponies has become abundantly clear to regular spectators and supporters at Windsor and the other grounds where he plays regularly. He always brings sugar for his ponies, and they soon learn to expect it, and look forward to it. The Prince will spend a great deal of time coaxing a new pony to take the sugar for the first time.

Pan's Folly is an example of the old saying that 'there is nothing a common horse can do, that a Thoroughbred cannot do better'. For this handsome gelding is out of a Thoroughbred, Molly's Folly, sired by the Thoroughbred Royal Hamlet out of Fair Molly. Molly's Folly had won races on the flat and had been bought and broken to play polo by Judy Forwood, who was highly successful at finding and training youngstock for this demanding game. The mare was bought as a suitable pony for Prince Charles in his early seasons in the game, but she has certainly proved her worth as a brood mare since.

Probably the most successful of the polo stallions used by the Queen has been Sanbal, the son of Palestine, who was a sprinter, out of a mare by the Derby winner Tulyar. He is thus bred for speed, with a great deal of quality in his ancestry. This has certainly been well in evidence in his progeny. In 1985 Prince Charles had eight ponies by Sanbal in his stables. Sanbal was in his twenty-first year in 1985, and other stallions were being sought to replenish the stock. Floriana, a mature stallion who has bred a number of polo ponies in the Cowdray district, has been used.

Among the mares used in breeding polo ponies, the most successful has been Inez, one of Prince

Philip's former playing mares; she was a champion in the Argentine before he acquired her.

The importance of the 'bottom line', the mare, cannot be over-stressed in successful breeding. One of the main problems in British non-Thoroughbred breeding is the tendency to put common or unsuitable mares to first-class stallions.

The Queen has avoided this by choosing excellent mares, usually with an impressive record as playing mares before being retired to stud. Among the mares used in the Queen's polo pony breeding programme have been Carnarita, originally one of Archie David's best playing mares, and Gussie's Love, one of the best mares played by Lord Patrick Beresford. One of Prince Philip's playing mares, Choquita, has been a successful brood mare, being the dam of Orieland Chartreuse, both by College Green. Another was the mare, Betaway, by Ocean Swell out of Cassio.

OPPOSITE *Happiness in action with Prince Charles – 'She is the most beautiful chesnut lady there has ever been'*
RIGHT *With Pan's Folly, a superb example of a Thoroughbred polo pony, by Hapanui out of the mare Molly's Folly, who won races on the Flat before being introduced to polo*

In 1985 Prince Charles played wholly on ponies bred by the Queen when he appeared in the Cartier International Polo Day at Windsor. Producing ponies to play at high-goal level in this way is a remarkable achievement.

Where there are disappointments in polo pony breeding it is sometimes due as much to mistakes in training and breaking as to failings in the aptitude of the animal for the game. Trying to produce an effective high-goal pony is like trying to breed Classic winners for racing – it cannot be done every time. Fortunately, the horses which do not prove suitable for polo often exhibit a surprising versatility.

Prince Charles is himself keen to breed polo ponies at home at Highgrove, and was seeking the Queen's advice in selecting the right stallions.

The achievement in producing polo ponies in this country to take on the best of the imported animals from South America and elsewhere cannot be overstated. Some experienced players in the past would not believe that there could be any comparison between Thoroughbreds and South American-bred ponies.

Prince Charles is one of those who has proved that first-class results can be achieved. One polo expert, who has watched the Prince for many years, says he tends to play more effectively on horses which are not too much 'on the leg' (not long in the leg). Certainly, the more compact, short-legged animal tends to be more manoeuvrable. In the hunting field, too, it is noticeable that the Prince is inclined to look more at home on a horse not much above 16.2 hands, short legged, and with a compact conformation. This is true of many riders of the Prince's height and build. A rider needs to have particularly long legs to make a 17 hands horse, or higher, seem totally under control in the more ambitious realms of horsemanship.

Prince Charles has publicly referred to polo as 'my one extravagance', and it is certainly far more expensive than his hunting. Yet undoubtedly the use, as much as possible, of home-bred horses has cut his costs. As indicated already, he is more than aware of the escalating costs of importing ponies in current conditions.

The economics of polo are more than a little hazy to the outsider, but basically high-goal polo in Britain and elsewhere is a sport sponsored by wealthy individuals. They act as patrons, forming their own teams, for which they buy the ponies and pay all expenses. Ninety per cent of the regular high-goal players making up such teams with the patrons are paid either in expenses or a straightforward cash payment.

It was reckoned at the start of the 1986 season that perhaps only four players with a handicap of four could be called amateurs. Prince Charles is, of course one of them, because he supplies his own ponies and pays his own costs.

As anyone who keeps horses is well aware, VAT and rising labour costs have made a huge impact on horse ownership in recent years. It is nowadays estimated that to keep one racehorse in training costs the owner a minimum of £7000 per annum, not including entrance fees for big races. A hunter kept in a top-class livery stable will cost a basic £55 to £60 per week, plus shoeing and veterinary fees, and a polo pony would be in a similar bracket, Fortunately polo and hunting are highly seasonal sports; the polo pony lives out at grass, with supplementary feed, in the winter months; the hunter lives out in the summer, and needs little or no feed in addition to natural grazing. Training fees, in the full sense, are also absent from a polo pony or a hunter's costs. Stud grooms perform such schooling as is necessary for little or no extra cost.

Both sports are therefore far cheaper than racing where top-class bloodstock is nowadays a commodity market, with individual lots fetching telephone numbers in prices at the annual autumn bloodstock sales at Newmarket, in Kentucky and the West Coast of the United States.

For sixteen years Prince Charles had the services of Roger Oliver, the Queen's stud groom, to supervise the care of his string of polo ponies, comprising ten playing ponies, and a couple of youngsters to bring on.

In recent seasons the Prince's stud groom has been

Raul Correa, born in Argentina, but naturalized British over twelve years ago. He worked for two seasons for Ronnie Ferguson, and married the daughter of the Major's stud groom.

Prince Charles is especially careful about the conditioning of his polo ponies. One problem is that they can easily be too 'well done' – given too much too eat, and watered too frequently.

'I think you can be too nice to them, treat them too much as pets. I don't take much notice of this because I do love them dearly and they have become real friends. But it is essential to keep them at the right level of fitness, and the correct weight. Fortunately Raul Correa is extremely good at stable management. He breaks them for me as well, and he produces ponies for me extremely successfully.

It is most important to avoid polo ponies becoming too sleek and well fed. You can so easily have problems with their legs if they become too heavy in the body.

My ponies are brought in from wintering out at grass at the end of February. Of course they have to be got fit, just like hunters or 'chasers, with plenty of slow work at first, and their food intake has to be carefully planned to adjust to their increasing fitness.

But with polo ponies there is the special task of schooling them for the game. Raoul Carrera is splendid in working on a horse, and changing the bit or the bridle, until he has really brought about a tremendous improvement in its performance. For example Pan's Folly, being a Thoroughbred, loves galloping straight; he is a wonderful galloper. That is splendid, but a polo pony must turn and stop immediately when required. I told Raul that Pan's Folly had been "hanging on a bit", and he got to work on schooling him and changed the bit. The difference made by changing the bit was amazing the next time I played the horse; he was turning all over the place, just when I wanted to do so. The schooling work involves a lot of galloping, then stopping and turning. If it is not carried out correctly, it can do more harm than good.'

A groom for the Prince of Wales adjusts a martingale just before a chukka

Prince Charles sums up his own advice to young players with humorous reference to his own experiences of the joys and frustrations involved in trying to improve yourself in one of the most fiendishly difficult ball games in the world.

'I think if you can find somebody who is prepared to shout at you and give you some hints, that is an enormous help. Otherwise, you can ride around rather aimlessly, and lose the incentive to play properly sometimes. It is important to accept that you won't be brilliant straight away. You will go through phases when the game becomes maddening, or worse. You think, "Hell! I'm not any good at this."

You have got to accept those periods, I think. Try to learn the rules, the rights of way and everything else connected with the game. But there is no substitute for lots of practice, and playing the game. It is confusing to start with. Each stage you go through seems faster than you can manage, and you don't know what is happening. But it comes; it's like flying faster airplanes – you are one hundred yards behind the damn things!

I know that polo players are sometimes criticized by some others in the horse world for over-bitting polo ponies. The problem is that you need something to make your horse stop faster than is normal in any other branch of horsemanship. Fortunately, I have one or two ponies which have remarkable

ABOVE *Discussing tactics with fellow team member, Memo Gracida, the brilliant Mexican ten-goal player*
OPPOSITE *Pan's Folly in action: Prince Charles challenges as Stuart Mackenzie is about to clear the ball in a Towry Law Cup match*

mouths, very light. A great deal of the control in polo should be leg power, not hands. Those who are not so skilled at leg power tend to put far more pressure on the mouth, and after a while the mouth becomes deadened – so the horse is not going to stop anyway. I try very hard, as it were, to "pump" rather than just "yank" a horse in using the reins to stop.'

Prince Charles has obviously changed and adapted his riding style in polo considerably during the past twenty years in the game. He pays warm tribute to the recent influence and advice of Memo Gracida, the brilliant Mexican player with a ten-goal handicap who visited Britain in 1985. Prince Charles clearly works on the sound precept that a horseman never ceases to learn, and unlike some horsemen, who are too inclined to think they 'know it all', the Prince is capable of constructive self-criticism.

'Memo told me the other day, when he was giving me a few hints, that he thought I was sitting too upright, and I ought to get down a bit to get my head over the ball – which is probably true. I think I do sit up too much in the saddle, and I know I tended to do this too much when I was riding in races, but it is something you learn as you go along.'

William Loyd, former polo manager at the Guards Polo Club, who has played with Prince Charles, has paid warm tribute to the Prince's own help to less experienced players:

'As an example to young players, he is a paragon par excellence. He has made time out of a near-impossibly tight schedule to play low-goal polo with some aspiring Army officers. He has played exhibition matches at some of the smaller clubs, Kirtlington, Ham, Rutland, Scotland. He is philosophical in defeat (never bad tempered), and generous in victory; and on the polo ground he expects no preferential treatment – and gives as good as he gets.

'Diables Bleus' team captain, Julian Hipwood, gives controlled "rockets" to all team members when he thinks that they deserve them. It is no different with Prince Charles, except that Julian always ends the rockets to him with "Sir!"'

As we shall see, Prince Charles's early years in polo were to give him a full taste of the disappointments as well as the rewards of the game. Always his play was conducted in the glare of the media, who were mainly far more interested in looking for a 'story' than in accurately reflecting a young man's progress or setbacks in a highly competitive game.

Polo was always to be fun for Prince Charles – but it also proved to be one more testing ground in public for the resilience and resolution of a modern Prince of Wales.

5

FROM A CASUAL PLAYER – INTO A POLO PLAYER

*The captain can better criticize the play of his team by holding
a friendly post mortem after the game than by shouting at them and rattling them
when their attention should be on what they are doing.*

LORD MOUNTBATTEN OF BURMA
(An Introduction to Polo by Marco)

As a fifteen-year-old, Prince Charles was already well used to the demands of polo on and off the field. Both he and Princess Anne were given plenty to do in assisting Prince Philip in his arduous role as a five handicap player.

One of the many delights of polo is that novices can play in teams with far more skilled players in low and medium goal matches. In April 1964, Prince Charles was seen playing in practice matches on the Guards Club grounds at Smith's Lawn in Windsor Great Park. In the mid-summer school holiday he began to play in matches at Smith's Lawn, usually in a team captained by Prince Philip.

Some of the great pre-war players were still active in the game. Prince Charles recalls that he was never short of encouragement and friendly advice. Among those experienced stalwarts of the game was Colonel Humphrey Guinness, who had played in every international match at Hurlingham in the 1930s, and played with an Army team in the Berlin Olympic Games. They won the silver medal and marched past Adolf Hitler carrying umbrellas – and not giving the Nazi salute.

Fatherly advice for the seventeen-year-old Prince between chukkas at Windsor. Prince Charles was playing for Rangers against Chiesman's in the Chairman's Cup

Humphrey Guinness died in February 1986, aged eighty-three.

It is a great pity that polo has not been an Olympic sport in the postwar years. Prince Philip would almost certainly have been a member of our Olympic team in the 1960s, with the Prince of Wales as a contender in the eighties.

Prince Charles especially remembers 'a wonderful old boy called Archie David who had helped my father in starting the Windsor club after the war. He used to ride around playing chukkas at the age of seventy. Archie was a tiny figure on top of a horse, bouncing around, and my vivid memory when I started playing was everybody shouting, "Get out of the way, Archie!" Dear Archie used to come up to me after a game, and would invariably say, "Well, my boy. If you ever want any advice you always know you can come to me."'

In April 1965 Prince Charles rode in what was described as a 'gentle steeplechase' around Windsor Great Park, with Princess Anne and a group of friends, but the delights of cross-country riding were not to attract him for some years. Polo was the priority where horsemanship was concerned for the sixteen-year-old Prince.

In August that year Prince Charles played for a team called the Rangers in an American Tournament (a shortened form of tournament) at Smith's Lawn. His grown-up team mates were Lt Cdr Robert de Pass, John Cavanagh, Lt Col Alec Harper, and J. T. G. Withycombe. They played a team called Blacknest with a distinguished composition: Earl Rocksavage, Capt John Macdonald-Buchanan (later Senior Steward of the Jockey Club), Colonel Gerard Leigh (for many years Chairman of the Guards Polo Club) and J. W. M. Maunder.

Rangers won – and Prince Charles scored twice in their 7–3 victory. Playing at number one Prince Charles definitely 'showed promise' reported *Horse and Hound*'s delighted polo correspondent, Emma Pert, wife of the Guards Polo Club Manager, General Claude Pert. Her verdict was that Prince Charles 'has inherited his father's good eye for the ball – an essential quality for a polo player – and from his mother he has acquired sensitive hands which enabled him to establish a rapport with three very different ponies, namely the lovely looking liver chesnut Khyber, from Pakistan, Judy Forwood's grey Molly's Folly, and John Cavanagh's bay, Orgullosa (the Proud One) from the Argentine.'

The taste of triumph ... with champagne spilt on his polo shirt, Prince Charles and the Junior County Cup, won by his team from Windsor on the Cheshire Polo Ground in August 1967. The Prince scored the winning goal to wrest the Cup from the holders, Cowdray Park

At the end of the 1965 season the Prince was given a minus one handicap by the Hurlingham Polo Association. He left for Australia at the end of January 1966, aged seventeen. As has already been remarked, his schooling at Geelong included plenty of strenuous outdoor activities far removed from the polo field, but he did find time to play at the Yarna Glyn-Lilydale Club at Coldstream, near Melbourne, and the Australians were 'surprised at his prowess', more than an accolade when applied to a visiting 'Pom', even a royal one.

Prince Charles completed three years at university, leaving Cambridge with a BA honours degree in 1970. It had been a strenuous period in his life, including his investiture as Prince of Wales at Caernarvon Castle in 1969. The summer term before this he had spent at the University College of Wales, Aberystwyth, studying Welsh. As well as the huge pressures of the Investiture ceremony itself, the twenty-year-old Prince had to cope with Welsh Nationalist protests, and the sudden increase in media attention paid to him before, during and after this major milestone in his life. The Investiture had a television audience of some 500 million.

He had made his first public speech, on 10 December 1968, as Chairman of the Countryside in 1970 Conference, in Cardiff; he had attended his first Buckingham Palace garden party; and his emergence into the full glare of international publicity included his first radio interview, with Jack de Manio on Radio 4's *Today* programme in 1969, Interviews on television and with the press followed. Through all the inevitable ballyhoo, and the Nationalist anti-investiture furore, Charles won acceptance throughout Wales. His total sincerity and dedication to the service of others were clear to all, and his attractive personality was a considerable asset in winning the hearts of the vast majority in the Principality.

There had been time for some polo during the Prince's hectic university career, both at Windsor, and as a representative of Trinity College, Cambridge. In April 1967 the Prince experienced his first success in tournament polo. He played in the Windsor Park team with Prince Philip, Gerard

Leigh, and William Loyd. Prince Charles had a fall during the final against the Lowood team, but he remounted swiftly and both he and Prince Philip scored during the match, which concluded with a 6–4 victory. The Queen was watching and was more than pleased to present the Combermere Cup and the individual prizes. Prince Charles received his first polo prize – a car compass. There could hardly have been a happier start to an outstanding polo career. The presentation was held as formally as possible in the circumstances. Prince Philip presented Charles to the Queen, with the remark, 'This is one of my team mates, I believe you know him . . .'

Prince Charles's appearances for Cambridge in their annual match against Oxford were tremendous fun, and valuable experience, but they were not crowned with success. At the end of 1967 the Prince's handicap was raised from minus one to nought. The following June he achieved his half-blue for Cambridge in the sixty-fourth annual match against Oxford played in front of a crowd of over 3000 at Kirtlington Park, home of Alan Budgett, Chairman of the Hurlingham Polo Association. The

ABOVE *The great leveller, as Prince Philip has described the horse. Prince Charles receiving one of a lifetime of hard knocks in polo while he was practising a swing before the junior match at Cheshire in 1967*

BELOW *Early experience in the rough and tumble of polo. As a nineteen-year-old, Prince Charles was playing against experienced adults, often as a member of the Windsor Park team with Prince Philip*

Queen was present to see her son play. At nineteen he was the youngest of the Light Blue team, and was playing at number three. His team mates were A. N. C. Embiricos (Magdalen) at one, P. W. Leatham (Magdalen) at two and P. de Rivaz (Trinity) at back.

It was to be a memorable game. To tremendous applause, Prince Charles opened the scoring in the second chukka. He achieved this with a backhander out of a mêlée in front of the Oxford goal. Cambridge were suffering from mis-hitting, although Prince Charles was making some well-placed passes. Oxford's back, Clive Preston (University College), did a good job in breaking up the Cambridge attacks. Still, it looked like a Cambridge victory, until the Oxford captain, Julian Eeley, at number 3, scored an equalizer in the final minutes of the chukka.

The referees ordained extra time, with a 'sudden death' finish when 'either side scored. The goals were widened – doubled from 8 to 16 yards. After fifty seconds Eeley scored again for Oxford, and it was all over. The Queen presented the cup to Oxford and polo whips to the team members. The Oxford captain was reported afterwards as saying, 'Prince Charles will be a fine player one day, but before he becomes really good he will have to develop a ruthless streak.'

The 1969 Varsity match was played at Woolmer, and again the Queen was in attendance. This time Oxford secured a 4–1 victory. Prince Charles was captain of the Cambridge team the following year, when the match was played on Oxford ground at Kirtlington, with about 5000 people watching. At this stage Cambridge and Oxford had each won thirty-three matches in those played since the first Varsity challenge match at Hurlingham in 1878. Alas for Cambridge, Oxford were a match ahead

at the conclusion of the 1970 encounter. Their 5–0 score did not reflect the run of play, however, and *Horse and Hound* reported it as a 'magnificent' match. Oxford piled on the pressure in the second chukka and Cambridge were forced on to the defence. The Queen and Prince Philip were both watching, and Her Majesty said with a smile as she presented the cup to the Oxford team captain, 'This is the third time I have had to do this ... very well done.'

Even a cursory survey of Prince Charles's commitments as a young man emphasize that if ever a twenty-one-year-old needed and deserved a recreation which afforded him a total escape, it was the Heir to the Throne. Polo continued to offer just such an ideal recreation, and one of his twenty-first birthday presents, on 14 November 1969, which Prince Charles still recalls with special gratitude, was Pecas, a painted (skewbald) polo pony. This was presented by the Royal Warrant Holders Association, the group of traders entitled to use the 'By Appointment' phrase.

LEFT *On the losing side in University polo: playing for Cambridge in the annual match against Oxford at Kirtlington Park in 1968*
RIGHT *Riding Pecas, the skewbald Argentine bred polo pony given to Prince Charles as a twenty-first birthday present in 1969 by the Royal Warrant Holders Association*

He kept up the game as best he could, but there were challenges to be met in his programme of training and discipline. For the next five years he was to serve in the Royal Navy, and in the naval arm of the RAF. He had already won his pilot's licence (Grade A) at Cambridge. He undertook a five-month jet conversion course at Cranwell, and attended the RAF Parachute Training School in Oxfordshire. Prince Charles's first parachute jump was from an Andover 1200 feet above Studland Bay, in Dorset. Some of us in the horse world, who were to worry unduly about the Prince's falls from borrowed horses in strange hunting countries, should perhaps have been more than comforted by the reflection that this was a young man who had been through some of the most strenuous and demanding Services training available anywhere in the world.

Taking hard knocks was all part of the scene in his RAF and Naval years. This was a Prince who had flown Phantoms, Hunters and Provosts, and, as an Acting Sub-Lieutenant at the Royal Naval College, Dartmouth, had studied navigation and seamanship. His naval service included nine months in the guided-missile destroyer *Norfolk*; service as a gunnery officer in the frigate *HMS Minerva*, and in *HMS Jupiter*, another Leander class frigate.

He adored naval flying, and also went to the Royal Marine School at Lympstone for a commando training programme connected with his helicopter pilot's course, which he completed triumphantly in December 1974. This was a particularly hazardous phase in his military career. He served in the aircraft carrier *Hermes* in 845 Naval Air Support Squadron, and had a month's helicopter exercise with the Royal Canadian Forces, which included living under canvas in sub-zero temperatures in New Brunswick. His Service career concluded with ten months in command of the minehunter *HMS Bronington*, from February 1976. The 360 tons *Bronington* patrolled the North Sea locating mines and helping naval divers to dispose of them.

Some of Prince Charles's comments during his Service life certainly put into the context the 'risks' which the press made such a fuss about when he suffered falls on the polo field, and later as an amateur jockey on steeplechase courses. It was all too easily forgotten that he had experienced such ordeals as underwater escape practice in a 100-foot training tank at Gosport, and one emergency landing in a helicopter.

His published remarks included:

'If you're living dangerously, it tends to make you appreciate your life that much more and to really want to live it to its fullest.'

(On his commando training): 'It was very exciting, very rewarding, very stimulating and sometimes bloody terrifying.'

(Of his naval training): 'I have to try that little bit harder, to be as professional as possible, to assimilate all the vast problems rather more quickly.'

Prince Charles certainly took part in other sports, but polo remained his first love throughout his Services career. This was accorded some light-hearted recognition at RAF Cranwell when he went in to bat at number six for the RAF against the Lord's Taverners in a charity cricket match, in July 1971. The 10,000 crowd roared appreciatively when the Prince trotted to the wicket on a chestnut polo pony, carrying a polo stick. However, he dismounted to wield a bat and scored ten before being bowled by the former England star, Ken Barrington. Later Prince Charles bowled out Barrington and stumped Bill Edrich.

The following year Prince Charles appeared before a large crowd on a far more formal polo occasion – playing for Young England on the inaugural International Day at Smith's Lawn, when the major match was England versus America. England lost 6–3, and the younger England side was also to be defeated by Young America. Yet the crowd had seen high-goal polo at its best in the first match, and had much enjoyed seeing the Prince of Wales and his team in a creditable encounter in the later match, even though it was played in teeming rain.

Prince Charles was playing at back, where he

shone, and certainly had a good game, hitting the ball hard and accurately.

He demonstrated his hitting power when he put a 40-yard penalty shot between the posts to give England a 4–3 lead, but the Americans equalized in the last chukka and were then awarded a short penalty which brought them their fifth goal. With his 1972 handicap of two, the Prince was the lowest handicap player in his team, which also comprised Reddy Watt (three), Sandy Harper (four) and Mark Vestey (four).

Prince Charles certainly justified the three handicap which he received for 1973. That season he made his debut in high-goal polo with Mark Vestey's Foxcote team. Mark, brother of Lord (Sam) Vestey was devoted to polo, and one of the most popular figures in the sport. Their Stowell Park team based at Cirencester was tremendously successful in the 1970s. They dominated the high-goal game from 1973, winning three out of four Gold Cups for the English Championships in which they competed at Cowdray.

The brilliant Argentinians Eduardo Moore and Hector Barrantes provided the essential South American high-goal input, but the Vesteys and their English friends in their team maintained a remarkable standard, too. Eddie Moore was selling as many as 100 ponies a season, and he and Barrantes played high-goal polo in Argentina in the winter months before coming to Britain to impress and astonish the natives in the summer months. In 1978 Eddie Moore had his handicap rating raised to the maximum ten by the HPA in the mid-season handicap changes – the first time they had created a ten-goal handicap in this way for thirty-nine years.

Tragically Mark Vestey's riding career was ended in 1984 when a seemingly unexceptional fall in the hunting field with the Heythrop rendered him a paraplegic, confined to a wheelchair. He has fought back against the severe limitation on his life-style with all the courage and panache with which he graced the polo scene as a player.

It can be seen that the high-goal Stowell Park and medium-goal Foxcote teams were both exciting and full of pep. They provided an interesting and colourful stage in Prince Charles's polo career – but he still lacked the intensive coaching which would enable him to be fully at home in the higher levels of the game. This was yet to come from another source – Australia.

In 1973 Stowell Park beat Cowdray Park 8–6½ in the final of the Queen's Cup, and they won the Gold Cup for the English Championship. Foxcote won the Royal Windsor Cup. Prince Charles was not in the Vestey teams during these major triumphs, but the following May he returned to play at Smith's Lawn after a year's absence and played for Stowell Park there in a *Horse and Hound* Cup match against Peter Palumbo's Bucket Hill team. It was an excellent match, and Stowell Park won 9–8½. As well as Mark Vestey, both the formidable Argentinians, Moore and Barrantes, were in the Stowell Park team that day. However, it was Prince Charles, playing at number one who scored his side's winning goal.

There were signs that season that the rarified high-goal play of Stowell Park was more than enough for the twenty-four-year-old Prince, who was in the thick of a hectic Service training schedule. When he appeared for Stowell Park in a Queen's Cup semi-final match against Pimms in 1974, with the latter winning by a resounding 10–2, one experienced polo reporter observed that 'Prince Charles was rather lost in this high-class polo'. However, the Prince played for his Windsor Park side and Bucket Hill that season whenever his hard-pressed time permitted.

The Prince had the assistance from the early 1970s of one of the most dedicated polo players and officials in the English game, Major Ronald Ferguson. He and his family became much better known nationally in 1986 when his daughter, Sarah, was married to Prince Andrew.

A Hampshire landowner, Ferguson served in the Life Guards, and is a former Commander of the Sovereign's Escort of Household Cavalry. He retired from the Army in 1968 to run his estate at Dummer when his father died. A long-standing friend of Prince Philip, he was playing polo with a handicap of five in the early seventies in Lord Brecknock's Pimms team. Ronald Ferguson has

ABOVE *Major Ronald Ferguson, polo manager to the Prince of Wales, and father-in-law of the Duke of York. The Major, seen here as a polo referee, organizes most aspects of the Prince's polo season*

OPPOSITE *Playing for Young England against Young America at Smith's Lawn in 1972, the inaugural year of the annual International Day, organized by Ronald Ferguson. Prince Charles had a good game, playing at back, but his team lost 5–3*

been deeply involved in the postwar revival of the game, and had a vision of polo making giant strides towards ever greater popularity with the general public.

He has contributed much to this through his organization of the International Polo Day at Windsor. High-class polo is mixed with a brand of showmanship which is dignified but which certainly appeals to crowds of around 20,000 and earns regular television coverage. The international matches are preceded by a lavish, tented array of luncheons by the polo grounds where club and private parties enjoy themselves enormously, no matter whether the sun shines or the English summer weather is at its most uncooperative. Rain bucketed down before the matches at the 1985 International Polo Day, but blazer-clad gentlemen and their fashionably dressed ladies strode across the sodden turf in the downpour towards champagne and four-course luncheons with blithe disregard for the weather, many not even bothering to raise umbrellas.

Ronnie Ferguson and his staff are keen to see everyone back in their seats before the black and white striped shirts of the mounted umpires are in the centre of the ground to start the next chukka.

At the end of a match the staff hastily erect rope barriers to form a small square in front of the royal box. Alas, most of the large gang of press photographers present are more interested in candid close-ups of the Royal Family than in the result of the match. They are tactfully kept behind the ropes but their tele-photo lenses are kept trained on the occupants of the royal box. It has long been clear to Fleet Street that the polo ground is a special place to see the Royal Family relaxing in a comparatively informal setting – even if International Polo Day is the least informal of such occasions. The Queen often presents the prizes, and poses with the winning teams and the gigantic silver trophies so popular in high-goal polo. Smaller trophies, and sometimes presents from the sponsor, are presented to the players of the winning and losing teams.

The pretty girls sipping Pimms in the bar, the panama-hatted men languidly strolling in the sunshine, and the delightful picnics in the car park, are

simply adjuncts to a top-class sporting contest.

The hospitality tent of the current sponsor of the 1985 International Polo Day, the international jewellers, Cartier, was exotically adorned with sheer forests of orchids, and pink as well as pale yellow champagne seemed to be keeping up with the weather in its copious outpouring.

On the polo ground, the tall, slim, erect figure of Ronnie Ferguson, equipped with two-way radio transmitter, ensures absolute punctuality, and as much discipline as he can muster from the crowds in the all-ticket open grandstands flanking the royal box, which is more of a private grandstand than a box.

The mounted trumpets and drums of the Household Cavalry strike a note of pomp before the international teams parade, and the national anthems are played. An excited commentary accompanies the play, so that even the least polo orientated spectator cannot fail to know what is going on, and cannot succumb to a doze even on the warmest of these international Sunday afternoons.

Captains of industry, film stars, diplomats, some of the authentic international jet set are among the crowd. Yet there is more than a leavening of the older polo afficionados, who bring with them a tradition dating back to the pre-war Hurlingham polo tournaments. Veteran ex-Army officers and their memsahibs who enjoyed polo in India are to be seen, still savouring the pleasures of the game which was taken for granted as part of their lives.

The largest element in the crowd, however, points to the real progress polo has made since it was dismissed as merely a 'game played by peers on the far side of the ground'. There are a great many at Windsor who have never played the game, and never will, yet who thoroughly enjoy it as a spectacle, and as an afternoon out in beautiful surroundings. The same may be said of the programmes at Cowdray, Cirencester, Ham Common and elsewhere.

The presence of the Queen, Prince Philip and other members of the Royal Family at the International Polo Day obviously does help to attract larger crowds of spectators. Yet the privacy of the royal box is well preserved, and the Queen is clearly present as an enthusiast. The prowess of her husband, and now her eldest son, and her knowledge of the game and the breeding of polo ponies all ensure that nowhere on the ground is closer attention being paid than in the royal box.

Between certain of the chukkas the crowd is invited on to the ground to play a useful role in treading in the divots (clods of earth) raised by the ponies' shoes. Nowadays, such is the size of the crowd that only alternate sides of the ground are invited on to the field of play at one time.

The polo at this level is great entertainment once you understand the rules, know the players, and understand the tactical play. ITV broadcasts an edited version of the International Day. It is not too fanciful to predict that polo could one day be a major television spectacle; it is not long since such minority sports as snooker and bowls were not dreamt of as compelling TV sports programmes; now they draw huge audiences on the box. Polo is the second fastest team game to ice hockey. Its demands in skill, intelligence and toughness are high, and it is unique in its combination of man and horse in a ball game. Much will be owed to Ronnie Ferguson and others who have dedicated themselves to the game if these further frontiers of popularity are achieved by polo.

A great part of the charm of the game, however, lies in polo at club level. Prince Charles clearly enjoyed medium-goal polo and played mainly in this area during the years when his Service commitments, added to royal functions, made the heaviest demands on his time.

Prince Charles was serving with *HMS Jupiter* in 1974 and had to speed from occasional matches back to his ship. While waiting to join *Jupiter* he had managed to squeeze in a game in Singapore after arriving by air. His team lost 5–2, and it was not surprising that his polo made little progress that year.

Jupiter called at New Zealand for the Commonwealth Games, and its other ports of call included the coastlines of Australia, Suva, Samoa, Hawaii, Fiji and California. It was a 46,000-mile round the world trip, and *Jupiter* did not return to Devonport until April. True, this was at the beginning of the polo season, but this was the year the Prince undertook his helicopter and commando training. At the end of the polo season he was accorded a handicap of only two for 1975. Ronnie Ferguson, never one to flannel, said crisply to press enquirers that Prince Charles 'didn't play very often, nor very well' that season.

Prince Charles played medium-goal polo in 1975, and had enjoyable sport with the Bucket Hill team run by Peter Palumbo, an enterprising and highly successful property man. It was an ideal polo outlet for a young Naval officer; the team included others who were extremely busy in other fields, and who had to make the most of their polo when they could make time for it. Tony Devcich, the ebullient New Zealander who is nowadays such a good public address commentator on the game, was the highest handicap player in Bucket Hill, rated at six.

Their principal triumph in the 1975 season was during the delightful Goodwood tournament at

With the Queen, and the Crown Equerry, Lt Col Sir John Miller, at Smith's Lawn in 1975

Cowdray Park in August. When the weather consents to live up to Glorious Goodwood standards this is a real strawberries-and-cream-in-the-sunshine polo occasion on Lord Cowdray's beautiful Sussex estate.

The Bucket Hill team, with Prince Charles at number two, distinguished themselves by capturing the medium-goal Harrison Cup during the tournament. Prince Charles's polo manager was playing at back for Bucket Hill's opponents, Lea Grange. Prince Charles and Palumbo scored in the first chukka, but bad mistakes by Bucket Hill cost them three goals from penalties in the next two chukkas. Fortunately Devcich regained Bucket Hill's lead in the closing stages, and a goal from Peter Palumbo clinched his team's narrow $5\frac{1}{2}$ victory. Prince Charles, delighted with the result,

readily conceded afterwards at the presentations, 'We were very lucky.'

Prince Charles's best game in 1975 was probably for his Windsor Park side against the American Patricians during the Guards Club's famous Ascot Week tournament. The Prince played at number two, with J. E. D. Browne (nought) at number one, Tony Devcich, number three and Ronnie Ferguson (five) at back. Windsor Park were winners by 5–4.

It was a rousing match, and on this occasion the Prince excelled in a forward position. Although his team lost, his participation in a Royal Navy side against the Blues and Royals at Tidworth caused much pleasure among old naval polo hands – not least his 'Uncle Marco Polo'. On this occasion Lord Mountbatten had to hand the trophy in the final of the 'Captains and Subalterns' to the Army team, who

The 1977 season was to be crucial in Prince Charles's progress in the game. He gives much of the credit to the Australian player, Sinclair Hill, who coached him. Hill, a wealthy farmer from New South Wales, is a flamboyant figure and a superlative instructor. He has been described as having 'arms like tree trunks and a voice to match'.

A former ten-goal handicap player, Hill had all the technical skills necessary to succeed in the game at the highest levels. Best of all he possesses the ability to communicate effectively with young players. He proved to be a brilliant choice as a new mentor for Prince Charles.

Ronnie Ferguson says, 'Sinclair, being a fairly abrasive, down-to-earth gentleman from Australia, cut out all the waffle and made Prince Charles correct all his shots, and get much more aggression into his play. Sinclair unquestionably turned him from a casual player, into a polo player.'

Prince Charles's own memory of his coaching influence from the Antipodes is even warmer:

'Sinclair Hill was the greatest influence in my entire time playing polo. He was absolutely fantastic, and revolutionized my whole approach to the game.

He made me think about what I was doing, or wasn't doing, and he was the best instructor and encourager I have ever come across. He has a great gift for instruction. I am one of those people who believes in listening to what the instructor says, and trying to reproduce this exactly. I think Sinclair Hill found it quite encouraging to teach me, because I really tried to put into practice what he said.

I wanted to impress him, and to show him what I could do. Although I am not in the same league, I think it is the same for top-class tennis players; they all rely terribly on their coaches. You need someone to say, "Come on, you silly clot!" or, "You can damn well do it!" "Get out there and show them!"'

Sinclair Hill was not shy of bawling across the ground to his royal pupil. He was once heard to shout, 'Sir! If you had played a backhand shot on that ball, there would have been no whistle. You played a forehand shot and you got the whistle!'

won 5–1, but Prince Charles and his team mates were described as 'the best young Naval side in the contest for many years'. Prince Charles recalls that 'the Navy have bad ponies – whereas the Army are always better mounted and generally have more time to play.'

Months at sea, and hectic training commitments in the air, made both 1975 and 1976 comparatively barren of major polo experience. Having relinquished the command of *Bronington* at the end of 1976 and returned to civilian life, the Prince was at last able to provide continuity in his practice and play, although his heavy round of royal engagements ensured that he was always pressed to get anywhere near as much practice time as his contemporaries.

OPPOSITE The tough Australian player Sinclair Hill: 'the greatest influence in my entire time playing polo,' says Prince Charles

BELOW In 1977, the year he began playing for Les Diables Bleus, the Prince had a handicap of two, but was widening his polo experience. He displays balance and concentration here, in going for the ball during a match at Smith's Lawn

Yet if he was forthright and abrasive by English standards, Hill was – as Prince Charles recalls – a great supporter. He told the press: 'Prince Charles is fearless, has great positional sense, and a technique that is almost without fault. I am confident that within two years I can turn him into a six handicap player, and that he will be captain of the England team.'

Perhaps the Australian did not take into account the huge toll on his pupil's time that royal engage-

ments all over the world would be taking in the years ahead, and his forecast as to the Prince's fortunes was over-optimistic. Yet immediate, major improvements in his play were apparent when the Sinclair Hill 'treatment' was well under way. According to Willie Loyd, then manager at Smith's Lawn: 'In 1978 playing at back for Windsor Park (medium goal) Prince Charles had the tendency to try to dribble the ball round in defence, rather than giving it a crisp backhander. Hill put that right, and again during the following season corrected his timing and swing so that he got some strength into his shots.'

By 1981 Loyd commented that 'both in high-goal and medium-goal polo Prince Charles has been moved up to number 2 position where his controlled aggressiveness and powerful forehand shots stand both teams in good stead.'

Ronnie Ferguson says Sinclair Hill was a 'great believer that when you are young you have got to play up the front. When you are older you can go back.' Prince Charles played at back soon after Sinclair Hill ceased coaching him, but has varied this with useful play in the number two forward position.

Sinclair Hill was described by the eminent polo writer Sir Andrew Horsbrugh-Porter (who died in February 1986, aged 78) as: 'about the best number three in the Commonwealth. He plays orthodox polo and will put the ball up to his number one.'

In 1977 Prince Charles played with Sinclair Hill in the Golden Eagles team, one of four high-goal teams based at Windsor that season. Golden Eagles was sponsored by the pleasure-loving Argentinian, Luis Sosa Basualdo, who was then married to Lord Cowdray's daughter, Lucy. Basualdo earned from Hosbrugh-Porter an assessment as 'one of the most improved players in recent years, with great quality if not quantity in his team's stud of polo ponies...'

The Prince's game was improving markedly throughout 1977, and his handicap was sure to be raised for the following season. In June he formed his own Prince of Wales IV to play a Major General's IV. The match was in celebration of the Guards Club's twenty-first birthday. The Prince was described as having 'seldom played better', and scored four of his team's goals to secure a 5–3 victory.

A major trophy just eluded Golden Eagles that month when they were beaten in a memorable match 8–6½ for the Warwickshire Cup at Cowdray Park. It was played in a steady downpour, and Horsbrugh-Porter reported, 'I cannot remember a game played in such heavy rain, and I raise my hat to the tough young men who insisted on performing in such conditions...'

Prince Charles's 'civilian' role in 1977 meant an increase in personal royal visits overseas. He went to Ghana and the Ivory Coast in March, and later in the year visited Canada – inevitably being installed as a Red Indian Chieftain in Alberta. He returned from Canada in July just in time to play in the full glare of public attention at the International Polo Day on Smith's Lawn. It was Silver Jubilee Year, and all things royal were receiving even more attention than usual from the media. The Queen and Prince Philip attended the International Polo Day, and there was probably the largest photographic press group so far seen on this increasingly popular sporting occasion.

Unfortunately this was not to be England's year. The senior team was beaten by a strong South American side 7–6, and Prince Charles's Young England team succumbed to a French opposing four by 5–4.

There was some doubt as to whether it was wise for Prince Charles to play at number two instead of number one. The total French handicap, fifteen, was two more than the England aggregate, and this was perhaps reflected in the result. Nevertheless, had Charles been at number two his power as a big hitter, and his large Thoroughbred ponies, might have been effective in knocking the Argentine player Aguerro off his stride. Aguerro, with a four handicap, was the French team's most effective player.

One expert comment on both the senior and younger team games was that there was a 'phenomenal amount of whistle', and the verdict was that this was not the fault of modern umpiring: it was the 'modern player' who was to blame.

6

HIGH GOAL

*Hot, tired and frequently hurting, you make your way back to
the pony lines, thank the grooms, pat the ponies which did well and make friends
again with the ponies who did not. Then for a shower, a change and,
almost the best moment of all, a cooling and refreshing drink with friends
and kindred spirits to whom polo is not just a game but
the greatest game of all.*

THE DUKE OF EDINBURGH
(Men, Machines and Sacred Cows)

The major change in Prince Charles's polo in 1977
and 1978 was the beginning of his long and happy
association with Guy Wildenstein's 'Blue Devils'
team, concluding at the end of 1986. The team's
patron is the son of France's famous racehorse
owner, the distinguished art dealer, Daniel Wildenstein. Guy Wildenstein is himself a leading figure
in the art world, with business connections and
homes in France, England and the United States. He
is editor of his own art magazine, *La Gazette des
Beaux Arts*. A keen Anglophile, Guy bases his polo
team at Cowdray and brings it to Windsor to play
in sponsored games when appropriate. Playing for
Les Diables Bleus has also meant a long-term association with one of England's leading polo personalities, Julian Hipwood, currently rated with a
nine handicap.

In 1977 Prince Charles undertook the first of only
two foreign trips made in his lifetime solely to play
polo, visiting Deauville to play for Les Diables Bleus
in the French polo championship. It was to be an
enjoyable glimpse of the chic of continental polo.
Other high-goal polo players are quite frequently
able to accept invitations to sample the delights of
Deauville, and such other plush settings for the
game as Sotogrande in Southern Spain. Swimming,

picnics, parties, dances and barbecues fit in well
with the summer tournaments at these polo play-
grounds – and they do receive far more of that
ingredient which has mixed well with the game ever
since it was born: long days of bright sunshine.

Before the start of the 1978 season, Prince Charles
visited Brazil for the first time. The social side was
hectic and colourful. In Rio a special carnival was
staged for him and the world's press printed photographs of the Prince dancing with an uninhibited
young Brazilian lady in an exotic costume clearly
designed for wear in a warm climate. Fortunately
the trip did afford Prince Charles the opportunity
to taste polo in the South American setting where
so many of the best players and polo ponies have
been nurtured.

The Prince was in Australia briefly in May 1978
to attend the funeral of Sir Robert Menzies. It
was noted on Prince Charles's return that he and
Sinclair Hill appeared 'to be suffering from jet lag'
when they played for Windsor Park against
Sladmore. The latter were victors by no less than
$12\frac{1}{2}$–3!

That year the Prince began to get nearer his great
ambitions in polo, which continued to elude him up
to the 1986 season: winning the Queen's Cup at

Windsor, and the Gold Cup for the English Championship at Cowdray.

'I long to win them,' he told friends. And he once remarked in a television interview that 'I hope to play polo until I'm 50. I shall go on as long as I bounce when I fall off – which I think I still do.' There are clearly still plenty of opportunities to achieve these ambitions.

He was a member of the Les Diables Bleus team when they beat Galen Weston's Roundwood Park team 5–4½ in the quarter final of the Queen's Cup. Alas, in the semi-final Wildenstein's team met the Vestey brothers' Stowell Park at the top of their form, and the latter were 7–6 winners. Les Diables Bleus also came up against the formidable Stowell Park in the final of the Warwickshire Cup, played on the delightful Ivy Lodge ground at Cirencester. Prince Charles played at number one, with the eight handicap Argentine player Geurrico at number two, Julian Hipwood number three, and Guy Wildenstein at back. This was indeed an impressive combination, but so was the Stowell Park line-up: one, Lord Patrick Beresford; two, Mark Vestey; three, Eduardo Moore, and back, Hector Barrantes. It proved to be an excellent match, with Stowell Park prevailing by the odd goal, 7–6. Les Diables Bleus had their revenge over Roundwood Park when they met them during the British Open Championship tournament for the Gold Cup at Cowdray. Prince Charles played at number one and scored the winning goal for his team in a 9–8 victory.

The Wildenstein team next met Cowdray Park in the tournament, and a ferocious six chukka game ensued. It had to go to extra time, with the goals widened in the eighth period. Cowdray Park emerged 6–5 winners, but went on to suffer an 8–7 defeat by Stowell Park in the final. The British Open Championship started in 1956, with teams limited to a total handicap of twenty-two, and it is played on a league system allowing each to play at least four games.

The International Day in July at the Guards Polo Club ground at Smith's Lawn proved to be a triumph for Prince Charles and his team mates in the 'The Commonwealth' team. They beat an England

II side 5–3 in an exciting match which thrilled a large crowd, who needed some consolation after seeing England's first team trounced 10–5 by South America for the Wills sponsored Coronation Cup.

Prince Charles played at number one, with Tony Devcich at two; Sinclair Hill, three, and Ahmadu Yakubu, from Nigeria, as back. It was indeed a team which fitted its title, which is more than can be said for many a polo side. Playing for England II were Reddy Watt at one; John Horswell, two; Patrick Churchward three, and Ronnie Ferguson as back.

Devcich hit three early goals, and Prince Charles scored in the third chukka, and hit the winning goal in the final period. The Queen has never looked happier at a presentation than when handing over the handsome Silver Jubilee Trophy to her eldest son. Yakubu was praised as one of the most effective players on the ground. His own team, Songhai, was to meet Les Diables Bleus in dramatic circumstances the following season.

If 1978 had been a year of progress for Prince Charles, the following season could be described as his best to date. The immense improvement in his play wrought by the Sinclair Hill coaching was flowering remarkably. At Windsor he had some excellent matches with Bucket Hill. They reached the semi-final of the Royal Windsor Horse Show Cup in May. Later that month the Prince was playing for Bucket Hill when they won the Alitalia Trophy, beating the Ham Club's team, Travelwise Tortuga, by 7–6. Bucket Hill also secured the Lex Mead Trophy at Windsor.

The highlight of Prince Charles's season occurred at Cowdray Park where Les Diables Bleus reached the final of the British Open Championship. After hard-fought matches, Les Diables Bleus topped their league and they had every reason to be confident of success in the final where they were to meet the Songhai team, whose patron was Ahmadu Yakubu, who had played so effectively with Prince Charles in 'The Commonwealth' team the previous summer.

Ironically, Yakubu, who had learned his polo in Nigeria, could not play in the Gold Cup because he was suffering from an earlier polo injury. However, his distinguished twenty-two handicap team did not let him down. They comprised: one, Alan Kent (five); two, Alphonso Pieres (five); three, Gonzalo Pieres (eight); back, Oliver Ellis (four).

Julian Hipwood was suffering from a strained arm muscle, robbing him of full powers, but the distinguished eight goal player did appear for Les Diables Bleus at number three. Guy Wildenstein (three) was number one, with Memo Gracida (seven) at two, and Prince Charles (three) was the back. Alas, the lesser handicap total of twenty-one attached to Les Diables Bleus was reflected in the run of play, and the result. Gonzalo Pieres proved to be the best player on the ground. It might have been a closer final if Hipwood had been sound.

According to *Horse and Hound*: 'The Prince of Wales played a capital game at back, sound in defence and hitting well-placed backhanders. He was also quick into the attack when the opportunity offered. He is very well mounted and his ponies are beautifully produced by a notable stud groom who learnt her trade with Gerald Balding.' Songhai were 6–4 winners to capture the Gold Cup, but it had been a most worthwhile achievement for Les Diables Bleus, and valuable experience for Prince Charles.

The International Day at Windsor in July, sponsored by Imperial Tobacco in 1979, was a satisfying occasion for the Prince. England's first team beat Mexico 9–7, and Prince Charles and the England II side conquered a French side 5–2. Alan Kent, Patrick Churchward and Ronnie Ferguson completed the England II team, with the Prince at back. He thoroughly earned *Horse and Hound*'s assessment: 'Undoubtedly the most improved player on the side was Prince Charles. He was hitting his backhander accurately and with great length, and he held the French number one in check – coming through to score the first goal of the match, and hitting a long pass up for Ferguson to score in the closing stages of the game.'

On 29 July Prince Charles played in a match which must count for an immense amount in his personal sporting memories, since he received the winner's trophy from Lord Mountbatten. No one

Receiving a polo award from Lord Mountbatten in July, 1979. On 27 August Mountbatten was assassinated by the IRA, when his boat was blown up near his Irish home, Classiebawn

could have been more proud and delighted than 'Uncle Marco Polo' when the Prince of Wales scored all four goals for his Naval team to beat the Army team 4–2 at Tidworth that day. Lord Mountbatten duly handed the Rundle Cup to his great-nephew, who was fast improving in the game which the former First Sea Lord had relished for most of his life. It was only twenty-five days later that Lord Mountbatten's distinguished life was to end tragically, murdered by the IRA when they blew up his boat at Mullaghmore, near his Irish home, Classiebawn.

Prince Charles had undertaken a lengthy overseas tour in March and April to Hong Kong, Singapore, Australia and Canada. He ended the year with a major visit to India and Nepal. His thirtieth birthday was celebrated on 14 November. The Prince of Wales ended the 1970s with an extraordinary range of experiences undertaken with immense resilience and energy: a great many challenges overcome.

In his recreational life, no less than in his official capacity, Prince Charles was well aware that the media's thirst for 'news' would inevitably focus on anything that went wrong. As he once smilingly told an assembly of Fleet Street editors and proprietors, 'Regrettably it does not make news to know that fifty Jumbo jets landed safely at London airport yesterday, but it does make news if one doesn't. I still believe, however, in the necessity every now and then of reminding people, metaphorically, that vast numbers of Jumbos *do* land safely – for the simple reason that we are all human and the maintenance of our morale needs careful consideration.'

Many of the photographs of the Prince on the polo field published in the press are anything but morale raising. During the summer months, the general public is given the impression that Prince Charles is constantly suffering heavy falls on the polo ground. The fact is that it is a tough game, and any player receiving the same volume of personal publicity would sometimes be pictured taking a spectacular tumble. Ronnie Ferguson says that overall 'Prince Charles has had remarkably few falls, but I truthfully admit that I am always relieved when the final whistle goes, because one always hopes – like anyone else – that if he has a fall it is not going to be a dramatic one.'

Polo players wear more sensible headgear than is sported in many other equestrian sports. One reason is that most patterns of polo helmet have a solid brim right round the head. This is invaluable in limiting the chance of a lateral blow to the side of the head where the skull is thinner. Ronnie Ferguson thinks 'the classic Prince Philip pattern Lock hat is as solid and as good as you are likely to get.' (Lock's are the famous hatters of St James's, founded in 1676).

Prince Charles in recent seasons has taken to wearing a safety mask with his helmet, which protects the face to some extent from blows from the ball or another player's polo stick. A polo ball can be travelling at 100 miles per hour, and a fall on the flat at speed can so easily involve a blow from a horse's feet, as well as the head striking the ground.

Polo ponies suffer knocks, too, but are seldom seriously hurt. Prince Charles was desperately upset when the six-year-old bay mare Norena fractured a hip joint making a sharp turn during a Gold Cup match at Cowdray Park on 14 July 1978, and had to be put down.

Horses are amazing in their strength and durability, yet paradoxically they are even more astonishing in their sudden fragility. All horsemen are bound to experience the agonizing loss of a partner and friend, but the shock of such a loss is always acute. Princess Anne suffered this when her marvellous European Championship winning horse Doublet had to be put down after he suddenly fractured a hind leg while she was exercising him at Smith's Lawn. The Princess described it later as 'quite the most ghastly experience of my entire life'. Prince Charles was later to suffer a similar loss with his first steeplechaser. Fortunately, such experiences are far outweighed in a horseman's career by the happy partnerships between mount and man.

At the end of the 1979 season Prince Charles wore his polo kit on one of the most amusing riding contests he has undertaken in public. He appeared at the Christmas international horse show at Olympia in December to compete in a celebrity show jumping class held in aid of the British fund to send our equestrian teams to the Olympic Games in Moscow the following summer. (Owing to the Afghanistan invasion by Russia, the British equestrian teams eventually declined to attend.)

Prince Charles displayed his accomplished horsemanship by accepting a ride on a top-class show jumper, no mean feat for a non-show jumping rider – and under the close scrutiny of BBC television cameras. He rode Sportsman, the brown gelding which has won many leading classes with former World Champion David Broome. Also in the team with Princes Charles were Broome, his sister Liz Edgar, Eddie Macken, the late Caroline Bradley and, from the polo world, Ronnie Ferguson, Paul Withers and Johnny Kidd.

Prince Charles acquitted himself well in the unfamiliar setting of the floodlit ring at Olympia, where the Royal International Horse Show had been born at the start of the century under the superb, arched roof of glass and metal girders.

For the Olympia crowd, and the huge TV audience, the major novelty came when the Prince of

Ready for anything – with camels: the sporting Prince delights the crowd by appearing in a camel race at the Olympia International Show Jumping Championships in London in 1979, to help raise money for Britain's equestrian teams competing in the Olympics the following year

Wales consented to take part in the camel race in the main ring. This was a slightly controversial attraction, since one well-known actress received damages for injuries received in the races which were played for comedy up to the hilt – and beyond. The Falstaffian figure of show jumper Ted Edgar presided, and he and his friends added to the mayhem by judicious misuse of brooms and ladders in ensuring that ascent on the the camels' backs was as difficult as possible for the celebrities rash enough to compete. Prince Charles did at least manage to sit astride Chipperfield Circus's camel Rosie, facing in the right direction – a privilege denied to all too many other riders – and he finished third, behind the flat jockey Willie Carson and polo player Johnny Kidd.

Early in 1980 Prince Charles endured what was probably his most dangerous polo experience – but it was not due to an incident during a game. He had visited Canada in April and flew down to Florida for a short polo visit on his way to a holiday in the Bahamas. Ronnie Ferguson was awaiting the Prince at the Palm Beach Polo and Country Club at West Palm Beach, which describes itself as the 'winter polo headquarters of the world'. The morning after his arrival, the Prince went on to the polo grounds to select six suitable horses from nine which Major Ferguson had ready for him.

It was already a very hot day, a sharp contrast to the conditions Prince Charles had experienced in Canada. After some practice play on these ponies the Prince returned to the Club and sat in the sun talking to his American hosts and friends. Alas, he overlooked the necessity to drink extra fluids and take salt tablets. By the time play began, the temperature had risen to 80 degrees, with about 95 per cent humidity. Afterwards, when Prince Charles returned to his apartment about two miles away, he collapsed with heat exhaustion and dehydration. Ronnie Ferguson and an aide quickly realized that the Prince was very ill. They summoned a doctor who ordered the Prince's immediate admission to a hospital. So worried was the staff by now that they did not wait for an ambulance. Prince Charles was put into a blue baggage truck, where he lay on a mattress, and was driven at top speed to the Good Samaritan Hospital at West Palm Beach.

State Troopers were called out to clear the road, but they had a difficult task in keeping up with the blue truck carrying the Prince of Wales. At hospital Prince Charles was given a saline drip and other treatment. His strength and resilience was amazing. Next morning he left hospital, and merely said with a smile to the waiting press, 'I'm all right, thank you ... ' However, the lesson was learned. Polo is an exceedingly demanding game, and when Prince Charles played later in the intense sunlight of Brunei's polo grounds he took full precautions against heat stroke.

Prince Charles entered the 1980s with his handicap raised to four. This was a remarkable achievement in itself. There were only twenty-three players with handicaps over four in the 670 players registered with the Hurlingham Polo Association in 1985. A four handicap is indeed high-goal and it takes a great deal of retaining. The other high-goal players in the English game are not only professionals in this country, they also spend their winters playing the game abroad – perhaps in Florida, Brunei, South America or some other hot clime. This is not only lucrative, but it also keeps their game at a high level before they return to the English scene in the spring. Prince Charles may, if he is fortunate, get some polo during an official trip abroad, but he certainly does not benefit from continuous play in the same way as the other high-goal players.

In the 1980 season Prince Charles played at Windsor at medium-goal level for the Pahang team of Prince Mahkota Pahang from Malaysia, and continued with Les Diables Bleus in high-goal matches. Howard Hipwood and Lord Patrick Beresford comprised the Pahang team, with Prince Charles and Prince Mahkota at the 'front end'. They were beaten 5–4 by Los Locos, Claire and Simon Tomlinson's team, in the Royal Windsor Cup contest. However, Pahang did well to win the *Horse and Hound* Cup, with a 5–2 victory over a strong Eaglesfield team, including the eight goal Hector Crotto. Prince Charles suffered a heavy fall in the second chukka but remounted quickly, and scored a goal. Howard Hipwood and Prince Mahkota scored two apiece.

In the high-goal tournaments that season, Stowell Park beat Cowdray 11–4 to win the Queen's Cup; Les Diables Bleus were beaten in the semi-final of the Warwickshire Cup by Cowdray Park and in the Cowdray Gold Cup for the British Open Championship, Stowell Park were the 10–7 winners over Cowdray Park.

Les Diables Bleus finished tenth in the leagues for the Championship, and Alec Harper observed, 'Julian Hipwood played brilliantly for Les Diables Bleus, in spite of an injured knee, and the Prince of Wales was a safe back. Alfonso Pieres did not always appear happy with his horses. On the whole the team did not do quite as well as one would have expected.'

The Prince's prowess in defence was also noted in the International Day at Smith's Lawn when he appeared in the England II side to beat France by 5–3 for the Silver Jubilee Cup. 'Steady as a rock' was one assessment of Prince Charles's play. Lord Charles Beresford (three) the nephew of Lord Patrick Beresford, played number one, with Alan Kent (six) at number two, and Robert Graham (six) at three. Alec Harper criticized the England forwards for 'not riding out the play – that is when behind, instead of galloping on ahead into the shot, they were pulling up to intercept, thereby giving the striker more time to make his shot. It is a modern fashion of doubtful value.'

The presence at polo matches of Prince Charles's fiancée, Lady Diana Spencer, had already caused enormous excitement among the media. All through 1981 there was a running news story about the 'risks' the Prince of Wales would be incurring by playing during the International Polo Day at Smith's Lawn only three days before his marriage at St Paul's Cathedral on 29 July.

He was to play for England II against Spain, and the more excitable newspapers conjured up pictures of the Prince limping up the aisle, or worse not arriving at all, because of a polo injury.

The best answer was given in characteristically terse terms by Major Ronnie Ferguson who was one of the selectors for the England II team, and of course the organizer of the matches: 'I am often asked whether it is right even to consider selecting Prince Charles to play on the International Day so soon before his wedding.

'Now that the selectors have decided to ask him to play, I can honestly say that I feel he is safer playing polo on that day with seven other very experienced players, than he is driving his car back to London on the M4 among many far less experienced drivers.'

Quite so. Nevertheless, the Major must have heaved a discreet sigh of relief when the Fates allowed Prince Charles to complete his international match without a scratch. Before that the Prince had had an extremely active season. The story that the future Princess of Wales was not keen on polo was fuelled by the inordinate attention which her attendance generated throughout 1981, making spectating less than pleasant at times. Nevertheless, Prince Charles pressed on with his full season, and put up some of his best performances in medium- and high-goal games. He played medium-goal for Galen Weston's Maple Leafs, and remained in Wildenstein's Les Diables Bleus, which saw the addition of the six handicap player Robert Graham. For the fourth year the Prince was therefore in a high-goal team aiming for the British Open.

With the impending royal wedding, there was inevitably extra attention being paid to all the Prince's activities. It was therefore especially appreciated when he played in exhibition matches – at the Rutland Club's ground at Oakham, Leicestershire; and at Ham Common, the popular club at Richmond, Surrey. Some of the Prince's many hunting friends in the Shires turned out to watch and to play when he visited the Rutland club. He played for Rutland against the team named Cream Gorse after a famous covert in the Quorn Friday country, and scored a good goal from a 40-yard penalty – but Cream Gorse won 2–1. At Ham he played in a Windsor Park team at medium-goal level against a Ham team with Guy Wildenstein as captain – and the Ham team won by 7–$5\frac{1}{2}$. The result hardly mattered to the appreciative crowd who so much enjoyed seeing the Prince of Wales playing one of the world's great games so expertly on their ground. Les Diables Bleus reached the semi-final of the Queen's Cup, but were beaten 5–4 by Stowell Park. It was reckoned that Wildenstein's team had been very unlucky. Alec Harper observed that Les Diables Bleus had not 'appealed' for infringements at all, whereas their opponents' goals came mostly from free hits which did appear to be the result of successful appealing.

Another *Horse and Hound* Cup victory was achieved in Prince Charles's polo records when he played for Maple Leaf against the Ipanema team from Cowdray Park. The Prince, at number two, was most effective in supporting Galen Weston at number one with accurate long shots. Prince Charles was among the scorers in his team's 6–5 win.

There was a disappointment for Maple Leafs when they reached the final of the Royal Windsor Cup and were beaten by Los Locos $5\frac{1}{2}$–4. This was a particularly good performance by the Tomlinson team. As *Horse and Hound* put it: 'The Tomlinson duo – Claire and Simon – have an uncanny knack of putting together formidable fighting machines in sixteen-goal polo.'

It seemed a good year for Les Diables Bleus in the British Open at Cowdray Park. They were in a commanding position, having beaten Centaurs 7–6, Julian Hipwood having scored the winning goal from a 60-yard penalty in extra time; they also beat Cowdray Park 9–4. However, their ambitions were halted by the Falcons, Alex Ebeid's team, who were on great form and included Hector Merlos, Gonzalo Pieres and Luis Amaya. Les Diables Bleus were leading 5–3 at half time, but the Falcons stormed back in the second half to win 9–8. In the final, Falcons ran rings round Ipanema to trounce them 13–3.

Although well used to the 'eyes of the world', Prince Charles must have been somewhat more aware of the media's gaze at the International Polo Day. The should-he-or-shouldn't-he debate had been nicely hotted up in the preceding few days. The Prince as usual lived up to the best traditions of his inheritance and training, and was not a mite rattled by any extra 'sense of occasion'. With him in the England II side were Robert Graham, captaining at number one, plus Martin Brown and John Horswell.

There *might* have been a little extra aggression in the Prince's play at back. The umpires awarded a '60' to Spain in the second chukka because they considered the Prince had been too rough in a ride-off against a Spanish player! There were more than a few gasps, too, when an English attack ended with a spectacular double fall, but it transpired that the fallers were Horswell and the Spanish back Rafael Echevarieta. Horswell had to leave the field, but returned, with his head bandaged, and led a spirited attack immediately which secured a successful '30'. England's drive resulted in three quick goals at the end to which Spain could only reply once. To huge cheers from the crowd of about 18,000, England II triumphed 10–5. No one was smiling more proudly than the Queen when she presented the Silver Jubilee Trophy to her son's team.

As history relates, the Prince of Wales attended his wedding unscathed by the hazards of polo. His 1981 season was completed; there was the matter of a honeymoon and settling into married life to be fulfilled. The Prince of Wales and his bride were to prove that a successful marriage *can* accommodate a season's polo. Prince Charles and Princess Diana did not comment publicly for some years about reports that Her Royal Highness had dismissed polo as a 'nothing sport'. But in a television interview in 1985 the Princess said firmly, 'I enjoy polo enormously. I mean, I go to as many matches as I can. So the myth about me hating it has really got out of hand.'

The factor which *did* change English polo for the Prince of Wales, and for everyone else in the game, was the Falklands War of 1982. The ban on Argentine polo players in Britain was still in force in 1986, even though the Football Association and the All England Tennis Club had long since lifted their embargo. The high-goal Argentine players had played regularly in Britain throughout the postwar years. Everyone paid tribute to their prowess, their ability to lift the English game, and their influence in importing excellent ponies.

As Alec Harper, Joint Hon Secretary of the HPA put it in 1982, 'There is no way the Argentinians can come here. It is an awkward situation. These chaps are our friends, and it is not their fault – their government has put them in this position.' The Hurlingham Polo Association considered the ban afresh every season after the Falklands War and came up with the same decision. The failure of the Argentine government officially to declare a cessation of hostilities was one key factor, and the presence of Argentine players would be especially embarrassing at the Guards Polo Club. The Prince of Wales is Colonel of the Welsh Guards. Three members of the Club fought in the campaign to recapture the Falklands, and there were many Guards casualties in the South Atlantic war. The solution was a greater role played by New Zealanders, Australians and high-goal players from the United States and South American countries other than the Argentine. Undoubtedly, this did have an impact on the English game. There were fewer high-goal teams, although the economic recession also accentuated this. Yet polo certainly remained more popular than ever, and the 670 registered players in 1985 represented a 6.5 per cent increase on the previous season.

Early in 1982 Prince Charles went to the Rhinefield Club at Brockenhurst, in the New Forest, for the first Mountbatten Memorial Day. Lord Mountbatten's family home, Broadlands, Romsey, is nearby. Prince Charles played for the local Foresters' side in the tournament which was won by Christian Heppe's European Polo Academy side.

Prince Charles and his friends in Les Diables Bleus reached the final of the Queen's Cup at Smith's Lawn that season, but his ambition to win this high-goal tournament was dashed by the team sponsored by the keen American patroness of polo, Mrs Helen Boehm. 'Well played, boys,' she would say encouragingly. Mrs Boehm is invariably described as ebullient, outgoing, and a multi-millionairess. Polo legend says that on one occasion a nought handicap player tried to persuade her to sponsor low-goal polo. The good lady replied, 'My dear, I can't count that small.'

Mrs Boehm's boys on this occasion were Lord Patrick Beresford (three), Howard Hipwood (eight), Stuart Mackenzie (seven) and the Hon Mark Vestey. They beat Les Diables Bleus 11–5. There had been a thunderstorm in the morning, and Julian Hipwood, star of the Blue Devils, is not considered to play his best in heavy going. Robert Graham was suffering minor injuries obtained while playing in South America during the winter. Prince Charles at back played reliably, exhibiting great strength in his backhand.

The British Open for the Cowdray Park Gold Cup was another disappointment for Prince Charles in 1982, but Les Diables Bleus nearly made it, and had much cause for satisfaction in their route to the final. Les Diables Bleus beat Cowdray Park in a particularly exciting match. At half time the Devils were leading 4–3, but Cowdray were one up at 5–3 in the fourth chukka. Prince Charles scored, but

Ready for anything with horses: demonstrating an ability to cope with harness racing after a polo match at Fife in 1983

Cowdray Park responded strongly and the teams started the fifth chukka level at 6–6. A great run up the field by Julian Hipwood, with brilliant approach work, enabled Wildenstein to score a winning goal. This victory entailed winning the Midhurst Town Cup, and the much heartened Wildenstein team went on to beat Falcons in their next Gold Cup match, 5–2. In the final, the Diables came up against David Yeoman's Southfields side, and a desperate struggle ensued. Les Diables Bleus were leading 5–3 at half-time, but Southfield achieved a 6–6 tie by the end of the fifth chukka. In the extra chukka, David Yeoman achieved the necessary 'sudden death' goal to secure a 7–6 victory.

On International Polo Day, 1982, the England first team beat New Zealand 6–4, but England II, with Prince Charles at back, were beaten by a United States II side by 6–5 for the Silver Jubilee Cup. Prince Charles's 1982 season concluded with a welcome victory in the Jaipur Trophy match at Smith's Lawn, against the Pegasus team.

In April 1983 he played before enthusiastic Australian crowds during his highly successful tour with the Princess of Wales. Charles played in the President's team in Sydney's Royal Easter Show tournament. 'Marco Polo's' memory was poignantly alive in Australia, too. Lord Mountbatten was patron of the Windsor (NSW) Polo Club, and had opened its ground. His daughter, Countess Mountbatten, had succeeded as patron. There could have been no more fitting inauguration to the first Earl Mountbatten Memorial Trophy match than the victory by the President's team, including Prince Charles. They were 5–5 against Richard Walker's Gold team at the end of the match, and won on a single goal in extra time.

At the start of the home season, Prince Charles had made a successful start with the Maple Leafs, winning the Gucci Challenge Cup at the Guards Club against Ingwenya 9–4½, and going on to cap-

ture the Towny Low Cup 6–4½ against Heppe's BBs. Prince Charles 'kept the back door well guarded' and went forward to score as well.

Les Diables had another exciting British Open campaign, but despite beating the strong Cowdray Park team, the Prince and his team mates failed to reach the final, which was won by Falcons 8–7 over Centaurs.

The Prince's International Day fixture was for England II against France, with the latter winning by a single goal on the bell in the last chukka, by 7–6. 'Red' Armour scored this goal for the French team by racing down field in a brilliant solo burst just as the final bell sounded for thirty seconds. On the whole it was one of the less inspiring International Day encounters.

Prince Charles's 1984 season was notable for the victory of his Windsor Park team in the medium-goal Royal Windsor Cup, at Smith's Lawn, during the Guards Club's medium-and low-goal week tournaments in June. Les Diables Bleus were unbeaten in three matches in the 1984 British Open, but failed to reach the final, which was won by Southfield.

The 1984 International Polo Day in July, sponsored for the first time by Cartier, was an exceptional success, taking place in bright sunshine before an 18,000 crowd. Prince Charles played for England II against Spain. His team mates were Lucas, Churchward and Horswell, and Spain included the two Domecq brothers.

By 1985 English polo had changed, but had settled down well since the absence of the Argentine players. Les Diables Bleus benefited from the introduction of two great Mexican players – the famous 10 goal Memo Gracida, and Jesus Baez, handicapped at five. Memo, brother of Carlos, was the only ten goal player in the English game that season. As we have seen already, Prince Charles greatly appreciated the opportunity to play with Memo Gracida and has paid tribute to the help and encouragement he has received from the Mexican in the never ending task of polo self-improvement.

In medium-goal, the Prince was still playing with Maple Leaf, and the Galen Weston side won the

---

One of the most demanding games on earth. Prince Charles in one of the bruising encounters called 'riding off', during an appearance for Galen Weston's Maple Leafs team at Windsor in June, 1985

1985 *Horse and Hound* Cup against the visiting American side, Kennelot Stables, 7–4½. Prince Charles put Maple Leafs into the lead with a stylish backhand and scored again in the fourth chukka off a pass from Devcich.

Les Diables Bleus fought their way to the final of the British Open in 1985, beating Los Locos 11–10 in a scintillating game on the way. In the final, however, Wildenstein's team met Maple Leafs, ironically the other team with which Prince Charles is so closely associated. It proved to be one of the narrowest and most hard-fought battles of his polo career.

Les Diables Bleus caught up after being 8–10 down to draw level at the end of the sixth chukka. A seventh chukka was played with neither team scoring. Memo Gracida for the Devils, and Julian Hipwood, this time for Maple Leafs, were doing tremendous work in the centre of the field. Gracida hit the post twice, but did not score. Prince Charles was thoroughly sound in defence and made several good attacking runs. The game went into an eighth chukka, with the goals widened. The excitement at Cowdray Park was tremendous. Was this to be the Prince of Wales's year at last? The vagaries of polo decreed otherwise. There was a 'sudden death' goal for Maple Leafs in the eighth chukka, and it was all over. Galen Weston was accompanied by Tony Devcich, Julian Hipwood and Martin Glue at back. If the horse is a 'great leveller', so is the game of polo itself. This was a tremendous disappointment, but taking the closest of defeats philosophically is an attribute needed in polo as much as in any skilled ball game.

Prince Charles had the satisfaction of a good victory on International Day when his England II side beat a Brazil team 6–5. He played at number one for a change, with John Horswell at two, Robert Graham three, and Lord Charles Beresford at back. One of the pleasantest moments of this Cartier International Day, however, was surely the presentation to the 'best pony'. The choice was Prince Charles's favourite, Pan's Folly. It was hard to judge whether there was more satisfaction at the award from the rider, or the breeder.

To some Prince Charles's 1986 season seemed in jeopardy before it had begun. While planting a tree in the grounds of Highgrove he struck the index finger of his left hand a heavy blow with a hammer. The end of the finger was badly injured, and for some time the Prince appeared afterwards with his left arm in a sling.

Fortunately, his usual resilience enabled Prince Charles to make a remarkably quick recovery, and he overcame the possible disability quietly and without fuss. The 1986 season proved to be the most successful in his polo career. Les Diables Bleus captured the Queen's Cup, giving Prince Charles the high-goal tournament victory he had longed to achieve for many years. In the same team he also reached the last stages of the British Open Championship, but Les Diables Bleus did not qualify for the final in which Anthony Embiricos's Tramontana team beat Cowdray Park 11–4 to win the Gold Cup.

However, Wildenstein and his 'devils' did win the subsidiary Davidoff Trophy in the tournament by beating Los Locos 13–11. It was a happy note for Les Diables Bleus to finish their twentieth and final season in England. Wildenstein wanted to spend more time with his young family, and had made his home in America where he intended to play in the 1987 season.

The victory of Les Diables Bleus in the Queen's Cup was described by William Loyd in *Horse and Hound* as 'the most exciting finals day in the history of the high-goal tournament.' Their opponents were Tramontana, who had been runners-up the previous year. They were an exceptionally strong side: Anthony Embiricos had only a two handicap, but his team was completed by the Mexican 'Chuey' Baez with a handicap of six, the ten-goal-handicapped Carlos Gracida, and Martin Brown at back who was considered under-handicapped at four.

A four-goal handicap player, with years of experience in the high goal game, the Prince of Wales still finds victory rewarding . . . and he values the game immensely as a form of recreation. 'If I didn't get the exercise, or have something to take my mind off things, I would go potty . . .'

The combination play between Gracida and Brown, who had played together in Florida in the winter, was an especially effective weapon.

The other ten-goal Gracida, brother Memo, was a major instrument in the eventual success of Les Diables Bleus. He was playing at number three; Wildenstein was number one, Rodrigo Vial was the other forward, and Prince Charles was the back. Tramontana dominated much of the early play, and were leading 7–4 by the end of the fourth chukka. Les Diables Bleus rallied remarkably in the next chukka, but could not score. Then in the sixth chukka Memo Gracida played magnificently to score three quick goals in succession.

Tramontana fought back but to no avail. Extra time was allowed, and in the first minute of this period Guy Wildenstein scored the winning goal. The excitement on the ground was tremendous. Prince Charles was resolute in defence as Tramontana strove desperately to draw level again, and there were to be no more goals.

Les Diables Bleus were winners by 9–8, and they received the Queen's Cup from Miss Sarah Ferguson, accompanied by her fiancé, Prince Andrew. The tournament, sponsored by Alfred Dunhill, had indeed provided a magnificent climax for Prince Charles's long and happy career as a Blue Devil.

In a particularly enjoyable season, Prince Charles had the pleasure of playing for the Royal Navy at Tidworth when they beat the Army for the Rundle Cup by 3–2. Prince Charles played at number three, and took the Navy into the lead by scoring from a penalty. He played yet again for England II during the 1986 Cartier International Day at Smith's Lawn, but they were beaten 5–3 by Chile for the Silver Jubilee Cup, after the senior England team had been decisively trounced 8–4 by Mexico.

At the end of the season Prince Charles brought enormous pleasure to his hunting friends in Leicestershire by visiting Oakham to play in the Rutland Polo Club Special Invitation Match. He played for the Quorn team which was narrowly beaten for the Colonel Sir Roland Findlay Trophy by the Rutland side. Afterwards Prince Charles attended a tea party given in the forecourt of their home, Burley-on-the-Hill, by Joss and Rozzie Hanbury. Joss, Joint Master of the Quorn and the Cottesmore, had invited a huge gathering of Leicestershire farmers and landowners to meet the Prince. It was one more reminder that the Prince's sporting interests are anything but private, solitary pursuits. He demonstrated yet again that he is well aware that riding on other people's land involves a real commitment to a rural community.

Prince Charles planned to hunt in Leicestershire in the 1986–7 season, and in the 1987 polo season he was to join a new high-goal team, called Windsor Park, with Geoffrey Kent, chairman of the tour operators Abercrombie & Kent, as its player patron. New Zealanders Stuart Mackenzie, handicap eight, and six-goal-handicapped Cody Forsyth were expected to play in the new team, and be based at the Guards Polo Club, Windsor.

What are Prince Charles's polo ambitions in the years ahead? As he says, he hopes to emulate his father in playing until he is at least fifty. He sums up his polo future briefly but emphatically: 'I would like to play even better – and I *do* love it.'

7

THE CHASE

'Tell me a man's a fox'unter and I loves 'im.' Thus spoke John Jorrocks, the Cockney grocer immortalized by R. S. Surtees as the comic hero of his sporting classic *Handley Cross* and other nineteenth-century masterpieces. It is something of an indication of the feelings of a great many country people throughout the British Isles when they learned that the Prince of Wales had not only been foxhunting for the first time, but apparently thoroughly enjoyed the sport and intended to keep it up.

As we have already seen, Prince Charles was a late starter compared with many horsemen when it came to jumping fences and revelling in the thrill of cross-country riding. Most young men receive their first experience of the Chase in the Pony Club. Christmas time meets for children are a regular part of country life. Boys do not always take to the hunting field as enthusiastically as their sisters nowadays, but they get their first experience of jumping hedges and timber in the hunting field. Some graduate to amateur race riding through the point-to-point, the annual race meeting held by each hunt.

Prince Charles would have followed early grounding in the hunting field with possibly some point-to-point experience in his teens if he had followed the pattern of many young British horsemen. Polo would have been an extra accomplishment.

The first news that he had started foxhunting was published in *Horse and Hound* on 28 February 1975 and came from the authoritative pen of none other than the modern 'Father' of the sport, the 10th Duke of Beaufort.

It had been a well-kept secret, and Fleet Street for once failed to grasp the significance of this new sporting venture by the future King. This was prob-

ably because the scribes did not appreciate the extent of hunting Britain's volume and intensity of support at many levels of rural life. It was just as much a source of interest in the smoky back bar of a rural inn where the terrier man was wont to drink his pint, as it was in the Members' rooms at White's Club in the West End of London.

The Prince's first excursion into the mounted ranks of foxhunters was to lead to a unique sporting royal tour of his future kingdom. Its significance has so far escaped any of the royal chroniclers, whether superficial sensation mongers, or serious reporters. At the time of writing Prince Charles has hunted with forty-six packs of hounds in Britain. He has ridden many different horses in widely varying terrains – from the huge enclosures divided by fly fences which may be taken at a gallop in Leicestershire, to the high stone-walled uplands of Derbyshire, the moorlands of Scotland, and the steep banks of his own Duchy of Cornwall. Anyone who has tried this form of equestrian adventure – and only a handful of hunting correspondents do it regularly – can testify that it calls for considerable resilience, a strong nerve and stamina, especially if you are expected to partake of some of the warm hospitality which hunting countries offer a visitor.

As pointed out earlier, hunting was certainly 'in the blood' in the Royal Family, although the notion that a love of the Chase is a purely hereditary family matter is nonsense. A love of hunting is every man's heritage if he has the opportunity to enjoy the sport when he is young enough to answer its challenge.

Prince Charles was twenty-seven years old when he first went hunting. Was it a whim on the spur of the moment? Did it just happen accidentally? We could have been forgiven for thinking this was the case. Perhaps it was an experiment: something to be tasted, but not a sporting experience to be savoured for many a year? How wrong were the doubters. They had overlooked hunting's appeal to an individual with an instinctive feeling for country life. Riding after a pack of hounds is a superb way of exploring the essential nature of rural Britain.

Driving along country lanes and peering over hedgerows affords little real appreciation of the terrain. Hiking does offer much more in terms of real exploration, of course, but the horseman has a vantage point at least 10 feet off the ground – the height of his head when he is mounted – and his equine partner enables him to encompass so much more country in the five to seven hours of a hunting day.

A deep affection for the British countryside goes hand in hand with a love for the sport, and the foxhunter who takes the trouble to understand the science of venery – the huntsman's skilled task in directing hounds – adds a major dimension to his pleasure in the hunting field. It was no coincidence that many of Punch's best jokes in the nineteenth century were directed at foxhunters, nor that among hunting's favourite writers were comic satirists such as Surtees and Ireland's inimitable Somerville and Ross.

Wearing a red coat and sallying forth into the rigours of Britain in the winter time has its extremely funny side. If you cannot laugh at yourself you will miss much of the fun of the hunting field – and Prince Charles showed from the first that he appreciated the humour as well as the romance and the challenge of the Chase.

'I had always wanted to hunt, ever since the days of the West Norfolk, when I was very small. I was taken to a meet there, or several, and I remember the extraordinary effect that it had when I heard the hounds and the horn. I have never forgotten the effect it had on me, so I always had this longing to try. It seemed such a romantic thing. Whatever you think about the merits of foxhunting, it definitely has an attraction.'

The longings created by those childhood visits to the West Norfolk meets during the Royal Family's regular winter sojourns at Sandringham could not be fulfilled earlier in Charles's life for perfectly normal reasons. The hunting tradition had missed a generation in the Royal Family. Prince Charles appreciated the significance of hunting as a perfectly normal rural recreation which children so frequently take up as part of family life.

Eventually family influence did offer Charles the opportunity to take up hunting. Princess Anne's marriage to Captain Mark Phillips – on 14 November 1973, Prince Charles's birthday – resulted in a reinforcement of royal interest in 'Beaufortshire'. Mark Phillips had been a member of the Duke of Beaufort's Pony Club. He and his family hunted with the Duke's famous pack from Badminton as a matter of course.

Princess Anne was to make her home at Gatcombe in the Duke of Beaufort's country and enjoyed all aspects of equestrianism in Gloucestershire, including hunting. The Princess continues to hunt, and has visited more than a few packs elsewhere. It would be fair to say, however, that Anne's enjoyment of the Chase appears to have far more connection with horse than with hound – although she certainly understands and appreciates the role of the pack, and indeed has judged hound puppies in the Dumfriesshire country.

The Duke of Beaufort's connection with horse trials has been a major factor in Anne's involvement in 'Beaufortshire'. The founding in 1949 of Badminton Horse Trials, still the greatest annual three-day event in the world, shaped the lives of so many of Mark Phillips's generation. Winning Badminton and the other leading events became a major goal. Gloucestershire and Avon is heartland of horse trials. Richard Meade, Michael Tucker, Toby Sturgis, and Virginia Leng are just a few of the sport's leading riders who live within the Duke of Beaufort's Hunt boundaries.

There was some inevitable flak in the press when the Princess appeared with hounds, but it was soon accepted that this was simply part of her normal life as Mark Phillips's wife in Gloucestershire. The

Watched by the Queen, Prince Charles sits astride the Master's hunter when he attended a meet of the West Norfolk foxhounds at Harpley Dams, near Sandringham, in January 1955, when the Prince was six years old. 'I had always wanted to hunt, ever since the days of the West Norfolk when I was very small,' the Prince recalls. Hatless, and holding a whip on the left is the West Norfolk's Master, a famous hunting man, the late Major Bob Hoare, who later won renown in the Cottesmore country. The Queen Mother is standing behind the railing to the left

equestrian connections were obvious.

To the hunting man the great Palladian mansion of the Dukes of Beaufort, and its nearby kennel, was the centrepiece of foxhunting England. Henry Hugh Arthur Fitzroy Somerset, tenth Duke of Beaufort, *was* foxhunting. It was easy to dismiss him as something of an anachronism: the epitome of the hunting squirearchy writ large, perhaps larger than life compared with most people's experience of the sport. The very size of Badminton and its kennel, the excellence of its hound breeding, the huge accompanying Hunt stables, and the formidable sight of the Duke out hunting his hounds followed by massed mounted ranks of subscribers in the distinctive Beaufort blue and buff Hunt coat, was enough to strike some awe into a visitor.

Yet although the Duke's temper could erupt swiftly, if rarely, he was not the possessor of a temperament so formidable that it forbade friendship with everyone in his domain. The word domain is not used without some significance, since for the sixty years of his Mastership he did exercise a form of benevolent rulership over his cherished hunting country.

His nickname of 'Master' was not derived from any autocratic strain in his personality. It was a childhood nickname which stuck.

'When I was eleven I acquired a new name when my father gave me a pack of harriers for my birthday. People would come up to me and say: "Good morning, Master. Where are you going to draw today?" It was from that little joke that the name by which I have been called ever since derives, for everyone now calls me "Master" and it is a name that I both like and am proud to have.'

It was not arrogance, therefore, but simply a wish to be friendly that inspired the Duke to write to Walter Case, then Editor of *Horse and Hound*, to declare, 'My dear Walter, We have known each other a long time. Please do not refer to me as Your Grace in your letters; just call me Master.'

The warmth of so many people's public and private tributes when Master died aged eighty-three on 5 February 1984 were some indication of his extraordinary contribution to English life at many levels. He exemplified one of the basic facts of foxhunting: that you only hunt on private land by carefully and meticulously maintained goodwill with the landowners and farmers. The Duke owned some 20,000 of the acres he hunted, but just like any other MFH he relied heavily upon the friendship of his neighbours for the continuance of his sport. He was just as warmly welcome in a village cottage, or farmhouse kitchen, as in a manor house drawing room.

The Duke's formal connection with the Royal Family was manifest: he was Master of the Horse from 1936–77, the longest of the seventy-six holders of this office since the fourteenth century. He was responsible for all official equestrian involvement in royal processions, and for three reigns rode in prominent attendance to the sovereign.

Yet Master's relationship with the Queen and her family was also on a far more intimate, informal basis, virtually that of a favourite uncle. He and the Duchess were childless, but Master adored children and was very good with them.

The Duchess was formerly Lady Mary Cambridge, second daughter of the Marquess of Cambridge, and sister of Prince George of Teck. She was therefore a niece of Queen Mary, wife of King George V. During the Second World War Queen Mary stayed at Badminton, occupying the same suite of rooms on the Church side of the house, in the south-east corner, which the Queen and her family were to use every April when they visited Badminton to watch the great three-day event. Thus for Prince Charles Badminton, and all that it stood for, were also potent influences in understanding the full implications of foxhunting as part of a way of life.

When Master was born, his father, the ninth Duke, was given the news in the hunting field. He announced the birth of his son to the mounted field, and the professional huntsman Will Dale then asked hesitantly, 'May we give three cheers, Your Grace?'

'Certainly not!' replied the Duke. 'You might frighten the hounds.'

The winter of 1974–75 was an unusually wet one. This brings good scenting conditions, and indeed sport had been good in most hunting countries. Unfortunately, the wet weather persisted well into the new year, and Master, ever mindful of the needs of his tenants and neighbours, had temporarily suspended his hunting fixtures because he was worried that large mounted fields would cause unacceptable levels of damage to growing crops and new grass. This decision would never have been taken at Badminton during the forty-seven years that the Duke himself actually hunted the hounds as his own amateur huntsman, wearing a coat of green livery instead of the blue and buff.

The decision to cancel Beaufort meets caused not

a little consternation in hunting England. It was not a policy which other hunts were keen to follow. Next door in the Heythrop country, Captain Ronnie Wallace – one of the keenest and most brilliant amateur huntsmen of all time – was still hunting five days a week. His policy was to keep going at all costs, but to tread warily in every sense, hunting those areas of the country where little or no damage could be done, and giving repeated stern warnings to his followers about the unusually wet state of the ground.

It was tactfully pointed out to the Editor of *Horse and Hound* that it would not be helpful if Master's decision was prominently published. Master, born in 1900, was increasingly subject to a certain impetuosity, inclined to take his hounds home somewhat early if he felt like it. His huge, devoted following bore his occasional drastic decisions cheerfully. They and their fathers and grandfathers had greatly enjoyed the Duke's passion for the Chase in his younger days when he was a superb Pied Piper across the thousands of acres of Gloucestershire grassland, flitting over the limestone walls dividing the fields on the hill country around his ancestral home, or launching over the big, hairy hedges in the deep riding vales of Sodbury or Dauntsey.

By the time Prince Charles began his hunting career it could be said that the fabric of Master's hunting paradise was shredding all too fast. The building of the M4 motorway through the country had been a major blow. Master had fenced the dratted road with link wire to stop foxes, and hounds, running across the motorway. The pack did make one very brief excursion on to the M4 owing to a hole in the fence. The prospect of this calamity ever occurring again, with the appalling risk of a major road crash resulting, haunted Master for the rest of his life. Hounds were kept as far away from the M4 as possible, thus curtailing all too many a hunting day. Other roads in his country also became busier than ever, and the reorganization of county boundaries even removed Badminton from the Duke's beloved Gloucestershire. It was technically in the new County of Avon, a fact which

caused not a few imprecations by 'displaced' citizens over many a dinner table.

Perhaps worse for foxhunting in Beaufortshire was the acceleration of the change from pastoral to arable farming. The green acres around Badminton gave way to autumn swathes of brown as yet more land fell to the plough. The introduction of Common Market wheat quotas led to a huge expansion in winter wheat, the worst crop of all for foxhunting since it removed even the prospect of riding across autumn stubbles. For all these reasons, Prince Charles's first experience of the glories of the Chase could have been low key, even disappointing. The Beaufort still had good days, but the restrictions were real ones. The Duke was no longer hunting hounds; he rode in the blue and buff now, at the head of his mounted field. Like Lord Scamperdale, in Surtees' *Mr Sponge's Sporting Tour*, Master was inclined to be all 'eyes, ears and fears' in the hunting field, keeping a very close eye on the activities of his professional huntsman, Brian Gupwell, young, good looking, a good rider, but with a vastly different style of hunting hounds to that demonstrated with such verve for nearly half a century by the Duke.

It was not until 1976 that Princess Anne and Phillips secured their permanent home in the Duke of Beaufort's country at Gatcombe. They lived in married quarters at Sandhurst but through Mark's family involvement in the Hunt they made frequent excursions in the Duke's mounted field. Prince Charles relied heavily at that stage upon his sister and brother-in-law for guidance and help in first riding to hounds. His problems were basically not much different to any other would-be enthusiast entering a deeply entrenched sport with its own etiquette, language and curious tribal customs. What to ride? How to tackle the country? What to wear?

Fortunately, the Phillips family were on hand to give help in all these matters. Details mean a lot in foxhunting. A day can be ruined by a knee button on your breeches rubbing hard against your shin bone inside your hunting boot. A bad horse is a disaster, especially if you are a beginner.

Captain Mark Phillips's parents, Major Peter Phillips and his wife Anne, who provided their family cob Pinkers as a first mount for Prince Charles in the hunting field. Pinkers proved a highly successful schoolmaster

Mark's parents, Major Peter Phillips and his wife Anne, had a lifetime of experience in the world of horse and hound. They gave Mark and his sister, Sara, a secure country childhood where hunting was simply something you did in the wintertime as a normal part of life. Anne Phillips certainly did not believe in mollycoddling her son. Family history has it that while hunting as a very small boy Mark screeched to his mother that he could not stop his pony. 'Well, what on earth do you want to stop for anyway?' replied his mother.

The redoubtable Aunt Flavia, sister of Major Peter Phillips, and living nearby at Great Somerford, Wiltshire, played a major supportive role in Mark's brilliant eventing career, not least by providing him with some of his early best horses, and affording stabling and grazing at her home – plus more than a little practical guidance. His first achievement on his aunt's horse Kookaburra in Pony Club events fired Mark's lifelong enthusiasm for eventing. Later Aunt Flavia was joint owner with Mark of Great Ovation, the gelding by Three Cheers with which he won Badminton two years running, in 1971 and

1972, plus securing an Olympic team gold medal at the Munich Games in 1972.

It was Anne Phillips who provided Prince Charles with the main essential for his first foxhunting day: a reliable horse. Pinkers was a family cob, but since this was the Phillips family, he was a cob who went hunting properly. Prince Charles was more than a little concerned about his latent fear of jumping fences. It is something like the difference between swimming and diving. Some enjoy the former but never manage to master the art of plunging into the water with style and total fearlessness from considerable heights. Many a lifelong horseman will confess to more than a few tremors when faced with jumping fences across natural country after a summer without riding regularly. Although jumping does cause injuries in steeplechasing and in the hunting field, the risks of a fall on the flat causing major injuries is far greater.

'A fall is a h'awful thing,' said Mr Jorrocks in his famous sporting lecture, and although the vast majority of falls over fences result in little or no damage to rider or horse, the possibility of an upset does account for much of the tension at the start of a day's hunting in a piece of country where jumping is inevitable. The worst 'h'awful thing' is the horse falling badly, giving the rider a kick in regaining its feet. Being struck by another following horse is another major hazard. 'Over-riding' the person in front of you, so that you land on top of them if they fall, is one of the worst sins in the hunting field, and one of the commonest.

The modern countryside probably offers more hazards than ever before. Riding on the roads is dangerous because the surface is frequently slippery. Even an experienced horse can all too easily fall on the road's desperately hard going, and all too easily break the rider's thigh, or worse. Farm lanes are increasingly concreted, and when it comes to crossing 'natural' country even the most fashionable hunting areas are far more likely to have barbed wire enmeshed in the fences, or guarding the fence as an 'oxer'.

Years of foxhunting teaches many a 'wrinkle' in avoiding or off-setting such hazards. You ride your horse on the roughened part of the road at the side; you learn to watch for wire. Experience tells you when your horse can clear both fence and wire safely. The need to kick on extra hard to ensure a big leap at a seemingly innocent obstacle is one of the many secrets of successful horsemanship in the hunting field. Even the artificial Hunt jumps erected here and there in most hunting country nowadays have special hazards. They are usually stout rails, or the famous 'tiger-trap', a pyramidal construction of rails, normally set over a ditch.

The queuing at hunt jumps is all too often made hazardous by the occasional young horse which tries to barge ahead, and then refuses. This can cause spectacular and painful pile-ups, especially in the 'cut-me-down' countries like the Belvoir in Leicestershire, where there is a considerable element of competitiveness after the more popular meets.

All these challenges had to be learned and coped with by Prince Charles. Inevitably, his every move in the hunting field would be watched, and discussed afterwards by people who had hunted since childhood and knew every facet of their own country; 'Couldn't ride our country,' is the remark expressed with just an element of glee after a visiting eminence has suffered an imperial crowner.

Nevertheless, everyone in the hunting field knows that, however skilled or experienced he may be, fate has more falls in store; luck as well as riding prowess will be needed to avoid a 'nasty'. There is, therefore, a genuine camaraderie in the hunting field, akin to that shared by all who partake regularly of genuine risk activities at any level. Go into the changing room at a steeplechase meeting to experience it at its best. Prince Charles was not only to meet the challenge of the hunting field but to taste the shared risks and thrills of 'chasing under Rules, something he would value and never forget.

Prince Charles recalls that he was more than aware of the jumping challenge awaiting him.

'I asked Princess Anne what sort of horse I could find. One of the things I wanted to do in the hunting field was to overcome my fear of jumping, because I had been rather put off when I was younger. I knew it was difficult to find the right horse. Princess Anne is a very good judge of horse character, and suggested this horse Pinkers which belonged to her mother-in-law. As it turned out she could not have made a better choice. It was a marvellous, sensible old thing, and jumped like anything. Pinkers made you feel safe, and before I went hunting I had a few practices on him. Princess Anne gave me a few lessons in the riding school at Windsor, which was a great help. I am a great believer in the fact that if a person knows what they are doing I will listen to them, and try to do as they say.'

Princess Anne also realized that her brother needed some outdoor training over natural country, as well as her 'brush up' equitation in the riding school. Years of playing polo had given Prince Charles a seat in the saddle, and a way of controlling a polo pony, which were not ideally suited to the formidable challenge he was now undertaking. The mysteries of 'seeing a stride' over a fence were probably too much to hope for immediately. Judging the exact stride on which to take-off over an obstacle is an essential part of the show jumper's technique. Yet it is important to be able to jump neatly and accurately at times in the hunting field, too. Unlike show jumps, most of the obstacles encountered out hunting do not break easily, if at all. Jumping a locked iron gate on to a metalled road is not unknown in some hunting countries. The Prince of Wales, from the start, was expected to ride 'up the front' among the thrusters. It is the place in the hunting field to see all the action, or as they sometimes say in Leicestershire, to 'enjoy the gas', but it does mean taking on anything and everything that the huntsman, or a hard riding Field Master, will tackle.

Princess Anne therefore took Prince Charles and Pinkers on a preliminary exploration of the Dauntsey Vale. 'Princess Anne used to shout at me sometimes. I think she shouted, "Sit back" – or something like that!' Prince Charles recalls.

Hounds have been kept at Badminton since 1728, according to the family records. In those days the third Duke hunted the stag, and it was not until

1762 that the fifth Duke accidentally hunted a fox after a disappointing day's stag hunting, and thereafter the Beaufort hounds were devoted to the pursuit of Reynard, or Charlie as he is more often known (a term dating back to the Whig politician Charles James Fox, 1749–1806.) Yet in all Badminton's long hunting history there could hardly have been a more significant meet than Monday, 17 February 1975.

The hounds had stopped hunting on Thurdsay, 6 February, because of the wet state of the ground, and Master had not planned to re-start until Monday, 3 March, two days after the hunt point-to-point.

It was on Sunday, 9 February that Prince Charles telephoned Master to enquire if he could come for a day's hunting on Monday week. Master had a problem, but with the aid of his Joint Master, Major Gerald Gundry, one of the great personalities of the sport, arrangements were hastily made for a special day. Such days seldom bring success. Diana, the spirit of the Chase, is seldom cooperative when special arrangements are made for a day which it is fondly hoped will produce top-class sport. Fox-hunters are well used to disappointment, delay and frustration. Equally, they are prepared to be surprised by joy when the worst covert in the country, surrounded by the least attractive terrain, suddenly produces the best run of the season.

Because of the suspension of normal meets, Master arranged to meet at the kennels at Badminton, with a mounted field of only about thirty, including 'my tenants over whose farms we were likely to run, and a few subscribers and farmers who have been particularly helpful to the Hunt during the present season.' Brian Gupwell was hunting hounds, with the veteran Dennis Brown as first whipper-in.

The Prince of Wales 'has no hunting clothes, so wore his polo boots, brown breeches, tweed jacket

'Master': the 10th Duke of Beaufort, known as MFH Number One, who encouraged Prince Charles to start hunting from Badminton in 1975. The Duke, who died aged eighty-three in 1984, hunted his own hounds for forty-seven years and was the senior Master of his pack for sixty years

and a bowler hat. He looked very smart, with a well-tied hunting tie and a gold pin,' reported the Duke later.

Lt Col Sir John Miller, the Crown Equerry, already had a hand in the proceedings, and his role in the early equestrian and hunting arrangements for Prince Charles was to become crucial. Born in February, 1919, Sir John came from an Oxfordshire military family; his father was a Brigadier General in the Royal Scots Greys. Educated at Eton and going on to Sandhurst before joining the Welsh Guards just before the outbreak of war, it might be thought that John Mansel Miller was simply a typical product of the old Army system.

John Miller is, in fact, a most remarkable personality, his steely purpose and ability to organize successfully being cloaked under a disarmingly modest manner. It is all the more surprising when he suddenly reveals a degree of disregard for personal safety which is positively alarming. He does not merely have strong nerves; he appears to have no nerves at all.

He had a most distinguished war, being awarded the DSO and MC after the Allied landings in Europe. His military career concluded when he was commanding the 1st Battalion Welsh Guards, and he was appointed the Crown Equerry in 1961. It proved to be a remarkably successful appointment, not only because of his organizing abilities, but because he is an exceptional horseman in every sense.

The Crown Equerry looks after all the Queen's horses, except the racehorses, and all the royal cars. It is an extraordinary task. Sir John is responsible for the horses in all the royal processions, and for the Queen's Birthday Parade. A bachelor, Sir John devotes himself to his royal duties to a singular degree, and he takes an immense interest and gives active support to equestrian sports and horse breeding in the wider horse world.

He was to visit over forty Hunts with Prince Charles, making all the arrangements for horses and travel. Sir John rode anything that came along if he could not take his own horses, and he was always to be seen somewhere near the young Prince of

Wales, for whom he was constantly helping to open new frontiers on the extraordinarily varied world of the British hunting field.

In more recent years the Prince's hunting arrangements have been assisted by James Teacher, a former Joint Master of the Quorn, one of the most affable and wittiest of personalities in the Masters of Foxhounds Association. James and his wife, Chloe, have accompanied the Prince on hunting trips.

Sir John Miller thoroughly approved of Mrs Phillips's Pinkers as being entirely suitable for Prince Charles on his first hunting day. It was to be such an unusual day's sport, so unusual in its content, and so significant in starting the Prince on his exploration of 'Hunting Britain' that it is worth reproducing most of Master's own report which he sent to *Horse and Hound* in a state of some excitement, and not a little glee.

'The morning of the 17th was warm with a light drizzle, which gradually increased to heavy rain throughout the day. We went straight to the Verge and soon found, but hounds, the bitch pack of $20\frac{1}{2}$ couple, hardly owned the line, so I think it must have been a vixen.

However, another fox was holloa away across the plough to Witheymore, and after crossing the Station Road, the fox swung back left-handed through the village and returned to the Verge.

He tried the earths and came away on much the same line but left Witheymore on his left and crossed the railway near the Tunnel. He crossed both the Chipping Sodbury, and Tormarton roads, pointing for Faggot Pile, but swung left-handed over the Burton and Littleton Drew roads to Alderton Grove. He re-crossed the railway and ran past Hebden Farm, pointing for Allengrove, but scent gradually faded away.

To my surprise, Allengrove was blank for the first time for many seasons. So we changed horses in front of Badminton House, and went off to draw the kale in the middle of the Little Badminton Farm, found immediately, ran back to the Verge and away down the Seven Mile Avenue, and right again down the hard track to Little Badminton Witheybed.

On they went through Swangrove, Hinnegar Wood and Bullpark, and away over the open to Sopworth. Hounds worked their way over the cattle foil to Sopworth Brake, and away running hard over the brook and along the valley to Manor Farm and into the outskirts of Sherston.

Here to our amazement, fox and hounds disappeared into a deep cave, which the local inhabitants told us stretched several hundred yards to the Church. We could faintly hear the hounds baying, and it is not known if they killed their fox.

It took us the best part of an hour to surface the hounds, indeed the last one did not come out until noon the next morning. I have never known fox or hounds go into this cave before. It was a five mile point and hounds hunted excellently.'

Diana, Goddess of the Chase, had indeed smiled, and not for the last time in Prince Charles's life – on and off the hunting field. He had enjoyed a marvellous ride, and an experience of an exceptional hunt which was to remain in his memory as one of the best days he would ever achieve.

'His Royal Highness rode extremely well, jumping everything that came in the way and was always in the first flight,' reported the jubilant Duke, whose attention to detail in his account indicated that he might have had a useful career in journalism if he had not been born at Badminton.

He did not neglect to note that Charles 'rode back to Badminton soaked to the skin. He had a hot bath, and a good tea, and driving his own car set out at 4.30pm for Buckingham Palace, where he was due for a meeting at 6.30pm, which was to be followed by another engagement.

'I telephoned the next morning to inquire if he was stiff, and was not surprised to hear that he did not wish to be disturbed.'

The tenth Duke summed up the great occasion: 'It was indeed an honour that he should have his first hunt with my hounds, and I was more than happy that he should enjoy such an excellent day's sport. I know it is the hope of every foxhunter in the United Kingdom that his Royal Highness shall enjoy many more good days' foxhunting.'

8

WINDSOR UNIFORM

'My love of the Chase comes from the thrill and challenge of a ride across country; from the skill and effort of a good pack of hounds; of the pleasure of riding an experienced or promising horse; and especially from the cry of the hounds, from the sound of the horn, from a good holloa, and from the hours spent riding in a green countryside.'

The tenth Duke of Beaufort's description of his pleasure in foxhunting could well be applied to Prince Charles's wholehearted enjoyment of all aspects of the sport. After his initial experience from Badminton it would not have been at all surprising if he had merely continued to hunt in the same environment, perhaps making the occasional foray into a neighbouring country. This is how most people hunt; they become great 'experts' in their own patch, but few take the opportunity to explore hunting countries far afield. Young Army officers used to get such experience through being posted to the Midlands, the North, or East Anglia. The delights of hunting in Southern Ireland were a bonus of service in Ulster until the latest 'troubles' began at the end of the 1960s.

It surprised and delighted hunting Britain when it became clear that the Prince of Wales was using the sport as a means of exploring remote rural areas of his future kingdom on a horse. The friendships which Charles forged in nearly a decade of visiting Hunts made a great contribution to his love and understanding of the countryside. *Baily's Hunting Directory* lists 203 packs of foxhounds in the United Kingdom, plus twenty-six packs of harriers and eighty-three beagle packs which are followed on foot.

It is probable that some of the great hunting correspondents of the past did not see sport with more than fifty packs. Poor communications in the last century prevented such as Surtees and Nimrod (Charles James Apperley) notching up centuries in Hunt visiting. Even in the late twentieth century, however, the rigours of the British winter are a formidable barrier for the Hunt visitor, and the uncertainties of the Chase are certainly multiplied once the hard weather sets in.

Prince Charles philosophically accepted all the disappointment that frost and fog can wreak on even the best organized pack. You arrive at the meet to find the fields shrouded in dense fog; you wait, and wonder whether to unbox the horses. The fog appears to lift a little; the horses are brought down the ramps of the lorries. Some of the riders mount and ride about impatiently; the fog descends again. Hunting is off for the day. Frost which renders the ground rock hard can usually be assessed early enough to prevent hunting folk even going to the meet, but it is so easy to make a long journey in our small island only to find the local weather conditions totally different from those which you were experiencing at home.

Perhaps the character-building nature of hunting's risks and uncertainties was the reason why it was extolled by cavalry officers as an excellent training ground for war. It is more likely that the cavalry simply enjoyed the whole thing tremendously, and found the virtues of the sport a useful excuse to prolong their time in the hunting field. Yet it cannot be denied that constantly riding strange horses over strange pieces of country does either make or mar your nerve and your riding ability. Prince Charles set out to perform a programme of hunting tours which improved his riding enormously, and forever ended his fears of jumping fences.

'I did not have many falls at the start. I think they come when you start being more enterprising – and later I began to ride all sorts of different horses. People would lend me one for the day. I was terrified at first, but after a bit I learnt more about horses that way. And I actually don't mind getting on to a strange horse. You accept that every now and then you will take a fall. I will admit, however, that to start with, I used to think, "My God, what's going to happen?" Still it is extremely good for you to be able to discover what types of horses there are. They do tend to fall into certain types. Then you get to the point where you know the type you want – although I must admit that it is very hard to find.'

Despite having started late in the season, Prince Charles was keen to have more days hunting before that season ended, in mid-March. The problem of what to wear was solved at first by John Miller lending the Prince a blue and buff Duke of Beaufort's Hunt coat which fitted surprisingly well.

Charles also sported a hunting top hat. These are made of strips of calico dipped into shellac and shaped into the conformation of a top hat, then covered with a black fabric. The workshop near the Elephant and Castle where Mr Patey and his staff make top hats, riding hats, mortar boards and other curious headgear used to resemble a medieval tradesman's premises. A wooden staircase led up to the first floor workshop where you would find men and women busy stitching and shaping the headgear. Old dustbins of steaming hot shellack added to the unique atmosphere of a hatter's establishment, mingling with the steam from numerous old-fashioned flat irons heated up on gas jets to be used on the felt coverings of the widely assorted headgear.

Into the yard below there would clatter a carriage and pair, or even a carriage and four, either driven by the Crown Equerry from the Royal Mews, or despatched by him to collect some piece of ceremonial headgear for use on State occasions. Mr Patey's staff took such visits in their stride, and nonchalantly displayed the royal warrant at their entrance to their old workshop which appeared to have survived numerous wartime air raids, and actually had plants growing from the brickwork.

The top hat, although undoubtedly handsome in appearance, was being treated with grave suspicion both by doctors and safety experts, although many a lifelong hunting man swore that it was still the safest protection for the head in a heavy fall. The top hat's tendency to crumple on impact was hailed as an ancient form of insulation. This overlooked the fact that the said hat was all too likely to fall off before the wearer's head hit the ground, and that the costs of repairing the damaged hat were escalating fast. By 1985 a new made-to-measure hunting topper was about £250 in London; repairs could cost anything up to about £175.

Various experiments were made at Patey's with Prince Charles's top hats. Struts were inserted for strengthening but were deemed unsatisfactory. Much later Patey's devised a skullcap inside a top hat which no doubt made the wearer feel safer, but which would never qualify for a British Standards Institution specification.

The delicate problem in the hunting field was that only Masters of Foxhounds, Hunt staff, and farmers were officially allowed to wear velvet caps. The fact that a velvet cap is neater, warmer, probably safer and certainly cheaper than a top hat was discounted. It was all to do with the problems of recognition, hunting people were told. If every male out hunting wore a black velvet cap you simply would not know who was in charge, and that would never do. There was an element of tradition and kudos attached to the velvet cap, but its retention for Masters and their staff was justified entirely on 'practical grounds'.

What to do about the Heir to the Throne's head, and its protective covering? Fortunately there was ample precedent in the Royal Family for a special hunting 'uniform' to be devised for Prince Charles, and Prince Philip pointed out that the wearing of a special coat, the Windsor Coat, would be useful as a means of solving the problem of Hunt buttons. The Prince of Wales was frequently given the distinctive button of a Hunt he had visited, and could hardly accommodate them all on one coat. Normally the Hunt button is awarded to a subscriber

Royal hunting traditions: Prince Charles's great-uncle and grandfather, the Prince of Wales and the Duke of York, hunting with the Fernie in Leicestershire in 1924. Top hats were the automatic choice for gentlemen in the hunting field in those days. Insulated hunting caps with chin straps had not even been invented

by the Master as a special honour. The buttons worn by Prince Charles bear the Garter Star, as worn by George III when out hunting.

The Crown Equerry made careful researches, aided by librarians of the royal household. It can only be said that the result is not only practical, but is eminently smart and stands plenty of wear.

Prince Charles appears in the hunting field in a dark blue coat; it has a deep scarlet collar and matching scarlet cuffs. There are three metal buttons in front, three on each cuff, and two at the back, all bearing the Prince of Wales crest. With this Charles wears a very dark blue hunting cap with a high crown, similar to the Pytchley style hunting cap; plus a white hunting tie (*not* called a

hunting *stock* please!), secured by a gold hunting pin, bearing a discreet crest, and pinned horizontally; white cord hunting breeches, black hunting boots with tan tops, secured with white garter straps; and plain, 'dummy' spurs.

Prince Charles carries a cutting whip rather than a conventional hunting whip with a lash. The latter is 'correct' and has the added advantage of being useful in opening gates. Its large bone handle can be used to lift gate latches, and it is also used to ward off a swinging gate when it threatens to strike the rider's leg as he passes through. Only Hunt servants are supposed to use the lash to crack the whip, sometimes to hasten lagging hounds to join the pack, and occasionally to help rouse the fox in covert, through the noise, not by any contact, of course. Many people, however, carry a cutting whip instead in the hunting field. It is far easier to manage, and is particularly useful in slapping a horse down the shoulder on going into a fence. Hitting a horse behind the saddle is rarely done, except by jockeys riding a finish, and they frequently flourish the whip to match the horse's stride, rather than actually strike. Even in the hunting field there *are* occasions when a 'quick one' with the whip behind the saddle will ensure that a sticky jumper not only takes off, but also puts in that vital, extra effort over a big fence.

The unique hunting dress which the Prince of Wales wears is called 'The Windsor Coat', and its link with royal traditions is fascinating, although little known. George III, who succeeded his grandfather, George II, in 1760, is credited with creating the uniform. Despite his bouts of mental instability, he was held in warm affection by his subjects. He was a plain, downright character, and during his long reign he was known as 'Farmer George'.

'The Windsor Coat' is defined officially as 'a uniform introduced by George III, consisting of a blue coat with red collar and cuffs, and a blue or white waistcoat, worn on certain occasions by members of the royal household, and by royal or other distinguished guests by permission of the sovereign.'

It has been surmised that George III derived the idea for the uniform from his second cousin, Frederick the Great of Prussia. 'The Windsor Uniform' was described in 1854 by Countess Bernstorff, wife of the Prussian ambassador in London, as 'exactly like the undress uniform of the Prussian chamberlains', who corresponded to the English gentlemen ushers. George III apparently instituted the private uniform when he decided to make Windsor his home in 1788–89, and he had his family painted in the uniform by Gainsborough in 1782. There are illustrations showing George III wearing 'undress Windsor uniform' when out hunting with hounds at Windsor. Its sporting links are therefore impeccable. The equestrian element in all gentlemen's clothes was of course inevitable until the mid-nineteenth century. Certainly the Prince Regent, 'the Prince of Pleasure', sported the coat among the many gorgeous dress clothes he wore during his glittering Regency and reign as George IV. During Queen Victoria's reign the coat was worn by mem-

bers of the Household at receptions or garden parties at Windsor. In her younger days the Queen even wore it herself, as did Queen Charlotte. Since the accession of King Edward VII the coat was worn only as evening dress. All the photographs of Edward VIII and King George VI in the hunting field in Leicestershire and Northamptonshire show them wearing conventional hunting dress of red coats and hunting top hats in the 1920s and 1930s.

The introduction of a special hunting coat for Prince Charles was undoubtedly dictated mainly by practicalities. Its sober colour enabled him to hunt in the least ostentatious manner, and wearing a cap instead of a top hat was a sensible safety measure. He was certainly 'ahead of the game'. By the 1985–86 season, the Masters of Foxhounds Association had officially approved a hunting cap up to BSI safety specification for use by all men in the hunting field. Some Hunts insisted that it could only be worn in an unbecoming grey if the male wearer was not a farmer or a former Master. Nevertheless, increasing disquiet by the medical profession and coroners about the incidence of head injuries in the hunting field led to total relaxation of rigid etiquette on headgear.

The death of the Commanding Officer of the Household Cavalry, General 'Snip' Hartigan, lent much impetus to the change. He was killed instantly when his top hat came off before his head struck the ground in a fall by his horse on a slippery road whilst hunting with the Grafton in the 1982–83 season. It was no coincidence that the Army soon issued orders that serving personnel on Army horses should wear crash helmets with chinstraps when riding. Even Army officers riding their own horses began to wear caps instead of top hats in the hunting field.

Yet the velvet cap then worn by Prince Charles and most other men in the hunting field would not have earned the approval of the British Standards Institution. The made-to-measure cap was constructed of similar material to the top hat, strips of calico dipped in shellac, and it had a rigid peak. In a fall on the face this increases the whiplash effect to the neck, and tends to cause facial injuries. At the start of the 1985–86 season Prince Charles decided to 'do his own thing'. He appeared in Leicestershire wearing a modern BSI specification cap, with fibre glass dome, insulated inside, and with a semi-stiff peak which would bend on impact. The biggest break with tradition, however, was the Prince's wearing of a chinstrap with his cap. The BSI specification insists on a chinstrap to keep the cap on at the moment of impact in a fall.

Other hunting men who had thus broken with tradition and fashion had already earned the scarcely concealed contempt of the older generation of hunting women in the Shires. 'Hideous! I wouldn't be seen dead in a chin strap! Pure Pony Club!' These were some of the kinder remarks from this particular brand of female reactionary. The fact that these ladies had long ago broken with tradition by abandoning bowlers for velvet caps was ignored, or forgotten.

Prince Charles's chinstrap was discreetly flesh coloured, but it showed – and he firmly continued to use it. Those hunting people with wider priorities than their own prejudices warmly welcomed the Prince's decision.

In steeplechasing, the great jockey Fred Winter had been one of the first to declare, and to demonstrate, that it was not 'cissy' to wear sensible protective headgear with a chinstrap. In all other forms of organized riding, except show jumping and dressage, modern headgear was insisted upon by 1985.

Prince Charles was not only tacitly demonstrating that his responsibilities in life made it necessary for him to adopt a commonsense, rather than a fashionable, attitude to headgear; he was also giving a valuable lead in an area where the medical profession was still endeavouring to persuade more people to behave sensibly in protecting their heads whilst riding horses – which statistics were now proving to be the most dangerous sport in Britain, well above Formula One car racing or motor cycle racing in terms of annual fatalities.

Backs and necks remain heavily at risk in bad falls from, or with, horses, although there is increasing use of protective waistcoats in racing. The leading 'chase jockey John Francome, now a trainer, is a keen advocate of these. Yet head injuries continue to be a major area of concern in riding accidents. Doctors, who have now formed their own Medical Equestrian Association, say that modern headgear can reduce the risk of head injury from 60 to 15 per cent in a fall.

The Prince of Wales's distinctive hunting coat became known in many hunting fields, fashionable and distinctly provincial. He was to find the sport a unique form of relaxation, for no telephone messages nor other official communications are possible in the hunting field. Friendship and good fellowship are abundant – but there is also a lack of formality not possible in any other form of recreation involving groups of people of both sexes and ages ranging from eight-year-olds to nonagenarians.

Recognizing that it is actually the Prince of Wales you are crashing into as you thrust to jump a narrow gap in a hedge is not always possible. Realizing that the future King of England has suddenly arrived out of the blue on a horse on your farm is also beyond some people.

Prince Charles was the first to appreciate, and to enjoy, the informality of the contacts he would make in the hunting field. From the start he made it clear that he was prepared to spend just as much time chatting to the terrier man as to a top-hatted Duke, and he was more likely to meet the former on most of his hunting days. As the Prince said in a speech at the centenary dinner of the Masters of Foxhounds Association in 1981, 'I have met more farmers, and more ordinary British blokes than in any other exercise or sport that I have ever done.'

Prince Charles emphasized that apart from the sport itself he looked upon hunting as 'a way of life for many people; an integral part of Britain.' Through hunting he had seen the kind of British countryside which he would never have encountered in any other way. He hoped very much, he told the assembled Masters of Foxhounds and their wives attending the dinner at the Savoy Hotel in London, that he would be able to continue hunting, because 'in a small way it helps me to keep in touch with what actually happens in the British countryside'.

9

THE SHIRES

Give me the horse that ne'er turns his head
at a fence, nor a five-bar gate...

WILL OGILVIE

After his first day's hunting from the kennels at Badminton, Prince Charles's next excursion with hounds was in Leicestershire with the Cottesmore. Sir John purposely arranged a low-key visit on a Friday, with hounds meeting at the home of Sir Henry Tate, the Chairman and former Joint Master of the Cottesmore. On a Friday the largest mounted field in Leicestershire is in the Quorn country. It was early days, Sir John felt, for Prince Charles to cope with the full shock of the mounted charge when a fox goes away in the Shires. Charles was later to experience this phenomenon frequently, and still does so. He confirms the view that is it no place for a beginner.

'It is like the start of the Grand National. I had never seen anything like it, everyone pushing and shoving. It was terrifying to start with ... going for a fence you get knocked over. Now I know nearly everyone, and I know how to cope. Initially, if you are not used to it, and you haven't much experience, it is terrifying. I wouldn't recommend anybody to go anywhere near until they have done a lot.'

Prince Charles wrote an amusing foreword to the book *Magic of the Quorn* by Ulrica Murray Smith,

who completed a record twenty-six years as Joint Master, retiring in the spring of 1985. Prince Charles recalled that 'The great Duke of Wellington apparently used to encourage as many of his cavalry officers as possible to hunt in the Shires in order that they could acquire that particular brand of dash, fire and an eye for country which so distinguished the British cavalry in the eighteenth and nineteenth centuries.

'When you first visit the Quorn you can't help feeling, while being trampled in the rush, that the majority of the field are still in training for one of Wellington's campaigns! It doesn't, however, take very long to adapt to the environment – the only difficulty being to try and keep your head while others in the vicinity tend to be losing theirs!

'I remember on one occasion there was a frantic rush to "get forward" through a gap in a hedge and several people shouted at me in the mêlée: "Push on, Sir, push on!" I'm afraid my response was to maintain a strict calm and to observe that *someone* had to try and keep up the standard....! My view is that there is always opportunity for "dash and fire" if you have a reasonable horse, once you have got going, but displaying it in the gateway can be somewhat hazardous to all.'

The significance of Leicestershire in foxhunting is far more than the crashing and bashing of the mounted field. It is the cradle of the modern sport, and in historical terms foxhunting as we know it is comparatively 'modern'. Hugo Meynell, a sports-

Hunting with the Quorn in Leicestershire. Prince Charles keeps two hunters in Leicestershire and hunts whenever winter engagements permit, often with the Quorn or its neighbour, the Belvoir

At the 'sharp end' of a hunt. Prince Charles with the Quorn hounds, amid the undulating grass and jumpable fences of Leicestershire. With the Prince is Quorn first whipper-in Charles Watts, with top-class cross-country rider David Bland on the left

man born in Derbyshire, was the first to recognize the full sporting potential of the great swathe of land between Nottinghamshire and Market Harborough to the south. Undulating, without being too hilly, Leicestershire offers the horseman a remarkable view of the country ahead. The old turf is one of the county's great glories. On the wolds and many other higher pieces of land, the pasture dries remarkably quickly in the wettest of winters. Galloping and jumping on it is a memorable experience. It has a zing and a spring denied to the deep lying clay vales of the south of England.

The Leicestershire fly fence adds hugely to the thrills of the Chase. Blackthorn hedges march across the spare winter landscape, each one often accompanied by a drainage ditch. They are not as huge as those of the Dorset or Gloucestershire vales, but Leicestershire's fences are best jumped at a gallop, and preferably on a hunter with scope and quality. A common horse which 'fiddles' a fence can all too often fall into the ditch, and its lack of stamina will not permit it to gallop effortlessly across the huge enclosures, tackling each obstacle in its stride.

Hugo Meynell took a house and kennels at Quorn near Leicester and hunted the country north and south of Melton Mowbray for half a century. The Dukes of Rutland hunted the country to the east from Belvoir Castle, thus founding the Belvoir

Hunt, and the Fernie and Cottesmore packs, together with the Pytchley – which lies mainly in Northamptonshire – form the Shires packs.

Such distinctions have now become blurred and somewhat meaningless, but until postwar hunting evolved on different lines to adapt to the major changes in the countryside, the Shires was the 'capital' of foxhunting and all other countries were 'provincial'. It would not have been surprising if Prince Charles, like his great-uncle, Edward VIII, had virtually confined his hunting to the Shires. Charles clearly enjoys Leicestershire hugely, but it says much for his own wisdom and sporting enterprise that he chose to explore so many other hunting countries so early in his experience of the sport.

The factor which has mainly changed Leicestershire is the immense postwar switch from pastoral to arable farming. No longer could Leicestershire be described as a 'sea of grass' dotted only by the islands of the famous fox coverts, planted and tended by the Hunts for over 200 years. Winter wheat has been the worst problem for the Hunts, since it denies access to huge areas throughout the winter months. The increased mechanization of modern farming means that harvest time is followed all too rapidly by ploughing, and autumn seeding. There are virtually no stubbles to ride in the winter months nowadays. New crops of oil seed rape add still more to the problems of riding the country.

Yet Leicestershire retains its proud position as the most famous and popular hunting county because the great prize is still retained by the sport: the wholehearted goodwill and cooperation of the farmers. The vast majority of the land is open to the great Hunts. Their hounds are regarded as the main sporting interest of the rural community. The large mounted fields continue to include many 'carpet baggers' from outside Leicestershire. They pay much larger subscriptions than local folk. In the 1985–86 season, for example, the Quorn's two popular days, Mondays and Fridays, cost a non-resident some £1600 for the season.

There were still enough pockets, or blankets of grass, to enable the Quorn to provide plenty of sport on old turf. The Vale of Belvoir retains much grassland because of the demands of local dairies for milk in the making of the traditional local product, Stilton cheese. The Cottesmore has been hard hit by increased ploughlands, but retains some delectable grass country around the villages of Knossington and Braunstone, near Oakham.

More than one horse would be necessary if Prince Charles were to take up hunting regularly. Instead of buying a ready-made stud of highly expensive hunters, Charles from the first showed himself ready to ride just about any horse that happened to be available, never keeping more than two or three of his own, and sometimes less. As any hunting man knows, one of the most disappointing elements in the sport can be your horse. Finding the hunter which really suits you is difficult enough. The perfectionist rider across country is seldom ever satisfied for long. The ideal hunter must be perfectly behaved in a crowd; unlikely to hot up too much at inconvenient moments, such as queueing for a jumping place; able, however, to summon the courage to jump a horrendous obstacle without a lead; not too hard a puller, yet capable of galloping tirelessly all day in any going.

And apart from sheer performance, the good hunter must 'do well': must return from a day's hunting ready to eat a large feed and benefit from it; and then sleep soundly, and turn out fresh for another day's hunting that week. Too many well-bred hunters get so excited that they 'run up light', fail to keep flesh on their bones through neglecting to eat enough, and not resting sufficiently in the loosebox after a day's hunting.

Worst of all is the disappointment when your 'perfect' hunter is lamed by some apparently trivial accident, and cannot hunt again for weeks, months, or perhaps never again. Tendons of iron, and a constitution to match, are therefore the other essentials in your top-class hunter which will carry you for seven or more seasons. Such paragons are to be found, but they are comparatively rare. 'Be to his virtues ever kind; be to his faults a little blind' is the maxim which the hunting man has to adopt to his horse. Prince Charles learned all these problems, and his extensive experience of polo ponies still did not prepare him for some of the disappointments in store from hunters.

Some foxhunters, including the Editor of *Horse and Hound*, thought at first that it would have been better if the Prince of Wales had simply spent huge sums on a large string of 'safe' top-class hunters. They were wrong. Learning the hard way, putting up with less than perfect horses, frequently borrowing strange hunters, and occasionally finding a really good animal, taught Prince Charles an immense amount about horseflesh in a manner denied to many 'adequate' horsemen, whose experience is confined solely to their own horses, ridden regularly in their local hunting country which they may well have known intimately since childhood.

The hunting man or woman who can enjoy a day in a 'moderate' country on a borrowed horse just as much as a day in Leicestershire on a blood hunter will find pleasure in the sport for a lifetime, and will not be limited by the need to find just the right mount. Even riding in strange saddles is difficult, if not impossible, for some accomplished horsemen and women. Prince Charles learned early in his hunting travels to overcome all problems involving unfamiliarity with the horse and its tack.

The Duke of Beaufort lent Prince Charles hunters from his extensive Hunt stables at Badminton. The Prince also rode Mulberry Star and several other hunters belonging to Sir John Miller. Sometimes horses intended for driving at the Royal Mews prove to be unsuitable for this task, and find themselves in the hunting field with the Crown Equerry. In case anyone thinks this is simply a method of topping up Sir John's stock of hunters, it should be pointed out that most horses 'sweeten up' in the hunting field. Being herd animals, they thoroughly enjoy the comparative freedom of galloping and jumping in a group of other horses, and will often return from the hunting field to a more disciplined sphere of work in a far more cooperative frame of mind.

Thus a part-bred Cleveland Bay horse from Scotland destined for the Royal Mews as a carriage horse found itself carrying the Heir to the Throne in pursuit of hounds, all over Britain. Even a Swedish-bred driving horse named Mexico, driven with success in competitions by Prince Philip, became an excellent schoolmaster hunter and team 'chaser for Prince Charles. In the 1985–86 season old Mexico was still fit and working, being kept at Highgrove for Prince Charles to hunt sometimes with his home pack, the Duke of Beaufort's.

Prince Charles also benefited from his sister's intense involvement in international horse trials, although some people in the hunting field were more than a trifle anxious when he appeared on Candlewick, the mare which had given Princess Anne a severe fall in a novice event. Candlewick, foaled in 1969, was bred by the Queen as part of the highly successful part-bred breeding programme at Hampton Court, The 17-hands Candlewick was sired by Night Watch, and was out of Trim Ann, a hunter mare belonging to Princess Alexandra. Candlewick's half brother was the illustrious grey, Columbus, by Colonist II and also out of Trim Ann.

Owned by the Queen, Columbus was first ridden by Princess Anne, with whom she won an intermediate class at Liphook in 1972. The headstrong horse was then taken over by Mark Phillips with whom he achieved glory in winning Badminton Horse Trials in 1974, and was leading as an individual in the World Championships at Burghley later that year until he was withdrawn after slipping a tendon off a hock. Despite the injury old Columbus later did great service as a hunter, and took part in hunter trials and team 'chases. Not many people recognized him when Prince Charles rode him once out with the Belvoir as first horse, but he was not sound and sadly this was his last outing with hounds.

Candlewick was ridden by Princess Anne in the Portman novice horse trials in Dorset ten days after Badminton 1976. The mare struck the top of a fence, catapulted Princess Anne on to the ground, which was all too hard at the time, and then fell on top of her. Concussed and bruised, the Princess was taken to hospital in Poole, amid huge national press and television publicity. Candlewick was trained for Princess Anne by the brilliant horsewoman Alison Oliver, who had a very high opinion of the mare. After the fall, Candlewick was also very stiff and sore and was turned out at Hampton Court with Columbus. Princess Anne's own resilience and hardiness as a leading event rider was emphasized by a brilliant performance with her superb horse Goodwill at Bramham three-day event in Yorkshire in June, before going on to compete with Britain's Olympic team at Montreal in July.

Candlewick's original training as an eventer stood her in good stead as a hunter, but it says a lot for Prince Charles's perseverance in the hunting field – as a comparative newcomer to the sport – that he eventually formed an excellent relationship with the mare. He rode her frequently out hunting and later in team 'chases as well. When he was painted on a hunter, wearing his Windsor coat, Prince Charles chose Candlewick as his mount. The distinguished equestrian artist Susanne Crawford produced a most attractive equestrian portrait which you will see hanging as a print in many a home throughout the land.

Prince Charles also established an excellent relationship with another relative of Columbus, his grey full brother Collingwood, also of course bred by the Queen. Collingwood was often ridden by Barbara Tatlow, former wife of the highly successful show hunter and hack producer and rider, David Tatlow. Their yard near Stow-on-the-Wold enabled them to school their horses over the walls, timber and fly fences of the Heythrop country, hunted with such distinction for twenty-five years by Captain Ronnie Wallace. As we shall see later, Prince Charles's friendship with the Tatlows resulted in some of his happiest riding experiences in the booming new sport of cross-country team riding, invented by Douglas Bunn at Hickstead (see Chapter 13).

The Prince rode an excellent hunter lent to him for a season by Mr John Snowdon, who was one of the most popular Masters ever appointed by the Zetland Hunt. Prince Charles was to enjoy many happy days in this fine country in North Yorkshire and Durham.

Spills as well as thrills did inevitably occur in those early seasons of the Prince's foxhunting experience. One recalls Prince Charles steering a borrowed chesnut hunter into a hedge bordering the narrow lane at Old Hills in the Belvoir country. It was a brave try to take a short cut to hounds, but the chesnut 'did not get the message' and the royal rider was decanted heavily over its head when it got its knees under the top of the hedge and fell into the field adjoining the lane.

Prince Charles remounted and finished the day, as usual. A little more kicking? A little more impulsion? A straighter approach to the obstacle? That is how such lessons are learned in the hunting field. From a tendency to sit bolt upright in the saddle – something of a legacy of early polo experience – the Prince was 'getting forward' somewhat more. He still tended to 'point' his horse at a fence, and approach with a certain amount of speed and a great deal of hope. On an exceptionally good horse this usually works, because the horse 'makes his own arrangements'. Young, inexperienced horses will need more help – a kick or a squeeze from the legs to jump on the correct stride, firm but sympathetic guidance down the reins, but no suggestion of a jab in the mouth for the horse when its jumping action makes it stretch its head and neck forward, requiring more length of rein on landing.

As the old hunting prints reveal, our forefathers 'sat back' at every fence. The Italian expert, Caprilli, and others, preached the forward seat for jumping, and jockeys learned from America to shorten their stirrups and crouch on the horse's neck in steeplechasing as well as on the Flat. Probably the best seat in the hunting field is a 'modified' forward seat. Unlike organized competitions, the hunting field at its most challenging does present the unknown to the rider as well as to the horse. The drop on the far side of a seemingly innocent hedge may be vastly bigger than you had imagined on the approach. Too exaggerated a forward seat will not enable you to stay in the saddle if the horse pecks on badly poached ground when landing.

'Hold and kick' is a good maxim for jumping big hedges, but the modern hunting field increasingly calls for balance and control in jumping tricky timber, or locked iron gates – if you really aspire to take on anything in your path – and the virtues of 'good riding' are absolutely necessary in avoiding falls for your horse and yourself. Jumping in a balanced manner off a stride is perhaps even more important in the hunting field because the obstacle may not bend or break.

Prince Charles had a fairly spectacular fall on the landing side of a large hedge in the Cheshire country during a superb day from Cholmondely Castle. He and his horse 'got it right' only to hit a barbed wire oxer fence erected on the far side of the hedge. On a grey horse which he had bought in Cheshire, the Prince had a nasty spill out with the Quorn. Riding the superb pastures of Dr Tom Connors, the famous horse dealer, at Muxlow, Prince Charles put his horse at a straight-forward Leicestershire fly fence below the good doctor's house. Unfortunately, he had failed to note that other riders were avoiding this point in the fence because there was a large boggy patch on the landing side. The Prince's grey landed in the bog and turned head over heels. Prince Charles resumed his hunting with a particularly muddy countenance and a bloody nose.

Again, such mishaps are all part of a genuine cross-country rider's experience. Watching Prince Charles in the 1985–86 season, and the preceding season, one could see how much progress he has made, despite having had to 'snatch' his days' hunting from his increasingly busy programme of official engagements in recent years, plus his responsibilities as a husband and father.

Sometimes he will exercise his privilege to ride ahead of the mounted field, accompanying the huntsman. This is a great treat but it calls for expertise and nerve. There is a great difference between following just the huntsman or his whippers-in over a fence, to thundering over it in the wake of the Field Master. Your mistakes in the mounted field are fairly anonymous, being lost in the crowd. 'Up front' your jumping is all too easily under scrutiny and there is virtually no likelihood of a friendly gap being created beforehand.

In Leicestershire Prince Charles used the stables at Melton Mowbray of the Guards Saddle Club. There is a great tradition in the Shires for young Army officers, and soldiers, to ride with the leading packs on specially reduced subscriptions. They add some dash and fire to the hunting field, and they are particularly helpful in catching loose horses, picking up the wounded, and generally assisting in making the day more enjoyable for others. The Club has its own horses, as well as keeping officers' privately owned hunters at livery, and Prince Charles frequently rode the Club's splendid little strawberry roan mare, Reflection. She is fast, bold, and handy; all the virtues of a good hunter mare are hers. Prince Charles adored her from the start, and rode her frequently in recent seasons. Guards Saddle Club members were so pleased to see the Prince enjoying Reflection that they decided to ensure the mare became Charles's own hunter permanently. They have a framed photograph of the Prince and Reflection in the Mess at Melton Mowbray. It was taken by the veteran hunting photographer Jim Meads during a day with the Belvoir near Long Clawson.

Another horse Prince Charles has ridden frequently in the hunting field is Highlight, the Thoroughbred mare owned by Mr Geoff Brooks, who farms at Widmerpool, Nottinghamshire, and is one of the Quorn's keenest supporters. He is unusual in hunting thoroughly the stallions who stand at stud at his farm. Geoff is one of the few people still breeding large horses with quality and substance for the hunting field. It is not a lucrative trade compared with the Thoroughbred market where horses are bred for racing. Yet Geoff has the pleasure of performance testing his stallions, none of them Thoroughbred, and later he and his friends and clients prove the worth of their progeny in High Leicestershire.

He was riding a green five-year-old mare in the 1977–78 season when she was especially noticed by the discerning eye of the Crown Equerry. He asked if she was for sale, but Geoff is not a dealer; he sells comparatively few horses, and always keeps those he likes. Yet he is one of the most generous and outgoing foxhunters you could wish to meet. He has always been willing to lend a good horse to a friend, and so it was perfectly natural for him to offer Sir John the mare as a 'spare ride' for Prince Charles.

Steaming horses in a Leicestershire winter landscape – a pause during a hectic Saturday with the Belvoir. With Prince Charles is first whipper-in, Ralph Mankee

'But, mind,' he warned. 'She is very green. The mare is very sensible, but she has a lot to learn.'

Sired by the Hunters' Improvement Society Premium Stallion Raoul, and out of a Thoroughbred mare, Highlight stands a huge 18 hands. This is not a height which would appeal to many foxhunters as a handy mount for the Chase. Yet the writer can testify that Highlight broke all the rules as far as conformation is concerned. She rode much smaller than she looked; she was perfectly balanced at every fence, and had an immense, natural aptitude for cross-country work. Prince Charles loved her from the start. Geoff Brooks recalls that the first time the Prince rode Highlight he was asked by the Quorn's Joint Master, and Field Master in the Monday country, Capt Fred Barker, if he would 'like to go up with Michael'.

They were hunting near Willoughby-on-the-Wolds, south of Nottingham, where the fences come thick and fast in a run, especially if you are endeavouring to ride close to Michael Farrin, easily one of the best natural horsemen across country to be seen anywhere. He slips across fence after fence, making each obstacle look so simple because his horse is always beautifully balanced, even though his eyes are seldom off his hounds. Geoff Brooks was more than a little concerned to see his mare tested in this way, but she performed brilliantly and it says a lot for Prince Charles's horsemanship at that stage that he could ride a strange young horse so prominently at the front in a sharp hunt with success.

Highlight went with the Prince to Hunts all over Britain and performed excellently everywhere, gaining experience over a wide variety of fences, and coping so well with deep going, which is especially trying for a young horse's legs. Highlight was such a royal favourite that she received her own Christmas card from the Prince while he was away on a skiing holiday. There were repeated offers via the Crown Equerry to buy her for the Prince, but although she was always made available whenever required, Geoff preferred to retain her ownership. Although he farms a considerable amount of arable land nowadays, he was brought up on a dairy farm and is

essentially a stock farmer. He adores his horses, and has a sympathetic, caring attitude towards them that is not always easy to find in the more commercial areas of the horse world. His ambition, when Highlight finished hunting, was to breed from her at home at Widmerpool. As well as Prince Charles, her passengers in the hunting field included Mrs Ulrica Murray Smith, Joint Master of the Quorn.

Another to ride Highlight was *Horse and Hound*'s hunting correspondent, Foxford, and he agreed with the Prince and Mrs Murray Smith that this was a hunter of exceptional ability, and a great pleasure to ride. Since Mrs Murray Smith's slim figure makes her among the lightest of lightweights, and Foxford rides at over 14 stone and is 6 ft 2 ins tall, it says a lot for the mare's adaptability in pleasing riders. She was retired from hunting as a twelve-year-old and has already produced a splendid colt foal by the Irish Draught stallion Enniskean Pride which Geoff Brooks used to stand at stud at Widmerpool.

Geoff's favourite stallion was Calgary Gold, a huge Palomino, bred in Ireland. Always known as Tex – for his cream and gold seemed straight out of a cowboy film – the stallion was a brilliant and safe performer across the stiffest country in pursuit of hounds. Among his sons was a useful colt which Geoff named Botany Bay, after a famous covert drawn by the Quorn. In the 1985–86 season as a six-year-old Botany Bay was performing well in Leicestershire from Geoff's yard, and was nearly ready for his owner – Prince Charles. Geoff gave the colt to the Prince as a wedding present, and has reared him until he is ready to take his place in the hunting field. All Tex's sons show natural aptitude across country, and Botany Bay is no exception. He is a bold, but safe jumper – and should be a useful addition to Prince Charles's hunters when needed.

A horse which Prince Charles rode frequently in his early seasons in the hunting field was Chiffchaff, a five-year-old brown gelding, loaned by Mr John Snowdon, Joint Master of the Zetland. This was a young horse for a novice hunting man, but again the Prince struck up a rapport, and hunted the gelding for a couple of seasons in a variety of countries. John had bought the horse for his father, Mr Bill Snowdon, who was his Joint Master, but who had recently died. John, and his attractive wife, Sally, continued a most successful Mastership in the Zetland country, and it soon became one of Prince Charles's favourite venues.

In recent seasons Prince Charles has kept his hunters in Leicestershire at the yard of Mrs Barbara Rich, whose late husband Captain George Rich was famed in the Midlands as a judge, producer and dealer in hunters. Barbara continues all these activities with immense expertise and energy; there can be few more devoted and knowledgeable foxhunters anywhere. A top-class hunter livery yard is effective in keeping your horses as sound as possible, despite the biffs and bangs of the hunting field; it is also essential that the proprietor knows the local Hunts and the hunting country intimately. Sound advice from your livery on whether a winter's morning will permit hounds to hunt at all can save you hours of driving. In all such respects, Barbara Rich is impeccable, and the recap analysis of a day's hunting at one of her hunt teas is almost as enjoyable as the day itself.

After his gruelling tour of Australia, and visits to Washington and Florida on the way home, Prince Charles appeared in Leicestershire on the first available Saturday with the Belvoir in December 1985. His horses were hard and fit for the hunting field, and he had a special treat. His new hunter performed superbly for him. Sometimes the Prince hunts perfectly happily among the mounted field; on this day it was clear that he could go where he liked by virtue of his new horse's prowess over any type or scale of fence.

By Jack of Diamonds, the horse came from Mr Christopher Hindley, Joint Master of the Pendle Forest and Craven Harriers, who hunt the Ribble Valley and Craven districts of Lancashire and North Yorkshire. He had bought it from David Tatlow as 1a four-year-old. You meet 'a bit of everything' in terms of obstacles in the Pendle Forest country and clearly Prince Charles's new horse found Leicestershire no problem. The Prince could be seen

riding confidently behind the Quorn huntsman, Michael Farrin, or the Belvoir's young Scottish huntsman, Robin Jackson, way ahead of the mounted field. Sometimes Prince Charles would take an extra flight of fences in company with David Bland, the intrepid and expert horseman who is stud groom for Mrs Rich.

A true countryman, Prince Charles found no difficulty in making friends with professional Hunt servants. A huntsman has to be a naturalist, a superb horseman, and above all must be able to 'think like a fox', whilst maintaining an invisible thread of communication with his hounds. He controls hounds by his voice, and the signals he blows on his hunting horn, but unless he has considerable sympathy for and understanding of the fox and its environment he will never be a fully successful huntsman. Wind direction, the flight of birds, the behaviour of other wild-life and farmstock must all be observed and acted upon by a huntsman during a day's hunting.

Inherited instincts, and the pack's ability to teach each season's new intake of young hounds by example from the older hounds, ensure that a great deal of its activities are self-motivated. The huntsman knows when to leave hounds alone but must provide the essential direction, in the form of his 'cast', when his pack has checked on the line of a fox and can go no further by its own efforts to retrieve the line. The great huntsman achieves this with amazing accuracy and consistency.

All the subtleties of hunting have been observed at close quarters by Prince Charles in his privileged position 'at the front end'. As always, he has paid for his privilege by 'putting something back' in the form of service. His position as Governor of the Hunt Servants' Benefit Society is by no means treated as just an honorary role. He takes great interest in the work of this body, which provides pensions and accident payments to huntsmen and whippers-in, and presides personally at its annual meeting in London. Hunting people make donations to the Society to augment the benefits available to retired huntsmen.

Evidence of his personal friendship with huntsmen was provided at his wedding at St Paul's when the guests included some of the professional huntsmen with whom he had hunted most, including Michael Farrin of the Quorn, Jim Webster, who was still hunting the Belvoir then, and Brian Gupwell of the Duke of Beaufort's.

During the Masters of Foxhounds Association's centenary celebrations in 1981, Prince Charles addressed a luncheon given for Hunt Servants from all over Britain at the Whitbread Rooms in the City of London. He thanked them for the pleasures he had enjoyed in the hunting field, and he amused them with some hunting stories. Significantly, he also took the opportunity to give a firm warning that the future of the sport depended greatly on huntsmen maintaining standards of conduct. There are strict rules laid down by the MFHA and at their dinner Prince Charles had already warned Masters of Foxhounds similarly about the need to stick to them. Many packs are hunted by Masters as amateurs, and in any case, they are ultimately responsible for the conduct of the sport if they employ professionals.

Prince Charles has given ample evidence throughout his public and personal life that he is a serious, tough-minded person, able to give and take criticism. He has made it perfectly clear that although he enjoys hunting immensely, he has thought a great deal about its moral and practical implications which occasionally cause so much furore in the press and on television – with the encouragement of the small but vociferous abolitionist pressure groups.

OPPOSITE ABOVE *Polo at Jaipur during the Prince's 1980 visit to India. The Maharajah of Jaipur and his family are well known and popular members of the international polo scene. They run an annual tournament at Jaipur on the picturesque Rambagh Palace ground, with the imposing Moti Doongri Fort on the hill behind*
OPPOSITE BELOW *In the conditions which generations of Britons have relished for polo in India: Prince Charles playing at Delhi during his 1980 tour*

ABOVE *Belvoir Castle, near Grantham, Lincolnshire, ancestral home of the Duke of Rutland who owns the famous Belvoir foxhounds, one of the favourite packs of the Prince of Wales. The hounds are kennelled in the grounds of the Castle overlooking the broad sweep of the Vale of Belvoir, which still provides some of the best foxhunting country in the world*

RIGHT *Lt Col Sir John Miller, the Crown Equerry, hunting with the Quorn in 1986. Sir John encouraged Prince Charles to hunt, and organized many of his first days in the hunting field*

OPPOSITE ABOVE *Polo round the world: the Prince of Wales playing 'down under' in Sydney in 1981. Since his schooldays at Geelong in Victoria, Prince Charles has many happy memories of Australia, and manages to fit in some polo on all his visits*

OPPOSITE BELOW *With Les Diables Bleus, the superb high-goal team which was disbanded in Britain at the end of the 1986 season. Prince Charles is accompanied by Robert Graham, Julian Hipwood and the team's patron, Guy Wildenstein*

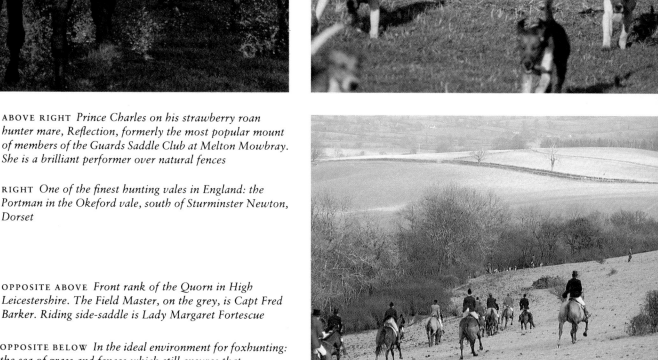

ABOVE RIGHT *Prince Charles on his strawberry roan hunter mare, Reflection, formerly the most popular mount of members of the Guards Saddle Club at Melton Mowbray. She is a brilliant performer over natural fences*

RIGHT *One of the finest hunting vales in England: the Portman in the Okeford vale, south of Sturminster Newton, Dorset*

OPPOSITE ABOVE *Front rank of the Quorn in High Leicestershire. The Field Master, on the grey, is Capt Fred Barker. Riding side-saddle is Lady Margaret Fortescue*

OPPOSITE BELOW *In the ideal environment for foxhunting: the sea of grass and fences which still ensures that Leicestershire is a magnet for foxhunters from all over the world*

OPPOSITE ABOVE *After overcoming his early fears about jumping fences, the Prince of Wales has become a bold cross-country rider, capable of tackling the toughest obstacles in the hunting field. He frequently goes ahead of the mounted field and takes fences without a lead from a horse in front*

OPPOSITE BELOW *'The Windsor Coat', worn by Prince Charles, was especially designed for him, and derives from a 'uniform' first worn by King George III*

RIGHT AND BELOW *A winter sport: the Bicester and Warden Hill pack hunting in snow near Barton Hartshorn in their country which lies in Oxfordshire, Buckinghamshire and Northamptonshire. Capt Ian Farquhar, now Joint Master of the Duke of Beaufort's, was hunting the Bicester hounds when the Prince of Wales was a visitor*

Beautiful Gloucestershire – enjoyed here by members of the Cotswold Hunt, cubhunting early on an October morning, near Rendcomb. They are standing on the bank opposite Old Park

HUNTING
AND CONSERVATION

The unspeakable in pursuit of the uneatable.

OSCAR WILDE

Wilde's famous definition of foxhunting has been used with varying degrees of derision, or scorn, by those who affect to despise the sport. What they do not know, or do not admit, is that Wilde made his witticism during an after dinner speech when he was the guest of a Hunt. His phrase was quoted with glee by hunting men thereafter, and spread from the hunting community to be used whenever the subject of foxhunting arose in public debate.

The moral question as to whether you wish to take part in a sport which involves the death of an animal is a personal matter. For society as a whole to denounce foxhunting on moral grounds is, however, the height of hypocrisy, since the killing of animals for pleasure in the form of non-essential meat eating, for clothing and footwear, is a huge national industry for which virtually the entire population is the customer.

Prince Charles has not sought to enter the public debate on foxhunting, but inevitably his name has frequently been dragged into the subject by those who wish to gain maximum attention from the media. Like all countrymen, the Prince is accustomed to the taking of life. Rearing animals for food production, killing pests, and hunting, fishing and shooting as recreations are all part of country life.

Prince Charles is well aware of the reservations of some people, mainly from towns, to foxhunting. He did not have preconceived ideas about the sport when he started to ride to hounds.

'I try to look at things with a reasonably open mind. It is not always easy, I agree. Sometimes it is very hard to square one's attitude to things. I believe it is necessary to have some form of control of the fox population because otherwise everything becomes completely out of hand. I know some think that it is cruel to inflict that kind of pursuit on an animal. But having seen the way foxes operate, I think the good thing about organized hunting is that at the end of a hunt there is either a dead fox, or a perfectly all right fox. There is nothing in between, in the form of a wounded fox. If you trap them, or shoot, or poison them, the kind of death you inflict can be slow and horrendous.'

One of the most important requirements of all wildlife is habitat, somewhere to live comparatively safely and the reasonably strict observance of a close season during the breeding period of the animal's life. Field sportsmen point out that they fulfil these requirements scrupulously in Britain. The woodlands, small copses and spinnies which dot the countryside were planted by sportsmen to harbour game for hunting and shooting. They add much to the beauty of the landscape; many were superbly sited by our forefathers who often had a great eye for aesthetic as well as sporting values in designing the countryside which is our heritage.

As a result of the policy of providing these wildlife habitats, Britain compares remarkably well with

the rest of Europe in possessing a large, balanced wildlife. There is absolutely no anomaly in the fact that Prince Charles and Prince Philip are lifelong field sportsmen, and are passionately concerned with wildlife conservation in Britain and abroad.

Prince Charles agrees that sporting influences do produce a useful counter-effect against a too ruthless commercial use of land, and therefore sport does aid conservation.

'I think this is absolutely true. Again, it is easy for people to say that this is just an argument, an excuse, to maintain field sports. But I honestly do believe that otherwise there would be no reason to prevent the countryside becoming a prairie. Why would you add coverts, little woodlands, hedges, and similar features, if you did not want to see wildlife? Unless there is a bit of shooting, hunting and fishing taking place why should such forms of conservation occur?'

Yet Prince Charles insists that field sportsmen *must* stick to the codes of conduct ordained by the ruling bodies of each sport. In foxhunting this means that a fox must be hunted 'in its wild and natural state'; this precludes such discredited practices as hunting 'bag foxes', which have been captured and then turned down in front of hounds to provide a hunt.

When a fox is run to ground, the Masters of Foxhounds Association's rules state that if a decision is made that the fox should be killed 'it must be humanely destroyed before being given to the hounds'. A gun is carried by Hunt staff for this purpose, although in Leicestershire and some other areas little or no digging for foxes marked to ground takes place. Much depends on the wishes of the farmers and landowners, and the density of the local fox population. In the West Country, for example, there is a particularly large fox colony in most

Enjoying the countryside during a day's hunting. The Prince of Wales appreciates the connection between conservation and field sports. He points out that sporting conservation of coverts benefits all wildlife

districts, and Hunts are expected to play an especially significant role in culling foxes. On Exmoor the Hunts are asked by farmers to hold special early morning meets in the spring to catch foxes which have been killing and worrying lambs.

Much has been made in the press in recent years about reports that Prince Charles had totally given up shooting. He has certainly not condemned shooting out of hand, but he finds the larger shoots of reared pheasants less attractive as a form of sport. It must be remembered, however, that organized shooting of reared game in Britain is one important factor in maintaining the rigid ban on shooting most forms of wild bird life in our countryside. There is ample alternative organized shooting, and even the least scrupulous shooting enthusiast finds no incentive to contravene our excellent ban on the shooting of song birds, hawks and eagles.

In foxhunting Prince Charles feels strongly that action must be taken if anyone attempts to break the Masters of Foxhounds Association's rules.

'Where exceptions to the rules occur, they should be cracked down on with the full weight of the controlling bodies, because it is unacceptable. All field sports have to be conducted properly. If you are fishing you have to make sure, if you catch the fish, that you dispatch it quickly and cleanly. Otherwise, I think it is unjustifiable. I find shooting much less easy to accept for myself nowadays because of the wounding that happens. I find with hunting it is much easier to justify it to myself because you are taking much more risk. You throw yourself over obstacles; you don't know what's coming; you have to shut your eyes and take a deep breath very often – I do. Whereas with fishing or shooting there is no danger in it. Someone *might* shoot you, but there is very small chance of that. With hunting, you have to get on the horse, and you have to ride it across country. It is not just a matter of sitting there, watching hounds tear a fox to pieces. It is easy to represent it as that, of course.'

Ulrica Murray Smith, one of the few Meltonians still hunting who can recall foxhunting in the fashionable 1930s, says that 'no one paid much

attention to the anti-hunting arguments' when the late Duke of Windsor and his brothers hunted before the war. Times have changed. Aided by a greatly improved communications system, the so-called animal rights movement – fragmented and contradictory though it is – makes sure that the hunting question does get aired when the Prince of Wales rides to hounds.

Prince Charles has observed the sport closely at many levels. He has thought deeply about hunting's ethics and practice, and he is keen that the toughest possible line should be taken against anyone who breaks the rules. The Masters of Foxhounds Associations has a disciplinary committee, and it can take sanctions in the form of expulsions of Masters proved to have broken the rules. The Association has censured Masters who have broken rules such as deliberately hunting a fox into a built-up area. It is easy to scoff that no one has actually been expelled in recent years. On the other hand there is ample evidence that the sport is more scrupulously conducted nowadays than ever before. It can truthfully claim to be the most humane form of control, and through its maintenance of fox coverts to play a significant conservationist role in the countryside.

Having a modern Prince of Wales as a keen participant in a sport which attracts controversies, is a privilege in the Britain of the 1980s. Yet this clearly involves heavy responsibilities as well – and even those who are the most ardent critics of foxhunting should be aware that Prince Charles's involvement has already been a power for good in maintaining standards – and will continue to be so, as long as he and other young men are impelled to answer the challenge of what the hunting poet Will Ogilvie described as 'riding keen to the flash of scarlet on England's green'. His poem *Carrying on* concluded hopefully:

Not in our day shall hunting die,
Or the day of our grandson's sons, say I.
If we rode the earth in a hundred years,
And looked at our land through a horse's ears
We should see the fields as we see them now
And foxhounds feathering over the plough.

Foxhunters of the 1880s might have found it exceedingly difficult to predict that a future Prince of Wales a century ahead would be enthusiastically riding to hounds. Many hunting folk then thought their sport was doomed because of the continuing spread of the railway system. In more recent years it was felt that motorways and the growth in arable farming and new towns would extinguish the sport.

Prince Charles's response to the enduring pleasures of exploring the countryside on a horse, answering the challenge of crossing natural fences, and watching a good pack of hounds work at the behest of a skilled huntsman, give the present day foxhunter some cause to think that, after all, a Prince of Wales *will* be visiting the Vale of Belvoir regularly in the latter part of the year 2087.

ROYAL HAPPENINGS

*'Untin', as I have often said, is the sport of kings – the image of war
without its guilt and only five-and-twenty per cent of its danger.*

MR JORROCKS
(*Handley Cross* BY R. S. SURTEES)

What 'goes on' in the hunting field is frequently a cause for mirth. Prince Charles has never been slow to appreciate fully the comic elements of the Chase. Here are a few examples from his own hunting tours.

High Leicestershire. The Quorn hounds are running hard. A particularly decorative Quorn lady has a mishap and is parted from her horse. She lies directly in the path of the Prince of Wales. Few Leicestershire hunting men dismount readily on such occasions. Many are inclined to look the other way. If someone actually catches your horse when hounds are running hard, then you *have* found a friend.

The 'politeness of Princes' prevails. Prince Charles dismounts and bends over the prostrate lady rider. He enquires about her condition with concern and offers her a refreshing sip from his flask. This is readily accepted, and the lady says she feels she will be all right.

'In that case I'd better catch up the others,' says the Prince, preparing to re-mount his own horse. 'Are you sure there's nothing else I can do?' he asks.

The Quorn lady replies simply, 'Just kiss me.'

(This story has become part of Leicestershire legend already. In some versions the lady received a peck on the cheek; in other versions she did not!)

Warwickshire. Hounds are running hard, and the Prince of Wales is at the front of the field following Warwickshire hounds in the Todenham area.

The Prince is indeed so near the front that he is able to follow one of the red coated whippers-in over a fence. The whipper-in's horse, alas, falls on landing. But Prince Charles has already started his take-off. He lands in a heap on the fallen whipper-in.

'I'm terribly sorry. I hope you're all right?' the Prince enquires.

'Quite all right, Sir,' replies the whipper-in. 'It was an honour.'

The Duke of Beaufort's. Prince Charles jumps a hedge. On landing his horse pecks badly and falls on to its nose. The Prince takes a fall over its head.

Lady Lettie Vernon, distinguished and veteran hunting lady, is next to jump. She and her horse land on Prince Charles.

'Good heavens,' says Lady Lettie. 'That's the second time I've landed on a Prince of Wales!'

The Belvoir. It is a Saturday afternoon. The Belvoir hounds are running hard in the grass vale below Long Clawson. It is possible to jump most fences on a wide front, but on Lord King's land near the Smite there is a jumping place, a set of rails installed by the Hunt.

Prince Charles has his hunter nicely balanced as he jumps neatly out of a covert during a day's hunting. He often accompanies the huntsman into a covert when hounds draw for a fox, while the rest of the mounted followers wait outside, as this young lady is doing

Members of the mounted field surge forward one after another to jump the rails. Prince Charles is in the mêlée and tries several times to take his place. Each time he is baulked by a queue-jumper.

Far ahead, hounds are running on. The hunt is getting further away every second. The Prince turns his horse and trots to the back of the queue once more.

'Ah well,' he says with a rueful smile. 'I can't do anything about it. I just wasn't brought up to barge.'

The Bicester and Warden Hill. Capt Ian Farquhar, the Joint Master and huntsman of this popular pack in Buckinghamshire, is famed for his skill in jumping bare barbed wire. His hounds are running hard, and Capt Farquhar has slipped far ahead of his mounted field.

Sharing the bliss of being virtually 'alone with hounds' on this occasion is Prince Charles. Unfortunately, hounds have run on to one of the very few farms in the country where the Hunt is not welcome. The distinguished amateur huntsman and Prince Charles ride into the farm yard on their way through, in pursuit of hounds.

'Get the hell out of here,' roars the farmer. 'You know you're not allowed here.'

'It's only the two of us. Would you mind if we go through?' asked Ian Farquhar.

'Of course, I mind. Get the hell out of here,' roars the farmer.

Ian Farquhar duly departed the way he had come. Prince Charles stood his ground and looked at the farmer.

'For once, I was hoping the penny would drop and he would let me through,' he recalled later.

But the farmer roared again, 'And you can clear off too! Get out of here. Back the way you came.'

The Prince of Wales duly retreated, and found the rest of the mounted followers by a circuitous route – by which time he was forced to continue the hunt at the back of the mounted field.

The Portman in deepest Dorset. A crowd of villagers is gathered at the meet in the Okeford Vale and is rewarded by the sight of the Prince of Wales riding with hounds. A chubby cheeked little boy waves at the Prince in the first field.

The Prince smiles, but asks, 'Shouldn't you be at school?'

'Oh no, I'm ill,' replies the sturdy child.

The Portman again. It is doubtful whether Prince Charles knows this story in full. Hounds produced a sizzling morning's sport in this deep-riding vale where the fields are divided by big hedges, planted on banks, and guarded by formidable ditches.

It had been a superb morning's sport, and an excellent ride. Yet this is a small area of hunting country, bounded by a high hill to the east, and the neighbouring Hunt boundary to the west.

There is virtually no covert in the district which the Hunt has not drawn. No matter, it has been highly successful, and the Masters and Hunt staff are preparing to blow for home. Their horses are nearly 'cooked' and they do not have reserves. Prince Charles, however, is met by a groom leading his second horse. He changes horses cheerfully and awaits the the rest of the day's sport.

Consternation! The Portman Masters, brothers Dick and John Woodhouse, hastily confer. Huntsman Geoff Harrison takes hounds to the tiny area of rough by a nearby duck pond. It is a slim hope. Hounds whimper; then there is a chorus of hound music. A fox runs – and the pack are away again.

The Portman Masters and a depleted field take in another hole in the girth buckle and ease their horses into a gallop again. It is fortunate that riders and horses know every Okeford Vale fence backwards. Another sharp, thrilling tour of the vale is completed. Hounds mark their fox to ground, and he is left in peace.

The Prince is offered tea in a farmhouse and accepts immediately, bringing joy to the Okeford Vale – and making a page of local hunting history in a country where two horses per ride are the exception rather than the rule.

The Duke of Buccleuch's country. It is a bleak winter's afternoon on the Scottish borders. Prince Charles and Sir John Miller have finished hunting, and have eaten their sandwiches and enjoyed a tot of whisky. Suddenly word reaches the parked horsebox: 'Hounds have found again!'

The Prince and Sir John, keen foxhunters indeed, hastily remount and make their way towards the pack, as directed by a foot follower. They encounter a gate, and Sir John stops to open it.

Prince Charles says, 'Why don't we jump it?'

'Of course you can if you want to,' replies the Crown Equerry.

The Prince's horse has *not* been fortified with sandwiches and whisky and demolishes the gate. (It has since been replaced by the Buccleuch Estates and is known as 'The Prince of Wales Gate').

Prince Charles and Sir John ride on. They see a hound – and enthusiastically ride after it, thinking that it is a tail hound (one left behind at the back of the pack). They ride on, and on, and on – across the heathery hills of the Borders of Scotland. The hound does not seem to be going anywhere definite, however.

Eventually the Prince of Wales and the Crown Equerry, disappointed and somewhat puzzled, return to their horsebox. On their return they learn that the huntsman, Sir Hugh Arbuthnot, has long since gone home. The lone hound was still out on its own – and with the Prince and Sir John had been one of only three individuals hunting in Scotland at the end of the afternoon!

James Teacher in February 1981 happened to meet Capt Ronnie Wallace, Chairman of the Masters of Foxhounds Association, in St James's, London's clubland.

'You've heard the news about Prince Charles's engagement?' James asked.

'Oh yes, very good news,' replied Ronnie.

Then he added a trifle anxiously, 'You don't think it will interfere with his hunting, do you?'

EXPLORATIONS

Not for the lust of killing, not for the place of pride,
Not for the hate of the hunted we English saddle and ride,
But because in the gift of our fathers the blood in our veins that flows
Must answer for ever and ever the challenge of 'Yonder he goes.'

W. H. OGILVIE

One of the glories of the British Isles is surely its incredible diversity. Drive a few miles and you find a striking change of scene, a noticeably altered local accent, and probably different weather. Such changes are especially enjoyable if you set out to tour a wide variety of Hunts at varying times of the season. Prince Charles experienced the joys, and the frustrations, of this form of discovery to the full in his first few seasons as a foxhunter.

His second day's hunting, referred to briefly in Chapter 9, was on 28 February 1975, with the Cottesmore. Simon Clarke was then hunting the Cottesmore country with great distinction, continuing a tradition of amateur huntsmen long preserved in this delightful area which included much of the old county of Rutland.

A private day was arranged at noon, meeting at Preston Lodge, home of the former Joint Master, and latterly the Hunt Chairman, Sir Henry Tate. Only the farmers and landowners over whose land the Hunt might run that day, and the Hunt committee, were invited to form the mounted field. Prince Charles had only just arrived back from a trip via India to Nepal where he had attended King Birendra's coronation. He was already displaying that special brand of resilience needed if you are to fit foxhunting into a life which involves much travel and duty outside the British countryside.

The Prince was accompanied by Sir John Miller,

and both wore 'ratcatcher', the tweed coats, buff breeches and bowler hats which are worn by fox-hunters during the cubhunting season before 1 November, but may certainly be worn during the season when occasion demands. Princess Anne and her father-in-law, Mr Peter Phillips, who wears the Duke of Beaufort's blue and buff, were also out hunting. Mrs Peter Phillips had again provided the reliable Pinkers for Prince Charles to ride. The cob proved just as effective over the grass and well-fenced Cottesmore country as he had at home in Gloucestershire.

'Prince Charles went terribly well; he later told me he thought he jumped more fences that day than he had in his whole life until then,' Capt Clarke recalls.

The small field enjoyed some of the cream of the Cottesmore country. There was a slowish hunt from the famous Little Owston cover to Lady Wood and back, and another hunt to Brooke. Near Knossington, the formidable Leicestershire hunting personality, the Hon Ursula (Urkie) Newton, fell heavily in front of the Prince of Wales: a sight once seen never forgotten. Another hunting lady fell at the same time.

Urkie, Secretary of the Melton Hunt Club, has a knack – mostly comprised of sheer courage and resolution – of surviving crumpling falls which would put others off the Chase for life. On this occasion she remarked cheerfully, 'I'm afraid the middle-aged ladies are not doing very well...' Later the Prince had a harmless fall, and soon after remarked to Urkie, 'I'm afraid I've just joined the middle-aged ladies.'

Although the country had been enjoined to strict silence on the Prince's visit, there was more than a slight clue at Lady Wood where a loyal farmer, the late Mr Sharpe, had erected a huge union jack by his drive. His explanation to the slightly peeved Master was: 'I only did it out of respect; I last flew it when we won the war.' The late Major Bob Hoare, one of hunting's great personalities who had been such a popular Master and huntsman of the Cottesmore, introduced the royal visitor to Mr Sharpe, and all was well. The Prince's ease of manner was noticed by all who met him that day; he would always be welcome of course wherever he hunted, but it was clear that he would make contacts and friendships with country people, far more worthwhile than mere courtesy demanded. That evening Prince Charles dined with the Queen Mother, and according to later reports 'the talk was of nothing but foxhunting.'

Eight days later, Prince Charles enjoyed his third day's hunting, this time with the Quorn. It was a Saturday, and hounds met at Hoton, but they soon drew into some of their best Monday country in honour of their visitor. Grass and fences abounded. Prince Charles experienced for the first time the special pleasure associated with jumping High Leicestershire where the extraordinary draining properties of the land provide such good going.

He told the huntsman, Michael Farrin, he was 'over the moon' at the end of the day. Since then, Prince Charles has re-visited the Quorn many times.

On 21 February 1976 Prince Charles had his first experience of hunting the fine, wild Border country of the Duke of Buccleuch's Hunt. It was founded by the fifth Duke in 1827, and includes pasture, hill and moorland in Roxburghshire, Selkirk and Berwickshire. Tragically, the ninth Duke, who has been Master since 1970, was seriously injured in a hunting accident and is unable to ride to hounds, but he continues to take a great interest in his

hounds, and often follows by car. The late Sir Hugh Arbuthnot was hunting hounds as an amateur when Prince Charles made his first visit, accompanied by Sir John.

The Duke of Buccleuch kindly provided me with this report of a memorable day:

'It had long been the tradition to move from the fertile farm land between and the Teviot, hunted on weekdays, to the wild hills known as the Saturday Country, west of a line from Hawick to Selkirk.

So it was on February 21 that hounds met at Borthwickshiels, about three miles west of Hawick. Within minutes of moving off, hounds found a big dog fox in some whins, and away they raced south west to Craik Forest, making a point of over eight miles.

For any man or horse unaccustomed to the hills, with every manner of hidden pitfall in the form of sheep drains to very large stone walls or dykes, as they are known, it is a daunting experience to go at anything but a sedate pace; to race over the hills as they did that day, with Prince Charles right up at the front, was an exhilarating and testing experience.

Although horses reared in these hills seem to

The fun of the Shires: jumping typical Leicestershire timber in the Quorn's Friday country at Cream Gorse

develop a third front leg to cope with the unexpected hole, ditch or bog, it must have been quite a contrast for horses from the Shires.

The hunt ended near a disused shepherd's cottage in the forest in just the most remote part of the whole Borders of Scotland. By an extraordinary coincidence the Duke of Edinburgh arrived by helicopter not long afterwards, to open it as a special centre in connection with the Duke of Edinburgh's Award Scheme.

There must have been some very tired horses by the time they boxed, in Harden Glen, some hours later, but I doubt if any of the intrepid sportsmen would have swapped one for a lift in a helicopter.'

This was the day, referred to briefly in Chapter 11, when Prince Charles and Sir John Miller remounted after riding back to Harden, the home of Lord and Lady Polwarth.

They returned to the Buccleuch country the following season, when Capt Clarke had moved north from the Cottesmore to hunt the Buccleuch hounds. The Hunt met on 29 November 1976 at Middle Third, Gordon, home of Mr Reg Tweedie, owner of Freddie, the great 'chaser who brought much

excitement to the Borders when he was second in the Grand National in 1965 and 1966.

Hounds ran hard in this fine, wild, open country, and the mounted field jumped a great many craggy stone walls. Prince Charles impressed the Mastership by his close interest in and knowledge of hound working and breeding. He experienced another drama to add to his hunting memories.

In jumping one wall off a road his saddle girth broke, or became detached, and the Prince parted company with his horse which jumped a very large stone wall back into the road, landing very close to the Dowager Duchess of Buccleuch, to her dismay. The horse galloped down the road and across country, and tried to jump a dyke with a barbed wire fence on each side, only to land upside down in the dyke between the two barbed wire fences – but extricated itself with hardly a scratch. Sir John had given his own horse to the Prince, and continued on the bolter when it was finally recovered.

That same month, on 8 November, Prince Charles had also hunted in Scotland with the Dumfriesshire. This is one of the most interesting packs in the world. The late Sir John (Jock) W. Buchanan-Jardine was a great breeding expert and created his own distinctive strain of foxhound, black and tan in colour and up to 29 inches in height, about 3 inches higher at the shoulder than most foxhounds. They have a distinctive booming cry, and contain some French blood in their breeding lines. The pack has stayed true to type for many years. Sir John's son, Major Sir Rupert Buchanan-Jardine, has been Joint Master and huntsman since 1950, providing splendid sport over their fine, open country near Lockerbie.

Prince Charles was then completing his tour of duty in command of the minehunter HMS Bronington. He had been patrolling the North Sea locating mines for ten months, but his ship was on the Clyde in mid-November and the opportunity of a day's hunting was too good to be missed. Later that month he was to sail his ship into the Pool of London just before his twenty-eighth birthday.

He arrived with the Dumfriesshire hounds at 12.30 pm and hounds found immediately at the first draw in Gimmenbie Glen. They achieved a very fast hunt of some twenty-five minutes before killing their fox at Cowdens. Later they found again in Burnswark and had another good hunt across Tundergarth and down the River Milk, catching their fox at Scroggs after a hunt of just over an hour.

At the end of November 1976, Prince Charles was back in the north, this time to hunt with the Percy which has a glorious, unspoilt country.

In the early years of his hunting experience, Prince Charles was extraordinarily lucky in visiting Hunts on good scenting days. No matter how good the area of country selected, a Master of Foxhounds cannot dictate the sort of scenting conditions his hounds will encounter. For a good scent the ground temperature should preferably be warmer than the air above, so that the droplets of scent left by the fox hang in the air and are easily detected by the hounds' noses.

Thus, the onset of colder weather usually provides good scent. Whereas when there is a frost on the ground and a warm sun is melting it, the scent droplets are usually carried high and evaporate quickly, producing bad scenting conditions for hounds. Settled weather is usually better for scent, too. All these rules are liable to be broken unexpectedly, and scent remains the greatest mystery in a sport where you can never be sure of the quality of the day's hunting until the huntsman blows the long drawn out note on his horn signifying hounds are going home at the end of the day.

The Duke of Northumberland, known affectionaly as 'Hughie Northumberland' to many sportsmen in his native country, where he is the largest private landowner, has been hunting his own hounds for nearly half a century, since he became Master in 1940. The Duke said afterwards that the day of the Prince's visit, 27 November, was 'one of the best scenting days I ever hunted hounds.'

Prince Charles, the Duke and Sir John Miller unboxed their horses at Humbleheugh Farm, where the Prince was introduced to a 'Percy Special', described as 'an invigorating cocktail of cherry brandy and whisky'! With the quality of the sport ahead, some invigoration was no doubt welcome. Mr Kit Graham, a keen hunting farmer, provided the Percy Special, and then the Prince rode over the hill to South Charlton where the Hunt was entertained by Mr Andy Bell, whose wife and daughter were keen followers.

Hounds found immediately in White House Folly whin and ran over Honey Hill, where several flights of rails on the downward slope brought grief to several riders. The fox bore right at Humbleheugh, over Murdie's Bog to Hefforlaw Bank Covert, and across the A1 road to Broxfield. Here the Duchess of Northumberland took a heavy fall, and had to abandon the chase with mild concussion.

Turning north, hounds ran very fast between Wisp Law and North Rennington to Rock Hall, where the fox was headed and a welcome check followed, giving the horses a chance to get their wind. Going back towards Wisp Law, hounds picked up the line of their fox and, passing through the covert, ran very fast up to Hefforlow Bank and over Rock South Farm, killing their fox by the lane running to Rock Midstead. This was indeed a fine hunt.

The day finished with a hunt of thirty minutes without a check, from Red Braes, finishing at Humbleheugh, where hounds caught their fox within 50 yards of where Prince Charles had unboxed his horse. Although it was only early afternoon, home was blown by the Duke after a day followers of his hounds will never forget. There had been more than enough work for one horse.

Just before Christmas, 1976, Prince Charles tasted the reverse in suitable hunting conditions when he visited the Grafton in Northamptonshire, from their meet at Halse. Fog came down during the day, and during a good hunt in the afternoon there was some alarm among the Masters when it was noticed that the Prince was no longer with them. Had he fallen, or simply got lost? Fortunately, he appeared guided by a local 'pilot' rider, perfectly safe and sound.

Arguably one of the best grass countries remaining in the Midlands is that of the Fernie, in South Leicestershire, around and above Market Harborough. Prince Charles first hunted with this pack on 5 January 1977, from Kings Norton. Prince Charles went into covert with the huntsman, the veteran Bruce Durno, and had the joy of being virtually 'alone with hounds' in the first hunt. It was a foggy morning and hounds slipped away from the field, running from Tamborough to the Skeffington Vale, followed only by the Prince, with Durno, a whipper-in and two lucky followers who had been on point (posted at one end of the covert to see the fox go away).

Prince Charles visited the Fernie again on 4 January 1978, from their meet at Ibston-on-the-hill, and this was a first-class day, with an excellent hunt from the famous Shangton Holt covert. Hounds ran

Taking a natural fence with a drop is one of the most exciting elements in a day's hunting. Prince Charles has developed a secure seat, and keeps contact with the horse's mouth, while allowing the horse's head essential freedom on landing

some fifteen miles, including a four-mile point (the furthest distance in a straight line from the start) in about two and a half hours. The Prince suffered one of the misfortunes of the Chase in being misdirected during the hunt, and missed the latter part. He hunted again with the Fernie on 15 November 1979 from Peatling Manor which was a moderate day's sport.

One of the best days Prince Charles experienced in his early hunting tours was with the Sinnington in the North Riding of Yorkshire, around Kirby Moorside and Helmsley. The Countess of Feversham has been the senior Joint Master since 1950. The country has some splendid moorland, and a good vale, but the plough has increased even since Prince Charles's first visit on 16 November 1977, when hounds met at Salton. The amateur huntsman then was Mr Willie Poole, one of the most engaging characters in the hunting field, and a gifted humorous writer on the subject.

From the Ness Waterholmes, a lovely area of rough grasses, hounds screamed away and eventually marked their fox to ground in a drain by Seamer

Wood, having achieved a superb hunt, with a six-mile point.

Willie Poole, whose girth is not his least noticeable feature, fell from his horse in front of the Prince during the hunt.

'Go on, Sir,' he yelled, 'to hell with my horse...'. But the Prince stopped and caught Willie's horse for him – not for the last time showing a willingness to sacrifice a good position in a hunt if it meant helping a faller. The excitement of the Chase does not always bring out the best in other foxhunters at such moments. Loose horses suddenly become 'invisible' to others still mounted.

A great day's hunting with the Sinnington concluded with hounds catching their last fox in the dusk near Sunley Court after running eleven miles. After the meet 102 horses had started the day – six finished, including Prince Charles.

A week later, on 23 November Prince Charles was down in the grassy, stiffly fenced Portman vale country near Okeford Fitzpaine in North Dorset (referred to briefly in Chapter 11). Hounds met at Belchalwell, and the Prince's visit has become part of local history here. They had a tremendous day, with the Prince tackling the huge Portman thorn hedges, guarded by very deep ditches, and often with high drops. The Joint Masters, who were brothers, the late John and Dick Woodhouse, recalled that in jumping one monster boundary fence into Lower Fifehead Farm, the royal visitor was heard to remark in mid-air, 'Bloody hell!' The fence has been known by this title ever since.

The last hunt of the day was the best, when hounds found a 'grand old silver fox' well known to the Hunt, who was in his usual place by Mr Robert Alner's brook. The fox ran a big circle round the vale, and escaped unscathed – to no one's regret, except the hounds.

On 5 December that year Prince Charles visited the Portman's neighbouring country, the South Dorset, hunted with much success by Alastair Jackson, nowadays producing great sport with the Cattistock. It was an appalling scenting day, but the mounted field enjoyed a ride in the Duntish Vale, always an adventure. Afterwards, Prince Charles

had tea at the Mitchell family's farm at Duntish. Neighbouring farmers, the Master and Hunt staff made up the tea party.

'Prince Charles stayed a long time – spoke to everyone (as he had done all day out hunting) and made himself late for an engagement in London,' recalls Alastair Jackson. As so often happened after a Hunt visit, an official letter arrived from an Equerry, but so did a hand-written letter from Prince Charles, several pages long, expressing warmest gratitude, and especially remarking on his pleasure in meeting so many farming folk 'at home'.

Prince Charles had indeed extended his exploration of rural Britain on horseback in 1977. His days included a visit to one of the most historic packs, the Fitzwilliam, in Northamptonshire and Huntingdonshire, hunted by the Earls Fitzwilliam for over 200 years. Hounds met at Moonshine Gap on the Bullock Road, famous in the last century as the site of illegal prize fights. Hounds ran well all day in this country near the A1. Afterwards the Prince had tea with keen hunting farmers Mr and Mrs Jack Martin and their family.

He stayed the night at Lord and Lady Fitzwilliam's magnificent house, Milton, outside Peterborough, where the Fitzwilliam hounds are kennelled, and were most carefully bred by the tenth and last Earl, the late (Tom) Fitzwilliam, to win prizes at Peterborough Royal Foxhound Show where he was the devoted Chairman until his death in 1979. After dinner the Prince inspected the Fitzwilliam stables and tack room, a remarkable example of early 18th century design, and looked at the family's fabulous collection of Stubbs's equestrian paintings not long before midnight.

Prince Charles was continuing a family tradition when he visited the Pytchley on 21 December 1977. As described earlier (Chapter 2) his grandfather, King George VI, was a keen wearer of the Pytchley white collar and enjoyed a great deal of sport with these hounds until 1931.

Edward, Prince of Wales, later King Edward VII, hunted with the Pytchley in 1870, paying a visit to Althorp Park, home of Earl Spencer. The Hunt in its present form owes its existence to the Spencer family; the first Earl was the first Master, in 1756. In the nineteenth century the fifth Earl played an immense part in the Hunt's fortunes, being Master for three separate periods. Prince Charles's family connections with the Pytchley are therefore especially strengthened through his marriage, The Princess of Wales being the youngest daughter of the eighth Earl Spencer.

Field Master, and Joint Master of the Pytchley for the past decade, is Dick Saunders, the great horseman who in 1982 won the Grand National on Frank Gilman's Grittar. Dick gives a wonderful lead to the Pytchley mounted field, and his Joint Masters and the popular huntsman, Peter Jones, all work hard to ensure that sport in this great country remains at a high level, despite the huge change from grassland to arable farming in Northamptonshire in the postwar years.

The Pytchley country was delighted when the Prince of Wales came out with their hounds, following a meet at Ashby St Legers. The Prince was given a warm welcome, and a busy day followed, but the Goddess of the Chase was not smiling on the royal visitor that day. He suffered two falls, one through being baulked at a fence by an adult – and the next through a small boy riding down a fence on his pony just as the Prince was taking off.

Also in 1977 Prince Charles hunted with the Derwent, near Scarborough in North Yorkshire. It was on 15 November, and Prince Charles had just mounted his horse when Mrs John Raines came running from her farmhouse at Garrow Lodge, Ryton, to tell him she had just heard on the radio that he was now an uncle. Princess Anne had given birth at St Mary's Hospital, Paddington, to her first child, and the Queen's first grandchild: Master Peter Phillips.

The Derwent was hunted then by Lt Col the Hon Nick Crossley, who has since taken the Mastership of the larger Yorkshire Hunt, the Middleton, and hunts those hounds. On this day, the Derwent pack hunted four foxes, and caught one. They finished in the dark by the covert known as California. In the middle of the day hounds crossed the River

Bill Lander, former huntsman of Sir Watkin Williams-Wynn's Hunt. Prince Charles has had some of his best hunting with these hounds. Here, hounds are standing with their huntsman during a cubhunting morning

Derwent to catch their fox by the Middleton covert, Marr Winn. A new by-pass bridge was being constructed there, and the workmen driving machinery and digging downed tools on recognizing the Prince of Wales, giving him a warm welcome. He spent some time talking to them – while hounds waited to draw the next covert.

This was also the season when Prince Charles first visited one of the finest preserved hunting countries in Britain, Sir Watkin Williams-Wynn's. This remarkable stretch of North Welsh Borders country has vistas of grassland, well fenced with thorn hedges, and delightful coverts, beautifully sited for hunting. Thanks to remarkable continuity maintained by the Watkin Williams-Wynn family, the enthusiasm of the farmers and landowners for hunting remains high. Few outsiders are able to visit the Hunt because its enclosures are not large enough to permit the size of mounted fields that can visit Leicestershire. On 26 November 1977 the Prince attended a day's hunting after a meet at Broughton,

having stayed the night at Eaton Lodge, as guest of Anne, Duchess of Westminster. Two years later, on 26 February 1979, the Prince hunted again with this pack, often known as the Wynnstay, where its hounds are kennelled near Ruabon, Clwyd. It was to be a tremendous day: hounds produced a remarkable eleven-mile hunt covering the best of the Wynnstay Vale in about seventy-five minutes.

Sir (Owen) Watkin Williams-Wynn, the senior Master since 1957, and his Joint Masters welcomed the Prince back to the Wynnstay country every season for some years. The huntsman until 1982 was Bill Lander, one of the most popular and effective professionals in the sport, and a great personality. Prince Charles much enjoyed a brilliant day from the Hunt kennels in Bill's last season. There were three splendid hunts, covering the best of the Park Eyton country. Prince Charles was piloted by a keen young farmer, John Fearnall, who gave a great lead, but during the day Charles had a fall following Fearnall over a drop fence. The Prince was by no means the only faller; the Cheshire huntsman Johnny O'Shea – a tremendous man across country – was visiting this day, and suffered a crasher.

After hunting, Prince Charles had tea with Bill and Eileen Lander in the huntsman's house. It was a jolly occasion, and Prince Charles offered to sign a print of himself which was hanging in the house.

Mrs Lander pointed out that as it was framed this would be difficult.

'Never mind that,' said Bill. Within seconds he had taken the picture outside, and there was an alarming noise of breaking glass. The picture had suddenly lost its frame, and was brought indoors to be signed by the royal visitor – later to be re-framed and hung as a prize possession.

Bill Lander was succeeded as huntsman of Sir Watkin Williams-Wynn's by the amateur huntsman, Mr Neil Ewart, who has continued to produce fine sport with this largely pure English-bred pack in a stretch of country which is living testimony to the conservationist influence of foxhunting: carefully maintained coverts amid 'old fashioned' grass or mixed farming, offering a paradise to foxes and other wildlife, but with a benevolently operated cull each winter to keep the top predator, the fox, at an acceptable level.

The aforementioned Johnny O'Shea hunted the Cheshire hounds on one of the Prince's 'red letter days' during his tours. Hounds met at Cholmondeley Castle, after six weeks of frost and snow, on 24 February 1979. The Master, Cheshire farmer Joe Heler, put the meet back until 11.45am because of the frost. No one expected much sport, with a thaw setting in, but *Horse and Hound*'s hunting correspondent Foxford, who happened to be out

The Cheshire field move off for a day's hunting near Cholmondeley Castle

that day, recalls it as one of the best he experienced in all his travels to over 170 Hunts.

The difficulties of riding a strange country as a visitor cannot be over emphasized, and Prince Charles impressed everyone by his courage and dash throughout the day. There are ditches guarding many of the hedges in this area; some tend to be misleadingly thin at the top, encouraging a horse to take chances, and occasionally a line of wire-free fences is interrupted by an unexpected wire oxer on the landing side which can bring down your horse.

This happened to Prince Charles, and he later wrote to the Master: 'I have a little Cheshire soil on my buttons to remind me of a very special day.' Foxford, who was very near at the time, remembers it as an especially heavy fall. Many would have pulled up or finished the day thereafter, but Prince Charles remounted and completed this fast hunt with tremendous zest. 'Over, under or through I will go' is one of the sayings of the hunting field. The Prince of Wales certainly lives up to this precept in a hunt – and they were indeed hard hunts on this Cheshire day.

Hounds found their first fox at Chapel Mere and marked it to ground at Peckforton Moss. They found next at Douse Green and ran over the cream of the Cheshire country to catch their fox in the open by Faddiley Common. Prince Charles was by

no means the only one to have a dirty coat. Foxford, riding a superb hireling called Basher, recalls fending off riderless horses (rather than catching them) at one stage. Basher continued to take on one obstacle after another with all the aplomb of a bicycle on a country lane.

Out of a field of 160 only a handful continued in the afternoon. Hounds found at Chesterton and concluded the day with a long, fast hunt over difficult country, ending at Bath Wood at 4.30 pm. Foxford, changing his boots by his car in a country lane, recalls hearing horses' shoes on the road. Round the corner came the Prince of Wales, riding next to Sir John Miller. They were at a sedate walk on two weary horses. The Prince looked supremely happy and relaxed.

It is impossible to convey adequately to anyone else the many challenges, small or greater, which you and your horse may have undertaken in a hard hunt; the excitements of watching hounds screaming across country on a good scent; the beauty of the British countryside in winter time when seen from the back of a horse.

'Once you've had a really outstanding day, well ... that's something no one can take away from you for the rest of your life,' said a distinguished retiring Master of Foxhounds. The Prince of Wales certainly appeared to have been in possession of such a day in Cheshire on that November February afternoon.

'In my five seasons as Master this was one of my most thrilling experiences,' Joe Heler recalled later.

In all his travels in the hunting field, Prince Charles looks back on a day with the Berkeley with special memories of a hard hunt. This is indeed a challenging country, especially for the visitor. The modern Berkeley country is just a fragment of the huge stretch from the Severn to London, originally hunted by the Earls of Berkeley.

The hounds are still kennelled below Berkeley Castle and belong to Major John Berkeley, descendant of the Earldom. The Marsh country between the Castle and the Severn is grassland criss-crossed with reens, or rhines: deep, water-filled ditches, with steep sides. If a horse gets into one of these reens it has great difficulty in extricating itself, and the rider will usually get a severe ducking. There are bushy hedges to be jumped, often with broad ditches in front or beyond. Boldness and skill are necessary to cope with this country if you are to stay anywhere near hounds in a good hunt.

Prince Charles has often hunted in the Berkeley country, and as Major Berkeley remarks, 'There are a lot of big, hairy fences in the Marsh, but the Prince of Wales makes light of them all, and has had remarkably few falls. He is now a very accomplished rider to hounds, with a natural eye for country.'

The superb huntsman Tim Langley was still hunting the Berkeley with much success when Prince Charles paid his first visit on 2 March 1978. Prince Charles recalls with relish the sport which followed the meet at the Hunt kennels:

'It was undoubtedly one of the best days I have ever had. I believe hounds ran something like twenty-two miles that day; I have never seen anything quite like it. We ended up with the huntsman and the whipper-in having dropped out at six o'clock in the evening. Hounds had disappeared and there were only four of us left on horses. We had to stand on the tops of gateposts, listening carefully, in trying to see or hear hounds – because they had just vanished.'

There had been a great deal of rainfall and the going was 'pretty punishing' for horses and hounds, Major Berkeley recalls. After a dry start, it began to rain and continued until dark. Hounds ran hard all day; there were a lot of foxes afoot in the Marsh, and there was a screaming scent. Hounds were eventually stopped just before 6 pm on Mr and Mrs Brian Savage's farm, Dayhouse, in the heart of the Marsh. The only mounted followers left were Prince Charles, Sir John Miller – who had suffered immersion in a reen earlier – Joint Master Mrs John Daniell and Major Berkeley. Tim Langley had 'got to the bottom' of three horses, and he and the whipper-in, Chris Maiden – nowadays the hunts-

man – had to take to a car to get to hounds at the end of the day.

'I do not think that I have ever seen hounds so tired; they had driven on relentlessly for six hours,' recalls Major Berkeley.

A year later, on 1 March, 1979, Prince Charles enjoyed another exceptional Berkeley day. They met at the kennels again, and spent most of the day in the Marsh, finishing in the dark at 6.30 pm, after covering a lot of ground – and a great many awesome fences and ditches. This sort of hunting is indeed a different experience from hunting over the more trim obstacles of the Shires on old turf.

When Prince Charles visited the North Cotswold country he had an opportunity to ride with one of Britain's leading amateur huntsmen, and certainly among the best horsemen in crossing natural country at speed, Captain Brian Fanshawe. They met at Laverton, on the edge of the Cotswold Escarpment, in bitter winter weather, with the hills covered in snow and shrouded in freezing fog.

The first fox found in the Broadway vale ran straight up into the hills. Hounds hunted in the 600 acres of Lidcombe Wood with some difficulty on a poor scent, and only one hound was able to own the line of the fox. She was a bitch called Tynedale Stamina (73) which Brian Fanshawe had bred in Ireland when he was Master of the marvellous country of grass and walls, the County Galway, always known as the Galway Blazers. Stamina was descended on the female side from a strain of hounds bred originally in Ireland's Carlow Hunt country. Fanshawe has always admired this line of breeding and tried to promote it. He carefully explained all this to Prince Charles as they rode down a wooded ride in filthy winter weather.

It was a brand of foxhunting again a long way removed from cantering across High Leicestershire's old turf, jumping well-kept hedges in the wake of a smart pack. The hound Stamina had a distinctive voice, and the huntsman pointed this out. Prince Charles listened closely, and appeared to be perfectly happy, but Brian Fanshawe confessed later he had feared the Prince was very cold and 'probably bored to tears with my ramifications'.

About two hours later the North Cotswold hounds were trying hard to find another fox in a thick covert at Burberry Hill. Suddenly one hound spoke, and Fanshawe doubled on the horn.

'Your bitch again,' said Prince Charles, immediately picking out the voice of Stamina from the pack. Probably the best definition of a 'real foxhunter' is someone who can enjoy this sort of hunting, in the worst of weather, and fully concentrate on what hounds are doing in woodland and thick coverts.

When the Prince visited the North Cotswold country again, on 16 January 1980, he thoroughly enjoyed a rousing day in the stiffly fenced Pebworth Vale. Hounds caught their fox at H.M. Prison, Long Lartin, after running about twelve miles in ninety minutes. Prince Charles had a tremendous ride on the grey Collingwood, of which more later. The North Cotswold followers were especially impressed when the Prince and Collingwood, his partner in team 'chases, cleared four strands of barbed wire as clean as a whistle near Cleeve Prior. Brian Fanshawe was especially pleased: his grandfather had bred Collingwood's grand-dam.

John Redfern, who had a lovely grass farm near Pebworth, leapt on his horse and joined in the hunt wearing his cloth cap and smock coat.

'You go well for a second horseman,' Prince Charles remarked later.

'I am not a second horseman; I am one of your landed gentry, Sir,' replied John Redfern.

The meet had been at Manor Farm, Aston Subedge, the home of a stalwart Cotswold farming farmily, the Organs. It happened to be the seventy-fifth birthday of Mrs Molly Organ, and the news of the royal visit had been kept from her, as a birthday surprise. Mrs Organ had a busy time serving the guests at the meet, and was not over pleased when her son, Richard, ordered, 'Come along, Mother. Two more coming; fetch them a drink, preferably in clean glasses.' Molly Organ duly held out a tray of glasses to the two strangers, took one look at Prince Charles, and dropped the lot!

Brian Fanshawe and his wife, Libby, moved to Leicestershire in 1981 when Brian took the Mas-

tership of the Cottesmore, continuing that Hunt's tradition of amateur huntsmen. Prince Charles has since had several days with the Cottesmore, the best again taking place in snow. Hounds met at Cold Overton, in the delectable stretch of grass country south of Oakham. Hounds ran straight to Whissendine, back to Langham, changed foxes, and hunted on through Preston, losing the fox in a blizzard. Preston and Whissendine are at least ten miles apart, and Brian Fanshawe says he cannot recall any day this side of the Irish Channel when he has crossed more country.

He sums up the feelings of Masters of Hounds everywhere about the royal visits: 'It is always an honour and a great pleasure to have Prince Charles out; his perception is amazing, and no one is more aware of the hospitality hunting receives from the farmers and landowners.'

In 1978 Prince Charles's visits included the Grove and Rufford country, around Retford, Nottinghamshire. During the day he met Will Jacklin, aged ninety-one, who had hunted the Rufford hounds for thirty-two years – and recalled hunting hounds in front of the previous Prince of Wales exactly fifty years previously, from Winkburn Hall.

There was a snowy day, on 13 January 1978, with the Tynedale, in their lovely grass and wall country, north of Newcastle. Prince Charles watched the snow fall heavily the night before, but hoped his hosts would still hunt the next day. They did, meeting at noon and setting forth to hunt on soft snow. Hounds were hunted by the Joint Master and highly experienced amateur, Geoffrey Gregson. The meet was at Col Neil Speke's White House, and on a cold, northern day a most enjoyable series of hunts continued until sport concluded in gale force winds at Mr Tommy Southern's farm, by which time the riders' coats were stiff with frozen snow.

Three days earlier in that northern tour, Prince Charles had hunted with the Zetland in North Yorkshire and Durham. This is an especially jolly, hard-riding Hunt and has been visited often by the Prince since his first day's hunting, from a meet at Summerhouse. Hounds were hunted by Cliff Standing, a professional with more than a touch of an artist

Michael Farrin, huntsman of the Quorn since 1968, seen with his hounds in kennel. Farrin, arguably the top huntsman in the world, is a brilliant exponent of hunting hounds over Leicestershire's grass and fences at high speed

in his handling of a pack in difficult conditions. He moved south to the Crawley and Horsham in Sussex in 1984.

The day included a hunt from Dobinson's nearly to Hampsterly Forest, with a point of seven and a half miles. The final run included some ten miles across country, with snow increasing in the faces of the mounted field. Scent usually improves markedly during the onset of snow, and it certainly did so on this day. There was a tremendous variety of fences, and the going was nearly all on grass. It was voted 'probably our best day for four seasons' by Joint Master John Snowden. As in the neighbouring Bedale country, the Zetland offers light going in general, and its fences are inviting – except that they are often laced with wire nearly to the top, and must be jumped with care and precision. Galloping on blithely and hurdling fences soon brings disaster, as some visitors have quickly discovered.

Prince Charles hunted first in his own Principality with the Glamorgan Hunt, on 5 December 1979. He stayed with Sir Cenydd and Lady Traherne at Coedanhydyglyn, and after dinner insisted on visiting his horse, Chocolate, stabled nearby at Tinkinswood, home of the Master and amateur huntsman, Anthony Martyn. The Prince took his carnation from his button hole and offered it to Chocolate as a late-night titbit. Hounds met at Cottrell next day, and had a busy and enjoyable day, catching one fox before home was blown as darkness fell.

Something of the immense variety of rural Britain is conveyed in even a brief survey of just some of the Hunts visited by Prince Charles. There were many other good days, not recorded here, and there were many middling days when hounds had to work hard to make the best of scenting conditions.

Prince Charles has hunted on many occasions with his home pack, the Duke of Beaufort's, continuing to appear since the major changes which followed the tenth Duke of Beaufort's death, with Capt Ian Farquhar taking over the hunting of the hounds from the professional huntsman Brian Gupwell. The eleventh Duke, formerly David Somerset, is maintaining the highest possible standards in the hunting field.

The Prince has hunted on his own Duchy of Cornwall land in Cornwall, Devon and Wiltshire, where he is especially well known among many of the farming communities. He has braved the challenge of the Blackmore and Sparkford Vale country, one of the most stiffly fenced in England – and has enjoyed the contrast of light turf and walls in harrier countries such as the Pendle and Craven Forest, on the Lancashire-Yorkshire borders, and the High Peak in Derbyshire.

There is a story that during a day with the High Peak the Prince happened upon the recumbent form of that keen foxhunter and team 'chaser George Goring, proprietor of the Goring Hotel, not much more than a stone's throw from Buckingham Palace. The faller's identity was irrelevant; the Prince exhibited his customary politeness and concern, and dismounted.

He leaned over, and was pressing the neck of his flask between George Goring's lips, when George opened his eyes. History relates that he looked up and recognized the comforter.

George groaned a little and rolling his eyes to heaven, said, 'They'll never believe me at home...'

13

TEAM WORK

If you can meet with triumph and disasters
And treat those two imposters just the same ...

RUDYARD KIPLING

It was in 1979 that Sir John Miller telephoned David Tatlow, hunting man and producer of superlative show hunters, hacks and cobs, to ask for his help in introducing the Prince of Wales to the new sport of team cross-country riding – or team 'chasing as its growing band of enthusiasts call it. This was an entirely different 'ball game' to the hunting field, even though Prince Charles had by then acquired considerable experience in riding natural country on strange horses.

Tatlow, who is based in the Heythrop country near Stow-on-the-Wold, is a tough-speaking, forthright professional horseman, son of a great producer of show horses. The Ratcatchers was the name of the team which David and his friends had formed to capture a large slice of the prize money in a tough, even rough sport. David admits that, with hindsight, he might not have been the ideal choice to give Prince Charles maximum fun in the sport. The Ratcatchers was designed to win, and tight discipline, with subordination to the Tatlow Plan for Victory was the order of the day.

'I was impressed that Prince Charles never questioned this from the start,' David Tatlow recalls. 'I soon realized that the Prince really wanted to win, and he was prepared to go to a huge amount of trouble to get things right. It was most impressive.'

Team 'chasing had been totally invented by Douglas Bunn, the founder and proprietor of the All England Jumping Course at Hickstead, Sussex, which he had created as a superb outdoor show jumping complex in 1960. In 1974 he devised a competition whereby teams of four rode a natural cross-country course one team at a time. Their score was the time of the third rider to get home, and the team with the fastest time on this basis was the overall winner. It is, of course, a race, but as it is not under Rules governed by the Jockey Club, the polite fiction has been maintained that it is *not* a race; hence the use of the word 'ride'.

The first team 'chases at Hickstead were televised and produced remarkable entertainment for spectators and huge TV audiences. Teams from the House of Lords, the Army, the hunting field and almost every known branch of equestrianism were amazingly keen to risk their horses and their own necks over Mr Bunn's daunting timber and reinforced hedges. Spectacular falls, and impressive feats of bravery – or foolhardiness, depending on your point of view – were the order of the day.

The riding fraternity usually made one basic mistake at first: they rode at the fences in line abreast. This resulted in extraordinary pile-ups when one horse ran down the fence, bringing down the others. Most horses were hunters, or competition horses, and had not been trained for racing over fences in company in the way that National Hunt 'chasers are prepared.

The teams soon learnt their lesson: they jumped singly. The best teams acquired techniques of cut-

David Tatlow, captain of the Ratcatchers Team 'Chase team, who assisted Prince Charles to make rapid progress in cross-country riding at speed

ting corners; they applied disciplines to ensure that the time of the third rider home was as good as possible. Only those with strong nerves and top-class horses prepared to jump timber and fences at speed and awkward angles or on gradients need apply to such teams.

The Hunting Farmers from the Zetland country and Ratcatchers from Gloucestershire tended to dominate the first placings in the early seventies. Such valiant groups as George Goring's Boring Gorings and the Coakham Bloodhounds gave brave opposition, and sometimes won. There were plenty of others keen to have a go – and very soon hunts realized that the new sport was something of a money spinner, and kept the thrusters happy on Sunday afternoons at the beginning and end of each season.

A national circuit of team 'chase courses sprang

up, and great fun was produced. It must be admitted that there was some serious grief too. Courses tended to be variable in quality; some appallingly trappy fences had to be jumped at speed on some bad courses. Large, natural hedges were best. Most of the serious injuries – and there was at least one fatality – occurred at artificial obstacles.

Royal participation came early from Princess Anne, often accompanied by Captain Mark Phillips, and their polished performances on horses with eventing experience aided the popularity of the sport enormously. Local sponsorships poured into the sport, and prize money of hundreds made it more lucrative for the victors than winning a point-to-point race, where the Rules severely restricted the prize to under £100.

National organization of the sport has been less than binding or comprehensive, and although most courses improved, by 1986 team 'chasing had settled down from its early fast growth. It was still popular and some courses were drawing large crowds, but there were far more novice competitions for ordinary horses, leaving the small group of leading teams to compete for the bigger money in the open classes which usually climaxed the programme.

Prince Charles made his first appearance in the sport in February 1978, at the Cheshire Hunt's event at Wardle, near Nantwich, after a rapid thaw had suddenly transformed a frost-bound course into a ridable one. It was a reasonably well-kept secret that the Prince was to appear in a team called The Earl of Chester's 'Chasers, one of the Prince's own titles. In the team also were Princess Anne, Capt Mark Phillips and his sister, then Miss Sara Phillips.

They tackled a course of twenty-six fences, mostly typical of Cheshire Hunt country, with plenty of hedges and timber. The Earl of Chester's 'Chasers clearly concentrated on an enjoyable gallop rather than the fastest round. Prince Charles and Sara Phillips both had to contend with refusals from their horses at an in-and-out fence called the Boddington Bunker. They managed to avoid impeding each other while they successfully jumped out and rejoined Princess Anne and her husband who waited patiently.

In this sport many of the fences are individually sponsored, so the royal team went on to contend with Steiner's Hair Raiser, Barclays Bank and the Whittles Warmer. More than a few previous riders had had stops at the tenth fence, a yawning open ditch with a brush fence sloping away. Prince Charles kicked on splendidly and galloped on to finish the course, third behind his sister and brother-in-law. Sara Phillips's mount had enough of the testing ground and was pulled up at the thirteenth. It had been an enjoyable and creditable start. The winners were the aforementioned Zetland Hunting Farmers from Yorkshire and Durham: Ernie Fenwick, Harry Johnson, John Ormston and Swanee Haldane. They were to be regular rivals of Prince Charles when he competed 'seriously' later on.

The following month Prince Charles appeared again in a team with Princess Anne and Mark Phillips, plus the experienced Gloucestershire rider, Toby Sturgis. They competed in the VWH event at Kemble, near Cirencester, on 5 March 1978, and rode the course in a good time – but not good enough to be among the top placings of the fifty-one competing teams. The winners were David Tatlow's Ratcatchers; he was accompanied by Althea Barclay, Ian McKie and Jaime Aladren, who was Joint Master of the Heythrop at the time.

That autumn Princess Anne and Capt Phillips, plus Toby Sturgis's wife, Gail, and the event rider, Andrew Hoy, scored a splendid victory as the Duke of Beaufort's team in the North Cotswold Hunt's cross-country event at Toddington, Gloucestershire. Princess Anne was riding Colman, a racehorse not long out of training, and Andrew Hoy was on the Badminton three-day event winner Columbus. They rode a scorching round, defeating the Zetland Hunting Farmers by six seconds – some indication as to how competitive the new sport had become.

Princess Anne and her Duke of Beaufort's team even beat the Hunting Farmers on their home ground at the Zetland event the following week. John White substituted for Capt Phillips on this occasion, and was left behind in the 'Swimming Pool' obstacle, but the Princess and Andrew Hoy, with Toby Sturgis, rode a brilliant round on superb horses to gain victory.

Among the skilled, the bold and the adventurous in the horse world, cross-country team events – or team 'chasing as they preferred to call it, despite the Jockey Club's dislike of the name – was all the rage. They chose quaint names for their teams: George's Angels, the Walthew Wanderers, the Nutcases, the Rank Outsiders, and many more bizarre titles. Boldness exceeded skill in all too many teams, but they were all learning, and they wanted to win. Prince Charles had already decided that he thoroughly enjoyed this form of cross-country riding. He wanted to win, too, and this meant joining a winning team.

'Oh Lord, I'm not looking forward to this nanny's job,' was David Tatlow's first reaction to the suggestion that Prince Charles should ride with his team. 'Thank heaven, it all worked out so much better than that,' he says now.

Prince Charles was first given a few schooling sessions. They used the old North Cotswold team 'chase course at Toddington.

'We had to teach the Prince to land and let the horse go round a bend on landing, and do the adjustments for the turn before you take off – not when you have landed, when it is too late,' says Tatlow. 'Lots of people who have ridden across country all their lives in the hunting field never learn such things.

'We never had any problems with Prince Charles in the first three-quarters of a course. At no stage did he ever get out of touch with the rest of the team. The whole unit went well. His problem at that time was basically a lack of physical fitness towards the end of a course when he would sometimes get tired. Don't forget that the rest of us were riding every day; he had to fit it into a very busy programme involving a lot of indoor duties. It was a tremendous thing to take on team 'chasing at top level for someone in public life.'

The Ratcatchers' team was at its best on courses which needed horsemanship 'rather than kamikaze' tactics, as David Tatlow describes it. They were

ABOVE *Candlewick, the former eventer bred by the Queen, and hunted regularly by Prince Charles. Here, they are competing in a jumping and obstacle class at Royal Windsor Horse Show. The mare jumped well but alas ...*

OPPOSITE *Candlewick let down her royal rider when he attempted to lead her through a narrow, fenced passage which was part of the course. The 'great leveller' was at work again*

always vulnerable to opponents on the more straight-forward courses requiring sheer speed. The other regular members of the team with Prince Charles and David Tatlow were Althea Barclay and Ian McKie. Althea, the slim, attractive blonde wife of businessman Victor Barclay, lives and hunts in the Heythrop and is a consummate horsewoman with strong nerves. Ian McKie farms and hunts in the Bicester and Warden Hill country and is a successful point-to-point rider, having been the champion men's section rider in 1980. Tatlow was champion point-to-point rider for four years running, from 1965 to 1968 and his great experience and skill in race-riding tactics undoubtedly had

much to do with the Ratcatchers' run of victories in team 'chasing.

David Tatlow offered Prince Charles a ride on the grey, Collingwood, which had been bred by the Queen, and was a full brother to the great eventer, Columbus, by Colonist II (referred to in Chapter 8).

Collingwood had soundness problems and had been the subject of insurance claims. The shrewd Tatlow bought the horse for £500 as a 'maybe horse' – and the big, bold gelding proved to be one of the most successful team 'chase horses on the circuit. Prince Charles thoroughly enjoyed riding Collingwood from the start.

'He was just about the best cross-country horse I've ever ridden. He was marvellous. If I could find another Collingwood I would not have stopped team 'chasing. You do need an exceptional horse to win nowadays.'

David Tatlow says that Collingwood was not the easiest of rides, and Prince Charles did well to get a good 'tune' out of him; the big grey was inclined to be lazy, and needed kicking firmly into his fences.

Prince Charles's first public appearance with the David Tatlow outfit was on 25 February 1979, in the Cheshire Hunt's cross-country ride. This was the day after his gruelling day's hunting with the

With a panorama of the beautiful stone wall country of the Cotswolds behind, Prince Charles and fellow team member, Mrs Barbara Tatlow, in the Earl of Chester's 'Chasers' team, swing sharply to take the next fence at speed

Cheshire from Cholmondeley Park (described in Chapter 12). He rode in the team called The Earl of Chester's 'Chasers. Althea, David and Ian made up the team with Prince Charles.

The going was wet after the recent thaw, and the new course on Lord Tollemache's land at Peckforton needed careful riding. Prince Charles's team unboxed at the farm opposite the course, and went about fifth in the running order, somewhat earlier than had been expected by some of the huge crowd who had come to see the Prince of Wales in this exciting sport. David Tatlow made a rare departure

from the saddle when his horse failed to negotiate the last part of a 'devil's dyke' complex – an in-and-out over a ditch, and up a bank. This happened very early in the ride, and David had time to make his way to the end of the course on foot, to cheer on the three remaining members of his team.

'Come on! Come on!' shouted David as the Prince approached the last obstacle on Collingwood, in third place.

'He's tired,' retorted the Prince, as his horse struggled in the increasingly deep going.

'He's not! Kick on!' was the rejoinder from the team captain. Prince Charles did just that – and the Earl of Chester's 'Chasers scored a victory. The Prince's personal prize was a Cheshire cheese.

Team 'chasing helped to improve Prince Charles's riding ability dramatically. David Tatlow felt that in the Cheshire Ride the Prince tended to sit on the back of the saddle, making his horse more tired than necessary.

'It wasn't the prettiest sight,' David recalls.

Nevertheless, the Prince was the toast of rural Cheshire. His exploits in the hunting field the previous day had achieved wide circulation locally. His team's victory the following day in the team 'chase confirmed the view that the Prince of Wales was indeed a 'good 'un to follow, and a bad 'un to beat' on a horse. Huge cheers went up as Prince Charles came forward to receive his cheese. The crowd had already much enjoyed seeing the Prince walking the course after his own ride, and observed him getting more excited, and pleased, as each new team failed to match that of his own team in which he had played a crucial part.

The day had not been without the sort of disappointment known all too well by the competitive horseman. Prince Charles also rode the course in another Tatlow team, but was eliminated when his mount, a hunter called St David, resolutely refused at a fence, and just as resolutely refused the Prince's urgings to take the obstacle at repeated attempts.

The following year, 1980, Prince Charles appeared again at the Cheshire event at Peckforton in The Earl of Chester's 'Chasers team. Everyone was thrilled when the Prince and his team-mates, David Tatlow, Ian McKie and Althea Barclay, achieved an early lead in a time of five minutes twenty-six seconds – and none of the following teams could do better. Prince Charles rode Collingwood again, and his storming round earned warm praise from the experts. David Tatlow's horse, Oliver, 'blew up' and he finished fourth in his team, with Prince Charles in third position. Runners-up were the Wynnstay Wanderers, a strong team from the neighbouring country of Sir Watkin Williams-Wynn's, where Prince Charles has enjoyed so many good hunting days.

Douglas Bunn, observing the 'progress' of the sport he had invented six years earlier, opined in *Horse and Hound* in the spring of 1980 that: 'On the whole team cross-country riding has helped to raise riding standards. The big lesson which people

soon had to learn was that you needed a good horse if you wanted to win. Far too many people were riding indifferent horses. They had underestimated the challenge of riding cross-country fences against the clock. I think the success of the sport has been marvellous for trade. Every week I get a dealer phoning me to ask, "Douglas, do you know where there is a good team 'chaser?"'

An indication of just how seriously winning was taken in the Tatlow camp was that on one occasion the Prince of Wales was nearly relegated to the reserves! The Prince had not been 'on song' at an event shortly before the Warwickshire event which the Ratcatchers badly wanted to win – having achieved victory twice before, and yearning to complete a hat-trick. There were to be two Ratcatchers' teams at the Warwickshire, and Tatlow was 'seriously thinking of dropping the Prince from the first team'.

Tatlow confesses: 'We were under a lot of pressure to win in those days. And I must say we have had a lot more fun since we ceased to care quite so much. We used to have strict inquests afterwards, and I admit that Prince Charles got a polite bollocking sometimes, just like everyone else in the team. He usually took it without a murmur, just like the rest of the team. Anyone who thinks he was treated differently from any other member of the Ratcatchers' is very wrong. He was provided with a fit horse, and he was expected to pull out all the stops to win at all costs. And he certainly did just that.'

At the Warwickshire 'chase, Tatlow recalls saying, 'I am afraid there was a very strong chance, Sir, that you were going to be dropped from the first team today.'

'Oh really?' replied the Prince, and laughed. 'Of course, it's your decision.'

Tatlow says the other team members persuaded him against the royal relegation. He recalls that at the Warwickshire the Prince showed his form by riding 'like a hero'.

'It was great stuff,' recalls the Ratcatchers' captain. 'You wouldn't mind going over the wire with him. He really kicked on, and showed us what he is made of. That TV programme *Spitting Image*

nowadays gives Prince Charles a lot of stick for being "wet". They just don't know what they are talking about. Wet? I've never heard such nonsense. You can break your neck in any horse sport, but team 'chasing is as risky as you can find if you are riding to win every time at top level.

'I tell you, Prince Charles is a man's man. If you can drag yourself off the floor when you've had some of the falls he's had, and remount to ride on, there's nothing wet about you.

'As a matter of fact, I used to tell the team members not to remount because if there was anyone behind a faller he could get run over by the man behind. "Well, there was no one behind me this time; you'd got well and truly lost," replied the Prince after the Fernie ride. And he was right of course.

'We used to get into some quite serious heat in our discussions about team tactics sometimes. It went something like, "Well, I did this, and you did that; and you should have done this, and you should have done that". It was all part of the way we ran the team. Winning was everything.

'The most vivid recollection I have of Prince Charles behaving like a man's man, for want of a better expression, was the very first time we rode together. We sat on the ramp of the lorry in the farm yard in Cheshire, and I said something like, "Look, Sir, it's a difficult enough job anyway doing this. And it's not going to make it any easier for us if you don't join in everything. After we've walked the course before the ride, we always have this team talk to discuss tactics. There are two golden rules that we have: one is there is absolutely no excuse for any of us interfering with another horse and rider on the course. It is difficult enough going as quickly as we have to; if we have to worry our other team members, it becomes a nightmare. The other rule is that there is no overtaking whatsoever, unless someone falls, and is out of the ride."

Prince Charles coming over the last fence on Collingwood in the Warwickshire Hunt team 'chase in 1980. 'Just about the best cross-country horse I've ridden,' was the Prince's opinion of Collingwood

'At first we thought about putting Prince Charles second or third in the riding order, and we decided against second in case he had a fall. So we put him third. We didn't put him fourth because in that position he wouldn't have had anybody to chivvy him on there.

'When I had said all this to Prince Charles, he was fine. He said simply, "I want to do this. I don't want to just go round for the ride. If I am going to do this I am going to compete." '

The Tatlow team used to work out ways of saving a second, or even half a second, at each of the twenty or thirty fences on the course. This would add up to ten to twenty seconds saved on the overall time: enough to win an event overall. Prince Charles was warned strictly not to cut in on the inside if he saw the rider in front taking a wide angle at a fence, because this would be part of a corner-cutting manoeuvre on landing.

The VWH (Vale of White Horse) Hunt in Gloucestershire has an interesting course which includes jumping in and out of a river – which visitors are surprised to learn is none other than the upper reach of the Thames. Old Father Thames claims many a watery victim, much to the joy of spectators and those team members who have negotiated it safely.

'We were on a high at the time,' says David Tatlow. 'It was not long after we had won at the Cheshire. I was some way in front of the other team members at the approach to the Thames; I powered my way into the river, and the next thing I remember is being under water. Something went wrong, and down went the horse. He must have lost his footing on the river bottom.

'Ian was next and rode past me – but Prince Charles was in third place, and he went straight to the bottom too. Collingwood made a rare mistake.'

Whether the historical significance of seeing a Prince of Wales fall into the River Thames for the first time was apparent to the crowd is not clear – but many went home that evening feeling they had certainly had their money's worth. Prince Charles emerged unbattered, but completely drenched.

'A good sport' was the general consensus, endorsing the spontaneous reaction everywhere to his ability to cope with the occasional lapses of 'the great leveller'.

'The most sterling ride Prince Charles put in, when he was a real hero, was at the Fernie cross-country,' David Tatlow recalls. At short notice Prince Charles had to ride Calico for the first time – 'A good horse, but not much more than just a good hunter,' Tatlow says.

The Fernie course in the Saddington Vale was very twisty, but much more of a hunter's course than many others. David Tatlow had a fall early in the Ratcatchers' round, leaving Prince Charles in third position behind Althea and Ian. It was vital that Prince Charles should stay in the ride and keep as close as possible to his team leaders. Alas, at the third last – to the huge excitement of the crowd – the Prince had a fall.

'He was great,' says Tatlow. 'He didn't let go of the reins, and leapt straight back on: a great performance because he has not always been the most adept at mounting swiftly. This was a lightning performance, by any standards. And thanks to this the Ratcatchers had the best time – and we fondly thought we had won the competition. We

had gone round early in the competition, but none of the following teams had a better time than Prince Charles's in third position. And we got more and more excited.'

Alas, one of the awful disappointments which so easily attends any horse sport was to befall the Ratcatchers. At the end of the competition they learnt with dismay that they had been disqualified. One of the stewards on the course had reported that Ian McKie had ridden the wrong side of a flag! Prince Charles's disappointment was as deep as the rest of his team's. The Ratcatchers were notable for their absence at the presentations that afternoon – and that included the royal rider.

At the start of the 1986 season the Ratcatchers had disbanded, but David Tatlow said he would continue to run a team in a lower key. They would be called the 'Has Beens'. Prince Charles was wistfully saying that, if only he had a spare horse, he would *love* to go team 'chasing again.

This chapter may easily *not* be the last chapter in the story of royal team 'chasing. If the Prince of Wales takes up the sport again it will certainly not be because he has anything to prove.

He has done it all . . .

14

TASTING THE TURF

.... that, by the Grace of God,
is the kind of Prince we are lucky enough to have.

LORD OAKSEY

'If the people could just understand the real thrill, the challenge of steeplechasing.... It's part of the great British way of life, and none of the other sports I've done bears any comparison.' This was Prince Charles's comment in March 1981 when his first explorations into one of the most demanding and specialist of sports caused sharply contrasting emotions among his many friends and admirers. It was perhaps inevitable that the cross-country riding experience he had gained with the Tatlow team should encourage him to try the 'real thing': race riding under Jockey Club Rules.

Probably the most sensible judgement on Prince Charles's much publicized adventures on the Turf came from Lord Oaksey, one of the great amateur riders and an eloquent writer and broadcaster: 'Opposition to the Prince's race-riding exploits takes two main forms. First you get the straight-forward "safety-at-all-costs" brigade – whose members regard steeplechasing as a nasty, dangerous pastime to the risk of which an heir to the throne should not under any circumstances be exposed.

'But there are also some people who affected shock and surprise when Prince Charles did not immediately ride in triumph into the winner's enclosure, behaving like a joint reincarnation of Lester Piggott, John Francome and Fred Archer.

'The quick answer to the first group is, of course, that they need an entirely different Prince – and to the second, that if he wanted instant, effortless

success he should have chosen an entirely different sport.'

John Oaksey noted that 'the highly infectious bug of riding over fences at speed has bitten him good and proper'. He praised the Prince's persistence and fortitude despite the risks and difficulties he had already faced, and remarked ' ... that, by the grace of God, is the kind of Prince we are lucky enough to have.'

The link between the hunting field and steeple-chasing is not merely part of history; it is just as alive today. Prince Charles was simply following the pattern of countless young men who have first enjoyed the thrill of riding fences in the wake of a pack of hounds, and then aspire to attempt riding such obstacles at speed in competition with others. The sport's birthplace was Ireland in the mid-eighteenth century when the gentry held 'pounding matches' across country, especially in Clare, Galway and Roscommon. In 1752 a Mr O'Callaghan raced Mr Edmund Blake over four and a half miles from the church at Buttevant, with the spire of St Leger church as the guide. Hence, 'steeplechasing' was born – and the term 'point-to-point' derives from racing from the point of one church spire towards the point of another on the horizon. In Leicestershire the Meltonians held impromptu races across country on the way home from hunting.

Point-to-point horses are still 'qualified' in the hunting field, having to appear with hounds on a stipulated number of occasions to gain a certificate from the Master before they can race in the annual point-to-point run by the Hunt. Under Rules on permanent racecourses administered by the Jockey Club, the hunter 'chase remains one of the glories of the winter jumping season.

Prince Charles recalls that 'talking to people out hunting I got rather excited by the idea of trying race riding – and also overcoming my anxiety about jumping at speed.'

Anyone who believes he is fit enough to ride hard in the hunting field, or even to take on team 'chasing, still needs to think again when it comes to race riding. Fortunately, Prince Charles was prepared for this immediate problem. As Brough Scott wrote after an interview, 'For all the Prince's head-tilted politeness, there is an almost evangelical fervour when he talks about fitness. ("I couldn't do my job if I wasn't fit.") And also about the mental disciplines of taking up challenges and conquering fear.'

In November 1979 Prince Charles began 'riding out' from Nick Gaselee's training yard at Lambourn, Berkshire. Nick, then aged forty, was an ideal contact in the world of National Hunt racing. He was brought up in Kent where his father was Master of the West Kent Hunt, and although this county south of the Thames is not well furnished with suitable foxhunting territory, it has exceedingly strong sporting traditions. Nick Gaselee rode out from the yard of the late Peter Cazalet at Fairlawne, who trained for Queen Elizabeth the Queen Mother. The Queen Mother's own colours, blue, buff stripes, blue sleeves, black cap and gold tassel, based on those of her grandfather, the Earl of Strathmore – were carried by some of the greatest jockeys and horses trained by Cazalet.

Nick Gaselee became a leading amateur jockey, and then gained training experience with Fulke Walwyn, who succeeded Cazalet as the Queen Mother's National Hunt trainer.

Gaselee had about forty horses in his string, but he fully understood the difficulties of finding a suitable horse for a keen young rider lacking in racing experience. Such a task would normally have occurred in helping a young man aged between eighteen and twenty-two. Often the route to racing over fences under Rules would be some experience in point-to-pointing. Prince Charles had missed these opportunities, and he was thirty-two when he undertook the challenge of steeplechasing.

Prince Charles recalls the first problems of attaining race-riding fitness. For a public figure with a packed diary of engagements arranged months beforehand it was anything but a minor commitment to fit into his life-style.

'When I rode out at Lambourn, it was rather a problem. It meant driving early in the morning from London or Windsor, and then trying to do things later in the day. Unfortunately, it was all too easy to fall asleep! I rode a bicycle for thirty or forty miles without sitting on the seat; I went for runs – and I did the John Hislop exercises before I went to bed; in a low crouch position!'

John Hislop wrote the definitive book on steeplechasing which includes precise instructions to aspiring jockeys on the best ways of strengthening back and leg muscles for the ardours of steering more than half a ton of horseflesh over fences and hurdles at speed. Hislop was a stylish amateur rider who gained a great reputation just before the outbreak of the last war. He continued to ride after the war, and then forged a reputation as a perceptive writer on the racing scene.

After his 1979–80 season's hunting, plus team 'chasing, Prince Charles had added still more to his store of experience in riding different horses over widely varying fences. He had worked as hard as possible at increasing his level of fitness, and in riding work at Lambourn he had begun to learn to use the shorter stirrup levels employed by jockeys. American influence led to British flat race jockeys shortening their stirrups to adopt the 'crouch' position in the 1930s. National Hunt jockeys and ama-

OPPOSITE *At the head of the mounted field. Prince Charles is well accustomed to the hurly burly of riding among the huge groups of up to 200 riders*

ABOVE *The Zetland hunting in their beautiful country, which lies in Durham and North Yorkshire. Here, hounds are hunting after a meet at Cockfield, near Bishop Auckland. This is one of Prince Charles's favourite hunting countries*

RIGHT *The Duke of Beaufort's hounds near Badminton. Left is the son of the 11th Duke, Lord Edward Somerset. Brian Gupwell is hunting hounds, and Roger Boulton is whipping-in. This is Prince Charles's home country – and the pack with which he first started hunting when the 10th Duke was Master*

OPPOSITE *The strongly fenced grass country of Okeford Vale, home of the Portman, offers a formidable challenge to horse and rider following hounds, as Prince Charles discovered on his visit there*

OPPOSITE *Riding Collingwood in the Cheshire Hunt's team cross-country ride at Peckforton in 1979 – when Prince Charles's team, the Earl of Chester's 'Chasers, were the winners*

RIGHT *Tackling a water obstacle with resolution on Collingwood at the Cotswold Hunt team event course*

BELOW *Candlewick, the mare bred by the Queen, and ridden unsuccessfully as an eventer by Princess Anne, proved to be a useful team 'chaser for Prince Charles. Here, they are competing near Cirencester*

TOP *Candlewick takes a Polo mint off the Prince's shoulder after a team 'chase. The Prince's horses are all treated as personal friends*

ABOVE *Prince Charles has often taken part in charity show-jumping contests, as seen here at Sandown Park, but it is not a sport he has participated in seriously*

RIGHT *Before the fall – Prince Charles riding Good Prospect in the Horse and Hound Grand Military Gold Cup over the stiff Sandown Park fences on 13 March 1981. Horse and rider parted company at the tenth fence*

teur riders continued to ride with longer stirrups into the postwar years, but the trend towards shorter leathers has considerably increased in jump riding.

John Francome, until his retirement as a jockey in 1985, demonstrated just how stylish steeplechase riding can be. He had earlier excelled as a show jumper, and his wider experience undoubtedly helped him to develop one of the most attractive and effective methods of riding fences at speed. The worst excess of bad jump jockeys is a tendency to treat the reins as handlebars to hold on with, rather than a sensitive means of communication with the horse. The ability to 'see a stride' is vital, even if the 'chase jockey does not always apply it. Asking for a 'big one' is part of the jump jockey's repertoire in surviving a stiff course such as Cheltenham. He must have the skill and experience to time his signal for take-off through his legs and heels. Giving a horse a severe jab in the mouth with the bit is one of the worst crimes of the rider who gets 'left behind' at a fence and uses the reins to stay in the saddle. When repeated frequently this 'crime' will stop even the best of horses. Riding a finish, using the whip to encourage a horse, rather than to punish it, and a multitude of other skills, which are part of 'jockeyship', all have to be learned by the novice if he is to make any progress on the racecourse.

An ideal opportunity for Prince Charles to gain his first race ride without the problems of jumping fences occurred in March 1980. He entered for the Madhatters Private Sweepstakes at the little Sussex course of Plumpton. The shrewd, sporting chairman of Plumpton, Isidore Kerman, had initiated a flat race for celebrities which would bring maximum publicity for his racecourse, and earn money for the Injured Jockeys' Fund.

The Prince's debut on the racecourse had more than a little to do with the doubling of the usual attendance of this meeting. He declined the use of a private changing room, and for the first time experienced the crowded camaraderie of the jockeys' changing area. Cheerfulness and the tang of embrocation are among the chief features of a National Hunt changing room. Prince Charles's mount was Long Wharf, a novice hurdler belonging to the great American sportsman and art collector, Paul Mellon. Long Wharf was trained by Ian Balding who also trains 'chasers for the Queen Mother. The Prince's lack of racing experience did not deter the great British public. Many risked a modest bet on his chances of victory. Long Wharf's starting price shortened drastically, falling from 3 to 1, then 6 to 4; at the off the Prince had the responsibility of riding a 13 to 4 favourite in his very first appearance on a racecourse.

At the paddock Prince Charles advised racegoers, 'Please don't waste your money in backing me.' It was to no avail. And the royalist supporters were to get a decent run for their money.

The Playboy Club's Victor Lownes, eventers Richard Meade and Lucinda Prior-Palmer (now Mrs Green), and Althea Gifford, wife of the trainer Josh Gifford, were among the famous starters.

Cheered as he left the weighing room in Mr Mellon's black and gold colours, Prince Charles mounted Long Wharf and faced up to the daunting prospect of starting his race-riding career amidst maximum public attention. Derek Thompson, the television racing commentator, riding Classified, trained by Nick Henderson, took the inside rail and set the pace for a circuit. On the second circuit, Prince Charles set off in pursuit, and made a lot of ground, but he had left his challenge too late. Classified won by two lengths, but the crowd was delighted with Prince Charles's performance in finishing second. Third was Althea Gifford on Glamour Show. Prince Charles said afterwards he had already learnt something new about racecraft.

'Next time I shall know a bit more about how to catch up,' he said cheerfully.

After the presentation he was suddenly handed the microphone by Mr Kerman, and the Prince 'apologized' to those who had 'put too much money on my horse. I apologize on behalf of the management.'

OPPOSITE *Riding just for its own sake. The Prince of Wales thoroughly enjoys non-competitive hacking in the British countryside he loves. Horsemanship can be a recreation which will last a lifetime*

It was that clear he had enjoyed himself, and he remarked, 'All I need now is my own horse.' Nick Gaselee was looking for this desirable acquisition, but first the Prince was to have his initial experience of racing over fences. Four days after his Plumpton ride, he appeared at the much more fashionable 'London' course, Sandown Park, near Esher. This was the second day of the famous Grand Military meeting. Its Patron is Queen Elizabeth the Queen Mother, and she is enthusiastic in maintaining the unique military character of the meeting.

The highlight is the *Horse and Hound* Grand Military Gold Cup, known as the 'Soldiers' Grand National'. The race was founded in 1841 at Little Billing, near Northampton, and had a variety of homes before becoming established at Sandown Park in 1887. Since *Horse and Hound* took over the sponsorship in 1976 conditions for the race have widened, but it is still essentially for horses owned by past or present members of the Services, and ridden by those currently serving in the regular or reserve forces.

This race was Prince Charles's main target in his projected riding career. The royal connection with the race through its Patron was to be emphasized in the years 1984 to 1986 when Queen Elizabeth scored a marvellous hat-trick of victories with her great 'chaser Special Cargo. At the 1986 meeting the old horse strode home to victory despite his rider, the brilliant young amateur, Gerald Oxley, having suffered a broken stirrup leather four fences from home. Oxley kicked his other foot free of the iron, and rode virtually bareback on the skimpy racing saddle to jump the four last fences triumphantly and win on the run-in. Queen Elizabeth had two more wins that afternoon – with her hurdler Insular, in the William Hill Imperial Cup, and her New Zealand bred 'chaser The Argonaut, in the Dick McCreery Cup steeplechase, so that she scored two hat-tricks.

The huge delight of Queen Elizabeth, and the Sandown crowds, made this an unforgettable royal racing occasion – and it certainly left no doubt where Prince Charles had inherited his love for the winter racing game. He was thrilled when he heard

the news of his grandmother's remarkable triumph. As a 'doer' rather than a watcher he spent the afternoon with the Belvoir, making the most of thaw after the long 1986 winter freeze, and enjoyed a great day, leading the mounted field in a series of thrilling hunts after hounds had met at Eastwell just above the famous Vale of Belvoir.

On 8 March 1980, his first appearance over fences in public, Prince Charles was to ride Nick Gaselee's ten-year-old chesnut gelding Sea Swell. This was an excellent schoolmaster for an amateur rider, staying well, and acting on any going. The previous May, Sea Swell had beaten Brod Munro-Wilson on Beeno at Warwick – and the combination had just won the *Horse and Hound* Grand Military the day before Prince Charles's debut on Sea Swell at Sandown Park.

Riding a 'safe' horse is no guarantee of a successful trip on any course, but especially at Sandown Park which is renowned for the testing series of 'railway' fences. The last three fences in the back straight stand below the main Waterloo railway line, and as Timeform puts it: 'of the eleven fences on a circuit seven are on the back straight, with the water jump in the middle of the line. The three fences after the water come in very quick succession and many races are won and lost here. From the home turn to 100 yards from the finish the climb is severe ... '

Again, there was huge public interest in the Prince's appearance on the Turf, but this time the betting public was more cautious. Sea Swell started at 16 to 1 in a five-horse race: The Duke of Gloucester Memorial Trophy (Past and Present Hunter 'Chase for Amateur Riders) over a distance of 3 miles and 118 yards, with twenty-two fences to negotiate.

The favourite was the 1975 Cheltenham Gold Cup winner, Ten Up, inclined to break blood vessels as a thirteen-year-old, but still a force to be reckoned with, and this rangy gelding was expected to like Sandown Park's heavy going that day. Second favourite was Coolishall, ridden and owned by Brod Munro-Wilson, the sporting City businessman who qualified for the Grand Military meeting as an SAS man. Andrew Patrick, ridden by Major Christopher

Prince, and Border Mark ridden by Capt John Evett completed the field. Sea Swell, by Sea Moss, looked well, and Prince Charles was as lean and fit as any rider you could see tackling this famous course which had so often proved the undoing of even the most experienced of 'chase jockeys.

It was greatly to the Prince's credit that he negotiated the two circuits successfully and finished in fourth place to congratulatory applause. Many a horseman would give a lot just to complete a ride at Sandown, and it would certainly rank among the sporting experiences of a lifetime. Coolishall took the lead two fences from home, and won comfortably, giving Munro-Wilson his second success of the meeting. (He was to ride Coolishall in the Grand National later that season, but had the cruel luck to have a stirrup iron shatter jumping the first fence; he was understandably ejected at the third.) Ten Up was second, with Border Mark third. Altogether, it had been a most exciting adventure, and the Prince's appetite was whetted for more racing over fences. Various experts were invited to give their views on his first performance, and it would not have been mere sycophancy which would have prompted the likes of the irreverent John Francome to remark that the Prince's style was 'very tidy'.

The great National Hunt trainer Fred Rimell observed, 'He has a good style for a new boy, especially when you consider he is in his thirties. On the basis of what we have seen here today he is the type of amateur who could go far.'

Learning to 'lay up' – to stay within call of the leading runners – is one of the most difficult tasks for the beginner, and Sandown had provided Prince Charles with an early opportunity to discover the problems involved in staying in touch during a race.

In May 1980 Prince Charles visited the Grand National course at Aintree for the first time. The great race was in dire trouble yet again, and the Jockey Club launched a fund to help buy the course and preserve it permanently for racing – which appears to have been achieved. The Prince's new enthusiasm for the sport encouraged him to write a foreword for a book extolling the race and its contribution – *Long Live the Grand National*. He remarked that 'it is only in the last five or six years that I have come to appreciate the real significance of the Grand National and its deep roots in the sporting life of Britain. It is indeed a typically British "institution". In other words, it developed almost by accident and in a very small way at the beginning ... '

Some indication of the Prince's awareness of the place of steeplechasing in the national character was contained in his further statement about the problems facing the race's future: ' ... we simply must not let these problems destroy something which is a glorious, and somewhat eccentric, part of our heritage.... we would lose something which is irreplaceable anywhere else; the whole racing fraternity would lose their greatest adrenalin producing challenge; many people's dreams and ambitions would be forever frustrated (after all, my great-great-grandfather, when Prince of Wales, won the Grand National in 1900 with Ambush II....!) and we would be denied the indescribable, tingling thrill of seeing those gallant horses fly over a series of astonishing obstacles.'

References to 'dreams and ambitions' and the 1900 victory of Edward VII no doubt fuelled speculation that Prince Charles was cherishing ambitions to ride in the National. It would have been entirely natural if this had been among his aims. Just completing the Aintree course has been the aim of many a Corinthian; the course lends itself to 'hunting' round, and the Grand National's list of victories since the race was born in 1839 include many illustrious amateurs, although not so many in the postwar years. Capt Mark Phillips rode an 'exhibition' round at Aintree on Columbus.

The Prince's immediate target was the 1981 Grand Military Gold Cup. This was already an ideal plan for an amateur with the Prince's degree of experience, and it must have appealed to him also because of its connections with the military – plus the patronage of his grandmother.

He recalls Sea Swell as a 'marvellous horse; he wasn't going to try very hard, but he jumped beautifully.' Clearly, a horse with more scope and speed was needed if the Prince was to finish 'in the frame' over the demanding Sandown Park course. What appeared to be a splendid solution was achieved in mid-summer 1980, when Nick Gaselee bought the ten-year-old brown gelding Allibar out of Ireland for Prince Charles. Tom Cooper of the British Bloodstock Agency in Ireland assisted in the purchase of the horse from Joseph McGrath, reportedly for some £15,000. This is by no means a vast sum for a horse to race successfully in good company over fences, but the figure was never confirmed and may well have been less.

Allibar had a busy, and creditable, early 1980 'chasing season in Ireland. At Leopardstown in January he won the Glencullen Handicap 'Chase over three miles, ridden by J. P. Byrne. In the light of the tragedy to come, it may possibly have been significant that this was a tough race on soft going. Allibar, a 20 to 1 outsider, won by only a short head over the 11 to 10 favourite Mighty Honour, ridden by Tommy Carberry.

At Leopardstown, again in February, Allibar finished sixth; he was fourth over three miles in heavy going at Navan in March; ridden by Tommy Kinane, he was a faller in the Irish Distillers' Grand National Handicap 'Chase at Fairyhouse on 7 April; about three weeks later he was second in the coincidentally named Prince of Wales 'Chase at Punchestown, putting up an excellent performance to be beaten only a short head by Colleen Rhu; and on 1 May, at Punchestown again, Allibar was second once more, by a length and a half, in yet another three-mile handicap 'chase, although this time on 'good' going at last. Allibar was by Bargello, out of a Vulgan mare, Gallic Star. He had certainly gained some experience during a strenuous season, and acted on any going. There were ample reasons for hoping for the best in his first season in England.

'In spite of all his other commitments, Prince Charles got to know Allibar really well and struck up an excellent relationship with the horse,' Nick Gaselee recalls. 'We planned for him to ride Allibar in public once in the autumn, and then for them to have a season of hunter 'chases and amateur riders' races. This would give the Prince a definite season for fitness (a three-month period) to aim for.'

Wisely, Gaselee engaged the professional jockey Richard Linley to give Allibar his first outing in England. This was on 11 October 1980, in the Geoffrey Eliot Memorial Handicap 'Chase over three miles at Worcester. Prince Charles had every reason to be pleased with his new horse's performance. Allibar led the field of ten runners from the second fence to the fourth; he proved somewhat one paced in this race, but kept at the front end, and finished second at 8 to 1, twelve lengths in front of the favourite, Mermaid, ridden by John Francome. The winner was Princely Bid, some eight lengths in front of Allibar.

A fortnight later, on 24 October, Prince Charles had the thrill of riding his own horse at Ludlow. He was competing in the Clun Handicap 'Chase for amateur riders over three miles. Ludlow is a charming setting for National Hunt racing, typical of many rural courses, staunchly supported by the local sporting fraternity. It has a stiff, right-handed oval-shaped track, with a 'chase circuit of about a mile and a half and a run-in of 450 yards. For the first time the Prince of Wales wore his own colours: scarlet with royal blue sleeves and a black cap. He rode Allibar in an Australian cheeker, a rubber noseband which fits over the bit rings on either side and then joins into a central strap running up the horse's face and fastening to an attachment on the headpiece of the bridle, right between the horse's ears. One aim is to lift the bit in the horse's mouth, making it more difficult for the horse to get his 'tongue over the bit', a form of evading action by the horse in avoiding the real effect of the bit. The other use of the cheeker is to deter a hard puller. There is reckoned to be some psychological restraint in having something running up the centre of a horse's face.

Whilst a horse which pulls has considerable advantages in jumping fences at speed, since there is no question of having to stoke him up at every fence, there are huge disadvantages in being 'carted' by a puller. The pulling horse will use up all his energy too soon in the race, and run out of steam before the final run-in. Prince Charles recalls that Allibar certainly did take 'a bit of a hold'. Yet in

With Allibar, his own 'chaser which he had thoroughly enjoyed riding into second place
at Ludlow in 1980. But the following February Allibar tragically collapsed
and died after being ridden at exercise by the Prince at Lambourn

this race he learnt a lot about his horse, and felt that he had a great deal of fun to anticipate later in the season with Allibar.

The experienced Irish 'chaser carrying the Prince of Wales soon showed that he was not taking much notice of an Australian cheeker. Up went the tapes, and Allibar set off firmly in the lead. His starting price was a fairly generous 10 to 1 considering his Irish form. The favourite was the moderate 'chaser Uther Pendragon, ridden by Tim Thomson Jones, and trained by Tim Forster. Second favourite was Vatican Express, ridden by Prince Charles's team 'chase comrade Ian McKie.

Prince Charles looks back on the Ludlow race with great pleasure.

'I had ridden Allibar out and schooled him over fences, but of course I did not know what he would be like in a race. He went off in front immediately, and terrified me. I didn't really know what was happening, but suddenly there was a whack down the side of somebody's horse and they all started to overtake me. It was a marvellous experience, but alas I was getting left behind.

Then the great thing happened. I asked the old boy to catch up – and he did. He was grand. We had nearly completed the second circuit by then, and had made up some ground. When I kicked him on he picked up speed. On the last run we actually overtook people like Tim Thomson Jones – and came second.'

Anyone who has ever ridden his own horse in public for the first time and achieved any sort of success will understand the glow of pleasure in which the Prince rode back to the unsaddling enclosure. It was only his second appearance in a race over fences, and many an amateur or professional has to wait for many rides, even several seasons, before achieving a placing. However, youthful inexperience was certainly not a bar to the winner's enclosure in this race. The winner was the 7 to 1 Hello Louis, a first victory for seventeen-year-old Keith Reveley, from Saltburn, Cleveland, who was riding his mother's horse.

Hello Louis took the lead at the thirteenth fence and kept in front throughout the second circuit. Allibar and Prince Charles led to the fourth fence, lost their place among the winners at the eleventh, and ran on from two fences out to finish in second place, six lengths behind the winner. In third place, half a length behind, was Ian McKie and Vatican Express. Tim Thomson Jones on the favourite could do no better than seventh, having made a bad mistake at the fourteenth.

'I am very pleased.' Prince Charles told the press. Asked the extraordinary question (by a non-racing reporter) would he try again? he replied, 'Hell yes! That's why I bought him.'

The non-racing press was fascinated far less by the race than by the presence among the spectators of Lady Diana Spencer who was reported to have backed Prince Charles and Allibar 'each way'. Increasingly that winter, after Prince Charles's return from India, the non-racing press was sure that it was 'on to a winner' in its speculation that the Prince of Wales and the Earl Spencer's nineteen-year-old daughter would become betrothed.

It was indeed sad, but a great source of support, that Lady Diana was to be present when there occurred what Prince Charles still recalls as an 'awful, awful tragedy'. Prince Charles had asked Lady Diana to marry him at the beginning of February. When the sudden, dreadful loss of his already much-loved horse occurred, his fiancée was able to share with him one of the worst experiences any horseman can undergo.

On 20 February Prince Charles was exercising Allibar on the Downs near Nick Gaselee's yard. The following day the Prince was due to ride his horse in the three-mile Cavalry Hunter 'Chase at Chepstow. A pipe-opener is essential the day before a race, and the Prince cantered and slow-galloped his horse about seven furlongs. Lady Diana was watching the training session from a Land-Rover, accompanied by Nick Gaselee's wife, Judy.

Suddenly, during the fast work Prince Charles realized that Allibar was not going normally. The horse ceased to take his usual firm hold, and showed a little distress. It was as if he had run much further, much more strongly, than a mere training gallop. The Prince slowed his horse immediately. He began to walk back towards Gaselee's yard. Then Allibar stumbled, and Prince Charles swiftly dismounted. His horse sank to its knees, rolled on to its side and died. The Prince knelt by Allibar; Princess Diana stood weeping nearby.

Allibar was dead long before a veterinary surgeon could arrive. The 'chaser, in his prime at eleven years old, was found in post mortem to have suffered a massive rupture of the aorta, the main artery into the heart. Horses are prone to heart problems, and they do occur with ghastly suddenness. To lose a horse so soon after ownership, apparently at the start of a successful partnership, is a cruel misfortune. Horses are 'tested for heart' when they are bought and sold, but a horse can be cleared on this count by a veterinary surgeon and yet still suffer a massive collapse, such as that suffered by poor Allibar.

The only possible comfort was that for the horse such an end was mercifully quick, and its perception of impending death was far less than that of a farm animal awaiting 'humane slaughter' in an abattoir. A heart failure during a race, either on the flat or over fences, can cause one of the ugliest falls imaginable, with special risks to the rider. At least this horrendous conclusion to Allibar's all-too-brief ownership by the Prince of Wales had not occurred.

This would have been a juncture when many a horseman would have deferred or cancelled his race-riding career. It says a lot about Prince Charles's character that he chose to press on. His public and private commitments were to be awesome in 1981. The royal wedding was to take place on 29 July. As always he 'fitted in' his sporting recreation, and never allowed it to interfere in any way with his public duties. Yet he had worked to get himself racing fit; he had proved that he could ride a horse over a three-mile steeplechase course with worthwhile results. If another suitable horse could be found, yes he would still 'kick on'. . . . would still ride in the Grand Military Gold Cup at Sandown Park in March.

Nick Gaselee is well aware that ever since the unfortunately named Good Prospect became bathed in the royal limelight, countless racing 'experts' and non-experts have expostulated: 'Can't think why on *earth* they put him on that!' It was blindingly clear to all concerned that Good Prospect was not the best choice for a substitute mount when he appeared on a racecourse, but it was not clear at the time, and it has to be said that the royal rider was reasonably satisfied after trying the twelve-year-old brown gelding over fences before deciding to purchase.

'He seemed all right, but nothing like Allibar. I suppose I really didn't know enough about 'chasers at the time,' Prince Charles recalls wryly.

On paper Good Prospect's credentials for producing a winning ride were excellent. Son of a tough, consistent stayer, Orchadist, Good Prospect was out of the dam Cagire's Plumage, who produced several other jumping winners, including the hurdler Lucy Swan, the selling hurdler Lucky Louis and the hurdler 'chaser Good Job. Good Prospect won the Coral Golden Hurdle Final as a seven-year-old and had a splendid 1979–80 season, winning five times over fences. He was still effective in the 1980–81 season, winning the Staveley Chase at Wolverhampton in November, in which he beat Tommy Joe and Prince Rock by four lengths and fifteen lengths at level weights. Timeform summed him up as a 'tough, genuine and consistent stayer'.

Altogether Good Prospect had run in ninety-two races, and had won twenty-five. He had never fallen, but had once unseated a jockey, Jim Wilson, after a blunder at Newbury.

Viewed by an amateur rider with limited experience, the prospect from the lightly framed gelding's saddle was less than good. One problem was that there was far less 'front' than Prince Charles had enjoyed on Allibar. A horse with a steeper shoulder and less neck is far less confidence-giving for the rider over fences than the animal with huge sloping shoulders and a swan neck. This comparison overstates the change between Allibar and Good Prospect, but it is relevant. To the novice it appears that there is virtually 'nothing in front of you' on some horses. This is particularly unnerving going into a big fence. The experienced horse will tend to drop his head going into a jump, which is an excellent habit, because it means he is more likely to see a ditch in front of it, and will not put his feet into it. He is also likely to judge the height of the fence more accurately, as it is believed that horses look 'up' a fence rather than 'down' it in evaluating height. Beware of the horse which takes its fences with head high in the air. This is why hunters are so often equipped with standing martingales in Leicestershire where most fences are guarded by ditches. The martingale operates restraint from a strap running from the girth to the noseband, and should keep the horse's head at the right angle on approach to an obstacle.

One other problem Prince Charles discovered was that Good Prospect rode completely differently. Far from taking a hold, the Prince found that 'he didn't give you a nice feeling; sometimes you had to push him into a fence. There was nothing of him compared to Allibar, and I realized how good Allibar was because this beastly thing didn't take a hold. The whole point was to work towards the Grand Military. After Allibar died I was desperate to get a horse. Allibar was a schoolmaster; he was brilliantly chosen by that wonderful man, Tom Cooper – and there just weren't any others available at short notice.'

These were the sort of lessons which every amateur rider learns, but not in the glare of publicity which was attending every aspect of the Prince's racing plans. Nevertheless, he rode as much work as possible with Good Prospect as soon as the purchase was made from the owners, John Edwards, the Ross-on-Wye trainer, and his wife, Virginia, who often rode the horse happily at home.

There was little more than a fortnight before the Grand Military – somewhat ominously looming up on Friday 13. Although there was some head shaking, the Prince's entry into the *Horse and Hound* Grand Military also received wide acclaim, especially in racing circles. The champion steeplechase jockey John Francome said in his column in *The Sun* that: 'Having watched Prince Charles at close quarters on the gallops last weekend, I know that the dreaded Aintree fences would hold no real

fears for him. He has really done his homework on horse racing and he certainly has style. I realize that, like me, he is more of a horseman than a jockey. Some amateurs look awkward, but not Prince Charles.'

Other encouraging headlines said, 'Charles really has a Good Prospect', 'Prince Charles is favourite for Grand Military', and 'Charles could be king of the track', although some struck a more sombre note: 'Prince runs double risk' in the *Daily Mail*, and 'The horse on which our future King will risk his neck' in the *Sunday Express*.

Nick Gaselee was reported as saying, 'He has been down to ride work, and school Good Prospect. However, all good horses take time to get used to. If he gets round successfully, and goes well, we'll all be happy, though this is not the carnival many people seem to think. Racing is a serious game, and the Prince realizes this.'

Queen Elizabeth the Queen Mother and Lady Diana Spencer were in the paddock at Sandown Park to see Prince Charles mount his 16 hands gelding before the Grand Military. At 11 to 2 Good Prospect was third favourite among the fourteen runners. Sandy Cramsie on Collars and Cuffs led the betting at 7 to 2. Prince Charles did National Hunt racing proud by giving interviews before and after the race to Brough Scott on TV. The Prince's infectious enthusiasm for racing came over splendidly. Those TV viewers for whom steeplechasing is about as remote as visiting the moon must have gained at least a clue as to why the Prince of Wales was risking his neck to ride fences at speed.

'The best way to understand something is to have a serious cut at it yourself,' was one of the Prince's remarks which is closest to the heart of the matter. It was perfectly clear that he had no illusions about the immense difficulties of succeeding in his latest challenge, but as he told Brough Scott, 'I have this awful thing of wanting to do things well ... '

There had been a lot of rain before the race, and the Sandown Park going was soft. The meeting had been in jeopardy until a seven o'clock inspection. Jim Wilson had won the Kim Muir 'Chase on Good Prospect in 1980, but Philip Blacker had pulled up the little horse when he was obviously unhappy in heavy ground at Chepstow. How would he fare today in soft going?

A record Grand Military crowd pressed close round the rails of the paddock as the Prince and Good Prospect were led round with the other runners. Both horse and rider knew the Sandown course and the perils of the railway fences on the back straight. There was every reason for optimism. Certainly the Prince, riding at 11 stone 7 lbs looked admirably confident as he rode out of the paddock amid shouts of 'Good Luck, Sir!' from the racegoers who on this Friday in the calendar include a large element of military families from all over Britain.

The runners filed down to the far left of the course, closely watched from the royal box by the Queen Mother and Princess Margaret, as well as the Prince's fiancée. For a few minutes the non-racing press present actually began to watch the horses.

The starter checked the girths on each horse, and returned to his rostrum. Starting stalls are, of course, not used in National Hunt racing; jockeying for position at the start hardly matters with a three-mile slog over twenty-two fences.

Up went the tapes and the field surged ahead, with The Drunken Duck immediately bearing Munro-Wilson's chocolate and yellow spotted colours to the front. Prince Charles kept Good Prospect well in touch, and very soon they had swung right to take the upright, 'quick' fences in the back straight. The little horse was jumping fluently, and proving that he certainly did 'act on all going'. This could not be said of all the other runners, and there was more than a little drama.

Three horses were tailed off in the soft going and were pulled up before they had gone far on the second circuit. Lt Col Sandy Cramsie on the favourite, Collars and Cuffs, fell at the ninth, and Major Baillie on Inkerman was lying third when he fell at the fourth.

Things were therefore distinctly 'select' as the depleted field thundered along the back straight for the second time. Prince Charles and Good Prospect had dropped back a little, but were working their

way back into contention. If they could stay on their feet there was an increasing possibility of success. The Drunken Duck was in front but was almost certain to be overtaken soon.

Good Prospect jumped the first two plain fences on the back straight and soared over the open ditch. The water jump was next, and again he made nothing of it. Next there was a plain fence, the eighteenth . . . John Oaksey explained in *Horse and Hound* what happened next, with the weight of his own experience as a finisher and occasional non-finisher of three-mile 'chases: 'Prince Charles, with perfectly understandable eagerness saw, or thought he saw, a longish stride at what turned out to be the fatal fence.

'Possibly he did not "ask" quite firmly enough – and then again, equally possible, Good Prospect would still have ignored the request if John Francome and Jeff King had made it together.

'Anyway, he fiddled half an extra stride, brushed through the top and worst of all, landed slightly off a true line.

'It does not sound much – and might not have meant much to Messrs Francome or King – but Prince Charles had followed his own instructions about the take-off and as he came down Good Prospect had somehow wriggled out from under.

'It happens to everyone and the only thing which varies is the time you take to learn to avoid it by reacting differently. As far as I can remember it took me about fifteen years, but my own guess is that the Prince will be a whole lot quicker. Anyway, all was well and jumping is fortunate indeed to have acquired such a heartfelt enthusiast.'

The Prince pitched out of the saddle, over the horse's shoulder, rolling over and coming to rest. Good Prospect obligingly did not continue the race, but was soon caught, and the Prince was given a leg-up. He rode back to the paddock with a noticeably bloody nose, but smiling cheerfully.

Another rider had later in the race suffered a far sharper disappointment than merely joining the ranks of 'u.r.' (unseated rider). John, Marquess de Cueller, son of the famous amateur rider, the Duke of Albuquerque, was riding Colonial Lad strongly

After landing over the 18th fence in the Horse and Hound Grand Military Gold Cup at Sandown on 13 March 1981, Prince Charles is in trouble ... the Prince parts company with his newly purchased steeplechaser ... and lands on one shoulder, as Good Prospect belies his name and gallops on. Prince Charles's only injury was a bloody nose – and he rode the horse again at Cheltenham the following week

and seemed likely to overhaul Munro-Wilson, drawing alongside The Drunken Duck. Approaching the second fence from last, Colonial Lad was struck by the riderless Collars and Cuffs. There was a gasp of disappointment in the stands as the Marquess and his horse were swept clean out of the race, missing the fence.

It was victory again for Munro-Wilson, with Major Faulkner on Brown Jock trailing in second twenty lengths behind, and another ten lengths back, Deep Memories in third place. Major Christopher Prince finished fourth on Beacon Time – and out of the field of twelve there were no other finishers.

Again, it would have been perfectly under-standable if Prince Charles had decided to hang up his boots for the season. Far from it, he decided to go ahead with Good Prospect's entry for the Cheltenham race the horse had won the previous year, the three-mile Kim Muir Memorial Challenge Cup Handicap 'Chase for amateur riders. This was really 'going at the deep end'. Cheltenham's fences are notoriously stiff, and the famous last half mile is uphill, with a run-in of 350 yards which provides such exciting finishes in the wonderful sporting atmosphere of the Festival meeting in March. The Kim Muir is part of the first day's programme. (Kim Muir was a noted military rider in the 10th Hussars who was killed in the war in 1940.)

There were twenty runners in the 1981 race, and the riders included the cream of the available talent among amateurs. One of the strengths of National Hunt racing is that so many young men, and an increasing number of women, enjoy racing over fences, with varying degrees of success, and later continue to give back vital contributions to the sport as owners, trainers or officials.

The last appearance in a race under Rules by the Prince of Wales – riding the Queen Mother's Upton Grey at Newton Abbott in May, 1981

OPPOSITE *Adjusting his chin-strap at Cheltenham before the biggest challenge in his all too brief racing career: the Kim Muir 'Chase*

Prince Charles's experience of riding the Cheltenham course was only to last nine fences, but his view of the great Festival of National Hunt racing is bound to have an extra dimension, compared with the vast majority of spectators, for the rest of his life. Good Prospect jumped off smartly when the tapes went up, and was placed in the early stages. This was the largest field the Prince had ridden in on a steeplechase course, and the pace was hotter than he had experienced at Sandown Park.

Prince Charles and Good Prospect took the first fence in third place. Jim Wilson was in the lead on the ironically named Another Prospect but dropped back after the fifth, and pulled up ten fences later. Good Prospect was lying about twelfth when they came to the tenth fence. This time there was no 'wriggling' as at Sandown. The gelding hit the fence good and hard, about half way up. He staggered through the top of the fence, pitching forward sharply on landing in a manner which would have unseated the best of jockeys. Prince Charles hit the ground harder than in his previous fall, and this time Good Prospect went on to complete the course on his own. The Prince dashed his racing whip to the ground in frustration as he lay there, but he was soon on his feet, limping and rubbing his back with one hand.

His much quoted comment was, 'It was a bloody nuisance. Now I've got to go back and face them all again. Oh well, we live and learn.' He was soon picked up by a Range Rover and driven back to the unsaddling enclosure. And his retort to a television reporter who said, 'Things did not go quite to plan?' was forgiveably ironic: 'How observant of you,' replied the Prince.

There were to be no more 'chasing opportunities that spring, although Prince Charles did appear suddenly, and somewhat unexpectedly, at the end of May, riding the Queen Mother's Upton Grey in an amateur hurdle race at the little Newton Abbott course in South Devon.

The visit is recalled with great pleasure by Newton Abbott's chairman, Claude Whitley, a great hunting man, who was Master of the South Devon hounds for over forty years, and by the course's faithful band of local supporters. But it was not a racing success in any sense for the Prince. The seven-year-old Upton Grey, trained by Fulke Walwyn, definitely did not like soft going, and there had been a great deal of rain before this meeting. The grey gelding, by Rugantino, squelched unhappily round the course, and was soon tailed off to finish ninth in a field of ten. Narribini was the winner, ridden by a housewife, Mrs Elsie Mitchell.

For Prince Charles there was to be an excellent season's polo, and despite the start of married life he was able to resume his hunting in Leicestershire at the end of the year. Should he also endeavour to re-start race riding? If Allibar, or some other suitable horse, had been available, it is highly probable that he would have ridden again during the 1981–82 season. He did not do so, and the Prince's steeplechasing ambitions remained unfulfilled. Yet he had tasted the thrills of the Turf, had demonstrated his courage, resolution and self-discipline, despite pressures far beyond those faced by other young riders. And he had taken up the sport in his thirties, a time of life when many a young amateur is thinking of reducing rather than extending his race riding under Rules.

By 1985 Prince Charles considered it 'highly unlikely' that he would ever resume race riding. Although he was much interested in entering the series of 'old time' races over natural cross-country courses which were being run at certain point-to-point meetings, 'If only I could be sure of having what I call a really good horse.'

For the National Hunt world Prince Charles's attempts at amateur race riding have been a wonderful bonus. Queen Elizabeth the Queen Mother has provided immense royal patronage as an owner in this great winter sport. If this tradition is maintained in the years to come by the Heir to the Throne, it will be an association much strengthened and enriched by his own personal memories of the Sport of Kings – in the saddle.

15

NOBLE HORSEMANSHIP

To turn and wind a fiery Pegasus
And witch the world with noble horsemanship

WILLIAM SHAKESPEARE
(Henry IV, Part 1)

Playing polo hard in the summer months, and hunting enthusiastically in the winter whenever other engagements permit, the Prince of Wales remains a consummate horseman.

One of the joys of horsemanship is that with luck and perseverance it can easily last a lifetime. The horse is such a versatile animal; there are so many sports in which it can be employed at varying levels. Prince Philip has demonstrated this with his highly successful switch from polo to combined carriage driving.

Prince Charles, like the Queen, is not one of those riders who *have* to be using a horse competitively to enjoy it. He thoroughly appreciates the pleasures of hacking in parkland or country lanes at any time of the year. As a countryman he is totally 'at home' on a horse's back, enjoying the unrivalled riches of the British countryside.

Popular press speculation that his marriage would lead to abandonment of his polo and hunting have been proved groundless. The Princess of Wales shares Prince Charles's deep affection for country life, and horses and hunting are just as much a natural part of her own environment and upbringing.

Some indication as to where his interests will lie when he can bear to do rather more spectating, is contained in his recent attempts to breed National Hunt horses at his Gloucestershire home, Highgrove, in the Duke of Beaufort's country.

Prince Charles purchased a mare, Spartan Legacy, by Spartan General, the great NH sire of John Thorne's famous partner Spartan Missile (John was tragically killed in a point-to-point in 1982). Spartan Legacy was put to the stallion True Song, and produced for Prince Charles a filly, Amethea, born at Highgrove. It was hoped Amethea might start hurdling in the 1986–87 season. Meanwhile Spartan Legacy has produced another filly foal by Sunny Boy, and there is other young stock at Highgrove which might one day appear on the Turf.

Monarchy is all about continuity, and if equestrian traditions are to be handed on, then every opportunity is being afforded to Prince William – and eventually to Prince Harry. Prince William, aged four, started his riding career on Smokey, a Shetland pony on loan from Princess Anne. Certainly some progress has already been achieved, since in August 1986 Prince William moved up the equestrian scale a few notches when there arrived at Highgrove a six-year-old Welsh pony mare called Llanerch Topaz, presented by members of the Welsh Pony and Cob Society.

Topaz is a Section A Welsh pony, which means ponies of no more than twelve hands. This delightful little grey mare was made available by her breeder, Mrs Phoebe Hambleton, former President of the Society. Topaz had a period of comprehensive training and handling by Mr and Mrs David Williams at Pentrebach, Brecon, before being handed

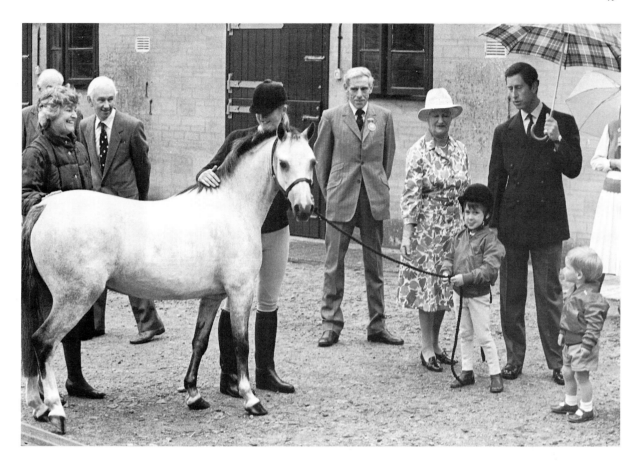

over to Prince William. The infant Prince, wearing hard hat and chinstrap, showed every sign of enthusiasm at the arrival of Topaz, and was happy to get mounted straight away.

Like his own parents, Prince Charles will not push his children into horsemanship, but ample

ABOVE *Prince William receives the Welsh Mountain pony mare Llanerch Topaz, from the Welsh Pony and Cob Society, at Highgrove, in August 1986*
OPPOSITE *Prince William on Smokey, the Shetland pony which Princess Anne's children used to ride. The string running from the bit up through the browband to form an extra draw rein is often used on children's ponies to discourage them from dropping their heads suddenly to graze, thus decanting the young rider over the head. Nanny Barnes is in attendance*

opportunities and encouragement to ride at the earliest possible age are being provided for the two robust little boys at Highgrove.

As we have seen, even in modern 'technological Britain', there is still much that the horse can contribute to the making of a man. And if that man should be a Prince there is still substance in Shakespeare's incomparable description of Henry V as Prince of Wales on horseback:

I saw young Harry ...
Rise from the ground like feather'd Mercury,
And vaulted with such ease into his seat,
As if an angel dropp'd down from the clouds,
To turn and wind a fiery Pegasus
And witch the world with noble horsemanship.

APPENDIX I

Polo teams

Summary of Prince Charles's principal years with teams.

Team	Seasons
Foxcote and Stowell Park	Occasionally from 1973 to 1974
Bucket Hill	1974–75
Golden Eagles	1975 (and intermittently later)
Les Diables Bleus	1976–86
Maple Leafs	1983 (still playing)

Summary of Prince Charles's progress in handicaps.

1964–67 **1**; 1968–70 **0**; 1970 **1**; 1971–72 **2**;
1973–74 **3**; 1975–77 **2**; 1978–80 **3**; 1981–86 **4**.

APPENDIX II

Polo – some of the principal rules

Under Hurlingham Polo Association Rules, polo is played in Britain on ponies of any height, which means that although referred to as ponies, most of the animals played are horses. (The division between horses and ponies is 15 hands high, and the mount of an adult polo player is usually well above this.)

A polo ground is up to 300 by 200 yards unless the side-lines are marked by boards, which tend to keep the ball in play, when the maximum is 300 by 160 yards. The use of boards at Smith's Lawn in recent years has greatly speeded up play on the principal grounds.

A polo ball must not exceed $3\frac{1}{2}$ inches in diameter, weighing between $4\frac{1}{4}$ and $4\frac{3}{4}$ ounces. Teams are limited to four players each, and there are two umpires on the field, and a referee off the field.

Play is forty-two minutes divided into six periods (chukkas) of seven minutes each, with a half-time interval of five minutes. The number of chukkas may be reduced.

In matches played under handicap conditions the higher handicapped team concedes to the lower handicapped team the difference in the handicaps divided by six, and multiplied by the number of periods of play of the match. All fractions of a goal count as 'half a goal'.

The goals, at each end of the ground, are 8 yards wide and at least 10 feet high. If there is a tie at the end of the final chukka of a match the goals are widened for ensuing periods. A goal is scored when a ball passes between the goal posts, and over and clear of the goal line.

The teams change ends after every goal scored, except where a goal is awarded as a penalty. Ends are changed if no goals have been hit by half time.

Throughout the game there is a 'right of way' extending ahead of the player entitled to it, and the direction in which he is riding. Other players are forbidden to enter or cross the 'right of way' except at such a distance where there is no risk of collision or danger to either player.

Players are forbidden rough tactics such as bumping at dangerous angles; zigzagging in front of another player riding at a gallop in a manner likely to risk a fall; pulling across or over a pony's legs, and riding an opponent across the 'right of way'.

Penalties for these and other fouls are as follows:

A penalty goal may be awarded for a dangerous or deliberate foul near goal in order to save a goal.
30-yard hit – a free hit at the ball from 30 yards from the goal line of the other side which has fouled; similarly, a 40-yard or a 60-yard hit may be awarded by the umpires.

There is also the award of a 'free hit from the spot' – that is from the position of the ball when the foul took place, but not less than 4 yards nearer the side-lines or boards.

Basically, anyone who has played soccer finds the rules of polo reasonably easy to understand, although the penalty system is more complicated and the change of ends after goal scoring is confusing at first.

At major tournaments the leading polo clubs employ commentators on the public address systems to overcome these problems, and the game is increasingly enjoyed as a spectator sport by people who have never played it.

APPENDIX III

Hunts with which Prince Charles has hunted

NAME OF HUNT *(foxhounds unless otherwise stated)*	MASTER OR JOINT MASTERS IN 1985–86 SEASON	COUNTY OR PARTS OF COUNTIES INCLUDED IN HUNTING COUNTRY
Duke of Beaufort's	The Duke of Beaufort Capt Ian Farquhar	Gloucestershire, Somerset and Wiltshire
Bedale	Sir Stephen Furness Mr David Dick Mrs A. Moore	North Yorkshire
Belvoir (Duke of Rutland's)	Mr Robert Henson Mr John Blakeway Mr James Knight Mr Charles Harrison	Leicestershire and Lincolnshire
Berkeley	Mrs J. Daniell Mr C. G. M. Lloyd-Baker	Gloucestershire
Old Berkshire	Mr Colin Nash Mr W. F. Caudwell Viscount Astor Miss C. Allsopp	Berkshire and Oxfordshire
Bicester and Warden Hill	The Hon Luke White Mr A. C. J. Preston	Oxfordshire, Buckinghamshire and Northamptonshire
Blackmore and Sparkford Vale	Mr and Mrs Trevor Winslade Mr Robin Cursham	Dorset and Somerset
Braes of Derwent	Mr Charles Stirling Mrs D. D. Aldridge	Durham and Northumberland
Duke of Buccleuch's	The Duke of Buccleuch Mrs R. A. Stobart Mr Jamie Innes Mr P. J. Scott-Plummer Mr R. B. Bruce	Roxburghshire, Selkirk and Berwickshire

Cattistock	Mr Alastair Jackson Mr George Pinney	Dorset and Somerset
Cheshire	Mr P. J. M. Boddington Mr J. G. Cooke Mr M. J. Dixon	Cheshire
Cottesmore	Capt Brian Fanshawe Mrs Joan Gibson Mr Joss Hanbury Mr Leslie Dungworth	Leicestershire and Lincolnshire
Cotswold	Mr Tim Unwin Miss J. Stevens Major M. T. N. H. Wills	Gloucestershire
North Cotswold	Mr M. R. Little Mr N. J. Stevens Mr E. A. Ward Mr J. Robbins	Gloucestershire and Worcestershire
Derwent	Mr S. Roberts Mr C. J. Swiers	North Yorkshire
South Dorset	Mr Robin Gundry Mrs F. C. Gordon	Dorset
Dumfriesshire	Sir A. R. J. Buchanan-Jardine Mrs E. Birbeck	Dumfriesshire
Fernie	Mr Joe Cowen Mr J. R. Millington Mr A. C. Hinch	Leicestershire
Fitzwilliam (Milton)	Sir Stephen and the Hon Lady Hastings Mr Rex Sly	Northamptonshire and Cambridgeshire
Four Burrow	Mr P. B. Warren	Cornwall
Glamorgan	Mr and Mrs A. S. Martyn	Glamorganshire
Grafton	Mr Michael Connell Mr Rodney Ward Mr H. C. Russell Col E. T. Smyth-Osbourne	Northamptonshire and Buckinghamshire
Grove and Rufford	Mr I. J. Youdan Mr R. Mitchell Mrs G. Vere-Laurie	Nottinghamshire, Yorkshire and Derbyshire
Hampshire (HH)	Mr John Gray Mr F. Momber Mrs S. J. Maxse	Hampshire

Heythrop	Mrs M. C. Willes Mr Oliver Langdale Mr Stephen Lambert Mr Richard Sumner	Oxfordshire and Gloucestershire
Ledbury	Mr James Daly Mr H. J. Baimbridge	Herefordshire, Worcestershire and Gloucestershire
High Peak (Harriers)	Mrs D. L. Turner Mr J. A. Brocklehurst	Derbyshire
Meynell and North Staffs	Mr David Meynell Mr Gerald Deville Mr and Mrs David Pennell	Derbyshire and Staffordshire
Middleton	Col the Hon R. N. Crossley Mr A. T. Preston Mr J. D. T. Megginson	Yorkshire
Morpeth	Mr Michael Cookson Mr T. R. P. S. Norton Sir R. E. Renwick	Northumberland
Pendle Forest and Craven (Harriers)	Lady Horsfall Mr Christopher Hindley Mr Michael Bannister Mrs A. R. B. Aspinall	Lancashire and Yorkshire
Percy	The Duke of Northumberland	Northumberland
Portman	Mr Edward Lycett Green Mr P. Stewart Tory	Dorset, Wiltshire and Hampshire
Pytchley	Mr and Mrs Dick Saunders Miss Louise Bates Mr A. E. Jones Mr P. F. Lee Mr W. S. Payne	Northamptonshire and Leicestershire
Quorn	Mr Jim Bealby Mr Joss Hanbury Mr Barry Hercock	Leicestershire and Nottinghamshire
North Shropshire	Mr A. Fox	Shropshire
Sinnington	Major A. G. Stewart Major J. S. Mangles Mrs C. Mackenzie-Smith	North Yorkshire
Spooner's and West Dartmoor	Mr T. J. Millar	Devon
Taunton Vale	Mr Martin Lee Mr A. Covey	Somerset

Tynedale	Mr A. C. Mann Mrs M. A. Anthony Mr G. J. K. Benson	Northumberland
Warwickshire	Mr J. L. Barnett Mrs R. D. Green Mrs D. E. M. Willson Mrs J. V. E. Way	Warwickshire, Gloucestershire Worcestershire and Oxfordshire
VWH (Vale of White Horse)	Capt Fred Barker	Wiltshire and Gloucestershire
Sir Watkin Williams-Wynn's	Lt Col Sir Watkin Williams-Wynn Mr Richard Matson Mr Neil Ewart	Denbigh, Flint, Cheshire and Shropshire
South and West Wilts	Capt Simon Clarke Mrs W. G. Whatley Mrs W. Blanshard	Wiltshire
Zetland	Mr J. V. Hodgson Mrs P. L. Westgarth	Durham and North Yorkshire

APPENDIX IV

Foxhunting Glossary

The language of foxhunting is one of its mysteries. On the whole this is an impediment nowadays, often leading to misunderstandings which damage the sport. For example, 'cubhunting' does not refer to the hunting of furry, baby cubs, but young adult foxes who are fully grown but in their first winter of active life.

Here are a selection of basic foxhunting terms which should add some understanding to the foxhunting chapters in this description of Prince Charles's life as a horseman.

ALL ON The expression used by the whipper-in to tell the huntsman that every hound in the pack is present.

AT FAULT This means the hounds have stopped during a hunt because they have lost the scent.

BINDER The top of a cut-and-laid fence; you may hear of a horse falling after 'catching its leg in a binder'.

BLIND The country is 'blind' in the autumn before the frosts arrive. Each ditch is usually filled with grass or weeds, and the unwary horse may easily put its foot, or feet, into a 'blind' ditch and take a fall.

BLOWING AWAY The huntsman's series of quick notes on his horn when hounds leave a covert, hunting the line of a fox. It is a most exciting sound when blown properly.

BLOWING OUT An appropriately less exuberant note on the horn which the huntsman blows to summon hounds out of a covert where they have failed to find a fox.

BLOWING FOR HOME At the end of a day's hunting the huntsman blows a long, somewhat mournful note, to signal that hounds are being taken home.

BRUSH The fox's tail. Sometimes a guest is presented with the brush at the end of a run; or it goes to a member of the mounted field who has done particularly well to stay at or near the front during the hunt. The brush is, of course, cut from the fox's dead carcase.

BYE-DAY An additional day's hunting to those normally hunted, and published in the Hunt's list of future fixtures.

CARRIES A SCENT The ground surface 'carries a scent' if conditions show that hounds are finding it easy to pick up the scent of hunted fox.

CAST The hounds' own attempt to recover the scent when they have lost it. They will cover the area with their noses down until, it is hoped, one or more pick up the line, and indicate this to the others by baying (or more correctly 'giving tongue'). The huntsman casts the hounds when they fail to find the line on their own. He indicates with voice and horn where he wishes the pack to search. An ability to cast correctly and quickly is the hallmark of a successful huntsman.

COUPLE Hounds are always counted in pairs; thus a pack may be fifteen and a half couple, which is thirty-one hounds. The name derives from the traditional practice of coupling hounds together in pairs by short lengths of chain connecting a collar worn by each hound. It is still done occasionally to young hounds during their training period on road exercise.

EARTH The earth is the fox's underground home. Gone to earth is the phrase used when the fox escapes underground during a hunt. Alternatively, the expression used is 'gone to ground'.

FIELD MASTER The Master, or someone he appoints, to be in charge of the mounted field (those following hounds on horseback). The Field Master must be capable of going first over any obstacle likely to be encountered. He must know the country intimately, avoiding growing crops and other problems, and he must liaise well with the huntsman who is ahead with the hounds. A Field Master's ultimate sanction against members of the field who disobey him and interfere with hounds, or ride on forbidden fields, is to send them home.

FOIL Any odour which obliterates that of the hunted fox; if a fox doubles back he is said to be 'running his foil'.

HARK FORWARD (pronounced 'Hark For-ard') The huntsman's cry to hounds indicating that one or several hounds further on have 'spoken' because they have picked up the line of a fox. He wants the other hounds to go ahead and join those who are 'on the line'.

HEEL To run the heel way, or to hunt the heel line, is to follow the scent in the opposite direction to which the fox is travelling – something the huntsman must be careful to prevent.

HOLLOA (pronounced Holler) The shout or screech given by someone who has just seen a fox and wishes to inform the huntsman and hounds.

HUIC HOLLOA (pronounced Hike Holler) This is shouted to warn the huntsman and hounds that someone else is holloaing further away, having seen a fox.

LAY ON To start hounds on a scent.

LIFT The huntsman 'lifts' his hounds when he calls them to him and takes them arbitrarily to another place where he thinks they can hit the scent off again, without having to try to find the scent over the ground in between. To lift hounds and then disappoint them is bad practice.

LINE The scent trail of the hunted fox.

NOSE To breed hounds for 'nose' is to breed them for their scenting abilities.

PAD A fox's foot.

POINT The distance in a straight line between the start of a hunt and its end; alternatively the furthest distance in a straight line between the opposite ends of a circular or oval route taken in a hunt. Hounds and their followers will have run far more than the point, hence 'The Blankshire made a four-mile point, ten miles as hounds ran ... '.

SPEAK Hounds 'speak' when they give tongue, or bay, which they should do on finding the line of the fox.

STERN A hound's tail.

UNENTERED A hound is unentered when it has not yet been 'entered' into the pack to go hunting.

WALK To walk a foxhound puppy is to rear it at your own home. This is commonly done by Hunt supporters, and each reared puppy is then returned to the pack for 'entering' in its first season's hunting.

WHIPPERS-IN The first whipper-in and the second whipper-in are the huntsman's assistants. Many Hunts dispense with the latter nowadays. Their tasks include 'turning' hounds to the huntsman, ensuring that the pack remains together.

APPENDIX V

Results of steeplechases in which Prince Charles has ridden under Rules

SANDOWN PARK, 8 MARCH 1980

Duke of Gloucester Memorial Trophy (Past and Present Hunter 'Chase for Amateur Riders), prize money £215.20; £102.60; £43.30. 3 miles 118 yards.

Coolishall 11-year-old carrying 12 stone 0 lbs, ridden by Brod Munro-Wilson	1
Ten Up (favourite) 13–12–7, Capt J. Hodges (4 lengths behind)	2
Border Mark 12–12–0, Capt J. Evett (7 lengths)	3
Sea Swell 10–12–2 HRH The Prince of Wales (4 lengths)	4
Andrew Patrick 9–12–0 Major C. Prince	0

Betting: Ten Up 4–9; Coolishall 4–1; A. Patrick 9–1; Sea Swell 16–1; Border Mark 33–1.

LUDLOW, 24 OCTOBER 1980

Clun Handicap Chase (Amateur Riders) £1,059; £294; £141. 3 miles.

Hello Louis 6–10–7 K. Reveley	1
Allibar 10–11–7 HRH The Prince of Wales (6 lengths)	2
Vatican Express 9–10–5 I. McKie (½ length)	3
Bankside 8–10–12 P. Webber (3 lengths)	4
Kabeau 10–12–4 (10 lengths)	5
Lismount VI 9–11–0 J. Cambidge (4 lengths)	6
Uther Pendragon (fav) 8–11–1 T. Thomson Jones	7
Sunday Evening 9–10–3 T. E. Pocock	8
Golden Autumn 8–9–11 B. Eckley	9
Hurrican Jules 8–9–13 S. Bowen	0
Queen Francesca 9–12–0 P. Dukes	0
Military Queen 6–11–1 R. Woolley	0

U. Pendragon 9–4; V. Express 9–2; Bankside 11–2; Kabeau 13–2; Hello Louis 7–1; Allibar 10–1; Lismount VI 11–1; Sunday Evening 25–1; Golden Autumn 33–1; Hurricane Jules 100–1.

SANDOWN PARK, 13 MARCH 1981

Horse and Hound Grand Military Gold Cup Chase (Amateur Riders) £2,438.70; £729.60; £349.80; £159.90. 3 miles 118 yards.

The Drunken Duck 8–11–2 B. Munro-Wilson	1
Brown Jock 13–11–10 Major R. Faulkner (20 lengths)	2
Deep Memories 9–11–8 P. Clifford (30 lengths)	3
Beacon Time 7–11–7 Major C. Prince	4
Collars and Cuffs (fav) 7–11–7 Lt Col A. Cramsie	0
Inkerman 6–11–4 Major H. Baillie	0
Good Prospect 12–12–0 HRH The Prince of Wales	0
Colonial Lad 8–12–0 Marquess de Cuellar	0
Mr Nobody 10–11–5 Capt C. Moore	0
Devon Mignon 11–12–0 W. Bethell	0
Tangled Knight 11–11–12 T. Voorspuy	0
Tanias Lad 7–11–0 Capt Lord John Fitzgerald	0

Collars and Cuffs 7–2; The Drunken Duck 4–1; Good Prospect 5–1; Brown Jock 11–2; Devon Mignon 10–1; Colonial Lad 12–1; Inkerman 14–1; Beacon Time 15–1; Deep Memories 50–1.

CHELTENHAM, 17 MARCH 1981

Kim Muir Memorial Challenge Cup Handicap Chase (Amateur Riders) £5,423; £1,627; £783.60; £361.80. 3 miles.

Waggoners Walk 12–10–3 C. Cundell	1
Hard Outlook 10–10–12 P. Webber (30 lengths)	2
Grand Cru 11–10–13 F. Code (neck)	3
Pongee Boy 8–10–4 E. McIntyre (15 lengths)	4
Lochage 10–10–7 T. Thomson Jones (1 length)	5
Martinstown 9–11–0 M. Batters (12 lengths)	6
Deer Mount 7–10–8 N. Babbage	7
Joint Venture 12–10–10 O. Sherwood	8
Roi de Frontiere 9–9–13 A. Madgwick	9

Kilkilwell 9–10–7 T. Walsing · 10

Choral Festival 10–9–12 H. Low · 0

Cedars Daughter 10–10–7 N. Oliver · 0

Midday Welcome 10–10–7 R. Treloggen · 0

Good Prospect 12–11–4 HRH The Prince of Wales · 0

Another Prospect 9–11–2 A. J. Wilson · 0

Shady Deal 8–10–9 T. Easterby · 0

Alpenstock 14–9–12 E. Pow · 0

Talon (fav) 6–10–0 T. G. Dun · 0

Indecision 7–10–5 C. Magnier · 0

Lustful Lady 9–10–0 N. Mitchell · 0

Talon 6–1; Grand Cru 13–2; Waggoners Walk 7–1; Shady Deal 8–1; Kilkilwell 8–1; Another Prospect 8–1; Lochage 9–1; Indecision 12–1; Pongee Boy 12–1; Hard Outlook 14–1; Joint Venture 16–1; Good Prospect 25–1

Bibliography

Books I have consulted include the following:

All the Queen's Horses, Bill Curling (Chatto and Windus, 1978)

An Introduction to Polo, Marco, with Foreword by HRH The Prince of Wales (J. A. Allen, 1982)

Badminton, Barbara Cooper (Westerham Press, 1969)

Charles, Prince of Wales, Anthony Holden (Weidenfeld and Nicolson, 1979)

Charles and Diana, Graham and Heather Fisher (Robert Hale, 1984)

'Chasers and Hurdlers 1981, 1982, 1983, (Timeform)

Competition Carriage Driving, HRH The Duke of Edinburgh (Horse Drawn Carriages Ltd, 1982)

Elizabeth R, Elizabeth Longford (Weidenfeld and Nicolson, 1983)

Fields Elysian, Simon Blow (J. M. Dent, 1983)

George and Elizabeth, David Duff (Collins, 1983)

History of the Althorp and Pytchley Hunt, Guy Paget (Collins, 1937)

Leicestershire and the Quorn Hunt, C. D. B. Ellis (Edgar Backus, 1951)

Long Live the National, John Hughes and Peter Watson (Michael Joseph, 1983)

Magic of the Quorn, Ulrica Murray Smith (J. A. Allen, 1980)

Majesty, Robert Lacey (Hutchinson, 1977)

Market Harborough, G. J. Whyte-Melville, with a Foreword by HRH The Prince of Wales (Country Life Books, 1984)

Men, Machines and Sacred Cows, HRH The Duke of Edinburgh (Hamish Hamilton, 1984)

Practical Polo, Lt Gen W. G. H. Vickers (J. A. Allen, 1958)

Prince Charles and Princess Diana, Michele Brown (Methuen, 1984)

Prince Charles, Douglas Liversidge (Arthur Barker, 1975)

Princess Anne and Capt Mark Phillips Talking About Horses, Genevieve Murphy (Stanley Paul, 1976)

Queen Elizabeth the Queen Mother, Godfrey Talbot (Country Life Books, 1978)

Royal Ascot, Dorothy Laird (Hodder and Stoughton, 1976)

Royal Champion, Bill Curling (Michael Joseph, 1980)

Saddlery, edited by Elwyn Hartley-Edwards (Country Life Books, 1981)

The Duke of Beaufort, Memoirs (Country Life Books, 1981)

The History of Hunting in Hampshire, J. F. R. Hope (Wykeham Press, 1950)

The History of Steeplechasing, Michael Seth-Smith, Peter Willett, Roger Mortimer, John Oaksey (Michael Joseph, 1966)

The Horseman's Year 1969, edited by Dorian Williams (Collins)

The Hunting Diaries of Stanley Barker, Stuart Newsham (The Standfast Press, 1981)

The Queen's Horses, Charles Mitchell (Macdonald, 1955)

Photographic Acknowledgements

The author and publishers wish to thank the following for permission to reproduce photographs:
All-Sport, page 50; BBC Hulton Picture Library, pages 14, 15, 17, 19 and 83; Camera Press, pages 10, 31, 76, 88, 103, 109, 120 and 121; Equestrian Sports Pictures, page 141; Tim Graham, pages 65, 98/99, 133 and 140; Jim Meads, pages 86 and 93; Stuart Newsham, pages 106/107, 111, 112/113, 116, 118, 122, 124, 144 and 145; Photo News, page 28; Photo Source, pages 21, 23, 24, 27 *above*, 46 and 78; Popperfoto, pages 27 *below*, 29, 30, 42, 44, 45 *above* and *below*, 51 and 73; Press Association, pages 53, 61 and 69; Mike Roberts, pages 2, 36, 37, 39, 40, 41, 47, 54, 55 and 66; Sport and General, page 59; Syndication International, pages 138 *above* and *below* and 139.

Colour sections
Section one: Camera Press, pages 2 *above* and *below* and 3; Tim Graham, pages 1 *above left* and *below*, 4 *above* and *below left*, 5, 6, 7 *above* and *below* and 8; Mike Roberts, page 4 *below right*; Universal Pictorial Press, page 1 *above right*.
Section two: Ace Photo Library, page 11 *above*; Alpha, pages 12 *above* and *below*, 13 *above* and 14 *above*; Tim Graham, pages 9 *above* and *below* and 10 *above*; Kit Houghton pages 11 *below* and 14 *below*; Stuart Newsham, pages 13 *below*, 15 *above* and *below* and 16; Mike Roberts, page 10 *below*.
Section three: Camera Press, page 17; Tim Graham, pages 20, 21 *above* and *below*, 22 *above left* and *below left*, 22/23 and 24; Stuart Newsham, pages 18 and 19 below; Roy Parker, page 19 *above*.

Index